For Ronnie Ruedrich

# Contents

# It's Catching

My friend Patsy was telling me a story. "So I'm at the movie theater," she said, "and I've got my coat all neatly laid out against the back of my seat, when this guy comes along—" And here I stopped her, because I've always wondered about this coat business. When I'm in a theater, I either fold mine in my lap or throw it over my armrest, but Patsy always spreads hers out, acting as if the seat back were cold, and she couldn't possibly enjoy herself while it was suffering.

"Why do you do that?" I asked, and she looked at me, saying, "Germs, silly. Think of all the people who have rested their heads there. Doesn't it just give you the creeps?" I admitted that it had never occurred to me.

"Well, you'd never lie on a hotel bedspread, would you?" she asked, and again: Why not? I might not put it in my mouth, but to lie back and make a few phone calls—I do it all the time.

"But you wash the phone first, right?"

"Umm. No."

"Well, that is just . . . dangerous," she said.

In a similar vein, I was at the grocery store with my sister Lisa and I noticed her pushing the cart with her forearms.

"What's up?" I asked.

"Oh," she said, "you don't ever want to touch the handle of a grocery cart with your bare hands. These things are crawling with germs."

Is it just Americans, or does everyone think this way? In Paris once, I went to my neighborhood supermarket and saw a man shopping with his cockatiel, which was the size of a teenage eagle and stood perched on the handle of his cart.

I told this to Lisa, and she said, "See! There's no telling what foot diseases that bird might have." She had a point, but it's not like everyone takes a cockatiel to the grocery store. A lifetime of shopping, and this was the first exotic bird I'd ever seen browsing the meat counter.

The only preventive thing I do is wash clothes after buying them in a thrift shop—this after catching crabs from a pair of used pants. I was in my midtwenties at the time and probably would have itched myself all the way to the bone had a friend not taken me to a drugstore, where I got a bottle of something called Quell. After applying it, I raked through my pubic hair with a special nit comb, and what I came away with was a real eye-opener: these little monsters who'd been feasting for weeks on my flesh. I guess they're what Patsy imagines when she looks at a theater seat, what Lisa sees lurking on the handle of a grocery cart.

They're minor, though, compared with what Hugh had. He was eight years old and living in the Congo when he noticed a red spot on his leg. Nothing huge—a mosquito bite, he figured. The following day, the spot became more painful, and the day after that he looked down and saw a worm poking out.

A few weeks later, the same thing happened to Maw Hamrick, which is what I call Hugh's mother, Joan. Her worm was a bit shorter than her son's, not that the size really matters. If I was a child and saw something creeping out of a hole in my mother's leg, I would march to the nearest orphanage and put myself up for adoption. I would burn all pictures of her, destroy anything she had ever given me, and start all over because that is simply disgusting. A dad can be crawling with parasites and somehow it's OK, but on a mom, or any woman, really, it's unforgivable.

"Well, that's sort of chauvinistic of you, don't you think?" Maw Hamrick said. She'd come to Paris for Christmas, as had Lisa and her husband, Bob. The gifts had been opened, and she was collecting the used wrapping paper and ironing it flat with her hands. "It was just a guinea worm. People got them all the time." She looked toward the kitchen, where Hugh was doing something to a goose. "Honey, where do you want me to put this paper?"

"Burn it," Hugh said.

"Oh, but it's so pretty. Are you sure you won't want to use it again?"

"Burn it," Hugh repeated.

"What's this about a worm?" Lisa asked. She was lying on the sofa with a blanket over her, still groggy from her nap.

"Joan here had a worm living inside her leg," I said, and Maw Hamrick threw a sheet of wrapping paper into the fire, saying, "Oh, I wouldn't call that *living*."

"But it was inside of you?" Lisa said, and I could see her wheels turning: *Have I ever used the toilet after this woman? Have I ever touched her coffee cup, or eaten off her plate? How soon can I get tested? Are the hospitals open on Christmas Day, or will I have to wait until tomorrow?*

"It was a long time ago," Joan said.

"Like, how long?" Lisa asked.

"I don't know—1968, maybe."

My sister nodded, the way someone does when she's doing math in her head. "Right," she said, and I regretted having brought it up. She was no longer looking *at* Maw Hamrick but *through* her, seeing what an X-ray machine might: the stark puzzle of bones and, teeming within it, the thousands of worms who did not leave home in 1968. I used to see the same thing, but after fifteen years or so, I got over it, and now I just see Maw Hamrick. Maw Hamrick ironing, Maw Hamrick doing the dishes, Maw Hamrick taking out the trash. She wants to be a good houseguest and is always looking for something to do.

"Can I maybe . . . ?" she asks, and before she's finished I answer yes, by all means.

"Did you tell my mother to crawl on her hands and knees across the living room floor?" Hugh asks, and I say, "Well, no, not exactly. I just suggested that if she was going to dust the baseboards, that would be the best way to do it."

When Maw Hamrick's around, I don't lift a finger. All my chores go automatically to her, and I just sit in a rocker, raising my feet every now and then so she can pass the vacuum. It's incredibly relaxing, but it doesn't make me look very good, especially if she's doing something strenuous, carrying furniture to the basement, for instance, which again, was completely her idea. I just mentioned in passing that we rarely used the dresser, and that one of these days someone should take it downstairs. I didn't mean her, exactly, though at age seventy-six she's a lot stronger than Hugh gives her credit for. Coming from Kentucky, she's used to a hard day's work. Choppin', totin', all those activities with a dropped *g:* the way I figure it, these things are in her genes.

It's only a problem when other people are around, and they see this slight, white-haired woman with sweat running down her forehead. Lisa and Bob, for instance, who were staying in Patsy's empty apartment. Every night they'd come over for dinner, and Maw Hamrick would hang up their coats before ironing the napkins and setting the table. Then she'd serve drinks and head into the kitchen to help Hugh.

"You really lucked out," Lisa said, sighing, as Joan rushed to empty my ashtray. Her mother-in-law had recently moved into an assisted living development, the sort of place that's renounced the word "seniors" and refers to the residents as "graying tigers." "I love Bob's mom to death, but Hugh's—my God! And to think that she was eaten by worms."

"Well, they didn't technically *eat* her," I said.

"Then what were they living on? Are you telling me they brought their own food?"

I guessed that she was right, but what do guinea worms eat? Certainly not fat, or they'd never have gone to Joan, who weighs ninety pounds, tops, and can still fit into her prom gown. Not muscle, or she'd never be able to take over my chores. Do they drink blood? Drill holes in bone and sop up the marrow? I meant to ask, but when Maw Hamrick returned to the living room the topic immediately turned to cholesterol, Lisa saying, "I don't mean to pry, Joan, but what is your level?"

It was one of those conversations I was destined to be left out of. Not only have I never been tested, I'm not sure what cholesterol actually is. I hear the word and imagine a pale gravy, made by hand, with lumps in it.

"Have you tried fish oil?" Lisa asked. "That brought Bob's level from three-eighty to two-twenty. Before that, he was on Lipitor." My sister knows the name and corresponding medication for every disease known to man, an impressive feat given that she's completely self-taught. Congenital ichthyosis, myositis ossificans, spondylolisthesis, calling for Cel-e-brex, Flexeril, oxycodone hydrochloride. I joked that she'd never bought a magazine in her life, that she reads them for free in doctors' waiting rooms, and she asked what my cholesterol level was. "You better see a doctor, mister, because you're not as young as you think you are. And while you're there, you might want to have those moles looked at."

It's nothing I wanted to think about, especially on Christmas, with a fire in the fireplace, the apartment smelling of goose. "Let's talk about accidents instead," I said. "Heard of any good ones?"

"Well, it's not exactly an accident," Lisa said, "but did you know that every year five thousand children are startled to death?" It was a difficult concept to grasp, so she threw off her blanket and acted it out. "Say a little girl is running down the hall, playing with her parents, and the dad pops up from behind a corner, saying 'Boo!' or 'Gotcha!' or whatever. Well, it turns out that that child can actually collapse and die."

6

"I don't like that one bit," Maw Hamrick said.

"Well, no, neither do I," Lisa said. "I'm just saying that it happens at least five thousand times a year."

"In America or the world over?" Maw Hamrick asked, and my sister called to her husband in the other room. "Bob, are five thousand children a year startled to death in the United States or in the entire world put together?" He didn't answer, so Lisa decided it was just the United States. "And those are just the reported cases," she said. "A lot of parents probably don't want to own up to it, so their kids' deaths are attributed to something else."

"Those poor children," Maw Hamrick said.

"And the *parents!*" Lisa added. "Can you imagine?"

Both groups are tragic, but I was wondering about the surviving children, or, even worse, the replacements, raised in an atmosphere of preventive sobriety.

"All right, now, Caitlin Two, when we get home a great many people are going to jump out from behind the furniture and yell 'Happy Birthday!' I'm telling you now because I don't want you to get too worked up about it."

No surprises, no practical jokes, nothing unexpected, but a parent can't control everything, and there's still the outside world to contend with, a world of backfiring cars and their human equivalents.

Maybe one day you'll look down and see a worm, waving its sad, penile head from a hatch it has bored in your leg. If that won't stop your heart, I don't know what will, but Hugh and his mother seem to have survived. Thrived, even. The Hamricks are made of stronger stuff than I am. That's why I let them cook the goose, move the furniture, launder the hideous creatures from my secondhand clothing. If anything were to startle them to death, it would be my offer to pitch in, and so I settle back on the sofa with my sister and wave my coffee cup in the air, signaling for another refill.

# Keeping Up

My street in Paris is named for a surgeon who taught at the nearby medical school and discovered an abnormal skin condition, a contracture that causes the fingers to bend inward, eventually turning the hand into a full-time fist. It's short, this street, no more or less attractive than anything else in the area, yet vacationing Americans are drawn here, compelled for some reason to stand beneath my office window and scream at one another.

For some, the arguments are about language. A wife had made certain claims regarding her abilities. "I've been listening to tapes," she said, or, perhaps, "All those romance languages are pretty much alike, so what with my Spanish we should be fine." But then people use slang, or ask unexpected questions, and things begin to fall apart. "*You're* the one who claimed to speak French." I hear this all the time, and look out my window to see a couple standing toe to toe on the sidewalk.

"Yeah," the woman will say. "At least *I* try."

"Well try *harder,* damn it. Nobody knows what the hell you're saying."

Geographical arguments are the second most common. People notice that they've been on my street before, maybe half an hour ago, when they only thought they were tired and hungry and needed to find a bathroom.

"For God's sake, Phillip, would it kill you to just ask somebody?"

I lie on my couch, thinking, *Why don't you ask? How come Phillip has to do it?* But these things are often more complicated than they seem. Maybe Phillip was here twenty years ago and has been claiming to know his way around. Maybe he's one of those who refuse to hand over the map, or refuse to pull it out, lest he look like a tourist.

The desire to pass is loaded territory and can lead to the ugliest sort of argument there is. "You want to *be* French, Mary Frances, that's your problem, but instead you're just another American." I went to the window for that one and saw a marriage disintegrate before my eyes. Poor Mary Frances in her beige beret. Back at the hotel it had probably seemed like a good idea, but now it was ruined and ridiculous, a cheap felt pancake sliding off the back of her head. She'd done the little scarf thing, too, not caring that it was summer. It could have been worse, I thought. She could have been wearing one of those striped boater's shirts, but, as it was, it was pretty bad, a costume, really.

Some vacationers raise the roof—they don't care who hears them—but Mary Frances spoke in a whisper. This, too, was seen as pretension and made her husband even angrier. "Americans," he repeated. "We don't live in France, we live in Virginia. Vienna, Virginia. Got it?"

I looked at this guy and knew for certain that if we'd met at a party he'd claim to live in Washington, D.C. Ask for a street address, and he'd look away, mumbling, "Well, just outside D.C."

When fighting at home, an injured party can retreat to a separate part of the house, or step into the backyard to shoot at cans, but outside my window the options are limited to crying, sulking, or storming back to the hotel. "Oh, for Christ's sake," I hear. "Can we please just try to have a good time?" This is like ordering someone to find you attractive, and it doesn't work. I've tried it.

Most of Hugh's and my travel arguments have to do with pace. I'm a fast walker, but he has longer legs and likes to maintain a good twenty-foot lead. To the casual observer, he would appear to be running from me, darting around corners, intentionally trying to lose himself. When asked about my latest vacation, the answer is always the same. In Bangkok, in Ljubljana, in Budapest and Bonn: What did I see? Hugh's back, just briefly, as he disappeared into a crowd. I'm convinced that before we go anywhere he calls the board of tourism and asks what style and color of coat is the most popular among the locals. If they say, for example, a navy windbreaker, he'll go with that. It's uncanny the way he blends in. When we're in an Asian city, I swear he actually makes himself shorter. I don't know how, but he does. There's a store in London that sells travel guides alongside novels that take place in this or that given country. The idea is that you'll read the guide for facts and read the novel for atmosphere—a nice thought, but the only book I'll ever need is *Where's Waldo?* All my energy goes into keeping track of Hugh, and as a result I don't get to enjoy anything.

The last time this happened we were in Australia, where I'd gone to attend a conference. Hugh had all the free time in the world, but mine was limited to four hours on a Saturday morning. There's a lot to do in Sydney, but first on my list was a visit to the Taronga Zoo, where I hoped to see a dingo. I never saw that Meryl Streep movie, and as a result the creature was a complete mystery to me. Were someone to say, "I left my window open and a dingo flew in," I would have believed it, and if he said, "Dingoes! Our pond is completely overrun with them," I would have believed that as well. Two-legged, four-legged, finned, or feathered: I simply had no idea, which was exciting, actually, a rarity in the age of twenty-four-hour nature channels. Hugh offered to draw me a picture, but, having come this far, I wanted to extend my ignorance just a little bit longer, to stand before the cage or tank and see this thing for myself. It would be a glorious occasion, and I didn't want to spoil it at the eleventh hour. I also didn't want to go alone, and this was where our problem started.

Hugh had spent most of his week swimming and had dark circles beneath his eyes, twin impressions left by his goggles. When in the ocean, he goes out for hours, passing the lifeguard buoys and moving into international waters. It looks as though he's trying to swim home, which is embarrassing when you're the one left on shore with your hosts. "He honestly does like it here," I say. "Really."

Had it been raining, he might have willingly joined me,

but, as it was, Hugh had no interest in dingoes. It took a solid hour of whining to change his mind, but even then his heart wasn't in it. Anyone could see that. We took a ferry to the zoo, and while on board he stared longingly at the water and made little paddling motions with his hands. Every second wound him tighter, and when we landed I literally had to run to keep up with him. The koala bears were just a blur, as were the visitors who stood before them, posing for photos. "Can't we just . . . ," I wheezed, but Hugh was rounding the emus and couldn't hear me.

He has the most extraordinary sense of direction I've ever seen in a mammal. Even in Venice, where the streets were seemingly designed by ants, he left the train station, looked once at a map, and led us straight to our hotel. An hour after checking in he was giving directions to strangers, and by the time we left he was suggesting shortcuts to gondoliers. Maybe he smelled the dingoes. Maybe he'd seen their pen from the window of the plane, but, whatever his secret, he ran right to them. I caught up a minute later and bent from the waist to catch my breath. Then I covered my face, stood upright, and slowly parted my fingers, seeing first a fence and then, behind it, a shallow moat filled with water. I saw some trees—and a tail—and then I couldn't stand it any-more and dropped my hands.

"Why, they look just like dogs," I said. "Are you sure we're in the right place?"

Nobody answered, and I turned to find myself standing beside an embarrassed Japanese woman. "I'm sorry," I said. "I thought you were the person I brought halfway around the world. First-class."

*

A zoo is a good place to make a spectacle of yourself, as the people around you have creepier, more photogenic things to look at. A gorilla pleasures himself while eating a head of iceberg lettuce, and it's much more entertaining than the forty-something-year-old man who dashes around talking to himself. For me, that talk is always the same, a rehearsal of my farewell speech: ". . . because this time, buddy, it's over. I mean it." I imagine myself packing a suitcase, throwing stuff in without bothering to fold it. "If you find yourself missing me, you might want to get a dog, an old, fat one that can run to catch up and make that distant panting sound you've grown so accustomed to. Me, though, I'm finished."

I will walk out the door and never look back, never return his calls, never even open his letters. The pots and pans, all the things that we acquired together, he can have them, that's how unfeeling I will be. "Clean start," that's my motto, so what do I need with a shoe box full of photographs, or the tan-colored belt he gave me for my thirty-third birthday, back when we first met and he did not yet understand that a belt is something you get from your aunt, and not your boyfriend, I don't care who made it. After that, though, he got pretty good in the gift-giving department: a lifelike mechanical hog covered in real pigskin, a professional microscope offered at the height of my arachnology phase, and, best of all, a seventeenth-century painting of a Dutch peasant changing a dirty diaper. Those things I would keep—and why not? I'd also take the desk he gave me, and the fireplace mantel, and, just on principle, the drafting table, which he clearly bought for himself and tried to pass off as a Christmas present.

Now it seemed that I would be leaving in a van rather than on foot, but, still, I was going to do it, so help me. I pictured myself pulling away from the front of our building, and then I remembered that I don't drive. Hugh would have to do it for me, and well he should after everything he'd put me through. Another problem was where this van might go. An apartment, obviously, but how would I get it? It's all I can do to open my mouth at the post office, so how am I going to talk to a real estate agent? The language aspect has nothing to do with it, as I'm no more likely to house-hunt in New York than I am in Paris. When discussing sums over sixty dollars, I tend to sweat. Not just on my forehead, but all over. Five minutes at the bank, and my shirt is transparent. Ten minutes, and I'm stuck to my seat. I lost twelve pounds getting the last apartment, and all I had to do was sign my name. Hugh handled the rest of it.

On the bright side, I have money, though I'm not exactly sure how to get my hands on it. Bank statements arrive regularly, but I don't open anything that's not personally addressed or doesn't look like a free sample. Hugh takes care of all that, opening the icky mail and actually reading it. He knows when our insurance payments are due, when it's time to renew our visas, when the warranty on the washer is about to expire. "I don't think we need to extend this," he'll say, knowing that if the machine stops working he'll fix it himself, the way he fixes everything. But not me. If I lived alone and something broke, I'd just work around it: use a paint bucket instead of a toilet, buy an ice chest and turn the dead refrigerator into an armoire. Call a repairman? Never. Do it myself? That'll be the day.

I've been around for nearly half a century, yet still I'm

afraid of everything and everyone. A child sits beside me on a plane and I make conversation, thinking how stupid I must sound. The downstairs neighbors invite me to a party and, after claiming that I have a previous engagement, I spend the entire evening confined to my bed, afraid to walk around because they might hear my footsteps. I do not know how to turn up the heat, send an e-mail, call the answering machine for my messages, or do anything even remotely creative with a chicken. Hugh takes care of all that, and when he's out of town I eat like a wild animal, the meat still pink, with hair or feathers clinging to it. So is it any wonder that he runs from me? No matter how angry I get, it always comes down to this: I'm going to leave and then what? Move in with my dad? Thirty minutes of pure rage, and when I finally spot him I realize that I've never been so happy to see anyone in my life.

"There you are," I say. And when he asks where I have been, I answer honestly and tell him I was lost.

# The Understudy

In the spring of 1967, my mother and father went out of town for the weekend and left my four sisters and me in the company of a woman named Mrs. Byrd, who was old and black and worked as a maid for one of our neighbors. She arrived at our house on a Friday afternoon, and, after carrying her suitcase to my parents' bedroom, I gave her a little tour, the way I imagined they did in hotels. "This is your TV, this is your private sundeck, and over here you've got a bathroom—just yours and nobody else's."

Mrs. Byrd put her hand to her cheek. "Somebody pinch me. I'm about to fall out."

She cooed again when I opened a dresser drawer and explained that when it came to coats and so forth we favored a little room called a closet. "There are two of them against the wall there, and you can use the one on the right."

It was, I thought, a dream for her: *your* telephone, *your*

17

massive bed, *your* glass-doored shower stall. All you had to do was leave it a little cleaner than you found it.

A few months later, my parents went away again and left us with Mrs. Robbins, who was also black, and who, like Mrs. Byrd, allowed me to see myself as a miracle worker. Night fell, and I pictured her kneeling on the carpet, her forehead grazing my parents' gold bedspread. "Thank you, Jesus, for these wonderful white people and all that they have given me this fine weekend."

With a regular teenage babysitter, you horsed around, jumped her on her way out of the bathroom, that sort of thing, but with Mrs. Robbins and Mrs. Byrd we were respectful and well behaved, not like ourselves at all. This made our parents' getaway weekend a getaway for us as well—for what was a vacation but a chance to be someone different?

In early September of that same year, my parents joined my aunt Joyce and uncle Dick for a week in the Virgin Islands. Neither Mrs. Byrd nor Mrs. Robbins was available to stay with us, and so my mother found someone named Mrs. Peacock. Exactly *where* she found her would be speculated on for the remainder of our childhoods.

"Has Mom ever been to a women's prison?" my sister Amy would ask.

"Try a *man's* prison," Gretchen would say, as she was never convinced that Mrs. Peacock was a legitimate female. The "Mrs." part was a lie anyway, that much we knew.

"She just says she was married so people will believe in her!!!!" This was one of the insights we recorded in a notebook while she was staying with us. There were pages of them, all written in a desperate scrawl, with lots of exclamation points and underlined words. It was the sort of writing you might do when a ship was going down, the sort that would give your surviving loved ones an actual chill. "If only we'd known," they'd moan. "Oh, for the love of God, if only we had known."

But what was there to know, really? Some fifteen-year-old offers to watch your kids for the night and, sure, you ask her parents about her, you nose around. But with a grown woman you didn't demand a reference, especially if the woman was white.

Our mother could never remember where she had found Mrs. Peacock. "A newspaper ad," she'd say, or, "I don't know, maybe she sat for someone at the club."

But who at the club would have hired such a creature? In order to become a member you had to meet certain requirements, one of them being that you did not know people like Mrs. Peacock. You did not go to places where she ate or worshipped, and you certainly didn't give her the run of your home.

I smelled trouble the moment her car pulled up, a piece of junk driven by a guy with no shirt on. He looked just old enough to start shaving, and remained seated as the figure beside him pushed open the door and eased her way out. This was Mrs. Peacock, and the first thing I noticed was her hair, which was the color of margarine and fell in waves to the middle of her back. It was the sort of hair you might find on a mermaid, completely wrong for a sixty-year-old woman who was not just heavy but fat, and moved as if each step might be her last.

"Mom!" I called, and, as my mother stepped out of the

house, the man with no shirt backed out of the driveway and peeled off down the street.

"Was that your husband?" my mother asked, and Mrs. Peacock looked at the spot where the car had been.

"Naw," she said. "That's just Keith."

Not "my nephew Keith" or "Keith, who works at the filling station and is wanted in five states," but "just Keith," as if we had read a book about her life and were expected to remember all the characters.

She'd do this a lot over the coming week, and I would grow to hate her for it. Someone would phone the house, and after hanging up she'd say, "So much for Eugene" or "I told Vicky not to call me here no more."

"Who's Eugene?" we'd ask. "What did Vicky do that was so bad?" And she'd tell us to mind our own business.

She had this attitude, not that she was better than us but that she was as good as us—and that simply was not true. Look at her suitcase, tied shut with rope! Listen to her mumble, not a clear sentence to be had. A polite person would express admiration when given a tour of the house, but aside from a few questions regarding the stovetop Mrs. Peacock said very little and merely shrugged when shown the master bathroom, which had the word "master" in it and was supposed to make you feel powerful and lucky to be alive. *I've seen better,* her look seemed to say, but I didn't for one moment believe it.

The first two times my parents left for vacation, my sisters and I escorted them to the door and said that we would miss them terribly. It was just an act, designed to make us look sensitive and English, but on this occasion we meant it. "Oh, stop being such babies," our mother said. "It's only a week." Then she gave Mrs. Peacock the look meaning "Kids. What are you going to do?"

There was a corresponding look that translated to "You tell me," but Mrs. Peacock didn't need it, for she knew exactly what she was going to do: enslave us. There was no other word for it. An hour after my parents left, she was lying facedown on their bed, dressed in nothing but her slip. Like her skin, it was the color of Vaseline, an uncolor really, which looked even worse with yellow hair. Add to this her great bare legs, which were dimpled at the inner knee and streaked throughout with angry purple veins.

My sisters and I attempted diplomacy. "Isn't there, perhaps, some *work* to be done?"

"You there, the one with the glasses." Mrs. Peacock pointed at my sister Gretchen. "Your mama mentioned they's some sodie pops in the kitchen. Go fetch me one, why don't you."

"Do you mean Coke?" Gretchen asked.

"That'll do," Mrs. Peacock said. "And put it in a mug with ice in it."

While Gretchen got the Coke, I was instructed to close the drapes. It was, to me, an idea that bordered on insanity, and I tried my best to talk her out of it. "The private deck is your room's best feature," I said. "Do you *really* want to block it out while the sun's still shining?"

She did. Then she wanted her suitcase. My sister Amy put it on the bed, and we watched as Mrs. Peacock untied the rope and reached inside, removing a plastic hand attached to a foot-long wand. The business end was no bigger than a monkey's paw, the fingers bent slightly inward, as if they had been frozen in the act of begging. It was a nasty little thing,

21

the nails slick with grease, and over the coming week we were to see a lot of it. To this day, should any of our boyfriends demand a back-scratch, my sisters and I recoil. "Brush yourself against a brick wall," we say. "Hire a nurse, but don't look at me. I've done my time."

No one spoke of carpal tunnel syndrome in the late 1960s, but that doesn't mean it didn't exist. There just wasn't a name for it. Again and again we ran the paw over Mrs. Peacock's back, the fingers leaving white trails and sometimes welts. "Ease up," she'd say, the straps of her slip lowered to her forearms, the side of her face mashed flat against the gold bedspread. "I ain't made of stone, you know."

That much was clear. Stone didn't sweat. Stone didn't stink or break out in a rash, and it certainly didn't sprout little black hairs between its shoulder blades. We drew this last one to Mrs. Peacock's attention, and she responded, saying, "Y'all's got the same damn thing, only they ain't poked out yet."

That one was written down verbatim and read aloud during the daily crisis meetings my sisters and I had taken to holding in the woods behind our house. "Y'all's got the same damn thing, only they ain't poked out yet." It sounded chilling when said in her voice, and even worse when recited normally, without the mumble and the country accent.

"Can't speak English," I wrote in the complaint book. "Can't go two minutes without using the word 'damn.' Can't cook worth a ~~damn~~ hoot."

The last part was not quite true, but it wouldn't have hurt her to expand her repertoire. Sloppy joe, sloppy joe, sloppy joe, held over our heads as if it were steak. Nobody ate unless they earned it, which meant fetching her drinks, brushing her hair, driving the monkey paw into her shoulders until she moaned. Mealtime came and went—her too full of Coke and potato chips to notice until one of us dared to mention it. "If y'all was hungry, why didn't you say nothing? I'm not a mind reader, you know. Not a psychic or some damn thing."

Then she'd slam around the kitchen, her upper arms jiggling as she threw the pan on the burner, pitched in some ground beef, shook ketchup into it.

My sisters and I sat at the table, but Mrs. Peacock ate standing, *like a cow,* we thought, *a cow with a telephone:* "You tell Curtis for me that if he don't run Tanya to R.C.'s hearing, he'll have to answer to both me *and* Gene Junior, and that's no lie."

Her phone calls reminded her that she was away from the action. Events were coming to a head: the drama with Ray, the business between Kim and Lucille, and here she was, stuck in the middle of nowhere. That's how she saw our house: the end of the earth. In a few years' time, I'd be the first to agree with her, but when I was eleven, and you could still smell the fresh pine joists from behind the Sheetrocked walls, I thought there was no finer place to be.

"I'd like to see where *she* lives," I said to my sister Lisa.

And then, as punishment, we did see.

This occurred on day five, and was Amy's fault—at least according to Mrs. Peacock. Any sane adult, anyone with children, might have taken the blame upon herself. *Oh, well,* she would have thought. *It was bound to happen sooner or later.* Seven-year-old girl, her arm worn to rubber after hours of back-scratching, carries the monkey paw into the master bathroom, where it drops from her hand and falls to the tile floor. The fingers shatter clean off, leaving nothing—a jagged little fist at the end of a stick.

"Now you done it," Mrs. Peacock said. All of us to bed without supper. And the next morning Keith pulled up, still with no shirt on. He honked in the driveway, and she shouted at him through the closed door to hold his damn horses.

"I don't think he can hear you," Gretchen said, and Mrs. Peacock told her she'd had all the lip she was going to take. She'd had all the lip she was going to take from any of us, and so we were quiet as we piled into the car, Keith telling a convoluted story about him and someone named Sherwood as he sped beyond the Raleigh we knew and into a neighborhood of barking dogs and gravel driveways. The houses looked like something a child might draw, a row of shaky squares with triangles on top. Add a door, add two windows. Think of putting a tree in the front yard, and then decide against it because branches aren't worth the trouble.

Mrs. Peacock's place was divided in half, her in the back, and someone named Leslie living in the front. A *man* named Leslie, who wore fatigues and stood by the mailbox play-wrestling with a Doberman pinscher as we drove up. I thought he would scowl at the sight of Mrs. Peacock, but instead he smiled and waved, and she waved in return. Five children wedged into the backseat, children just dying to report that they'd been abducted, but Leslie didn't seem to notice us any more than Keith had.

When the car stopped, Mrs. Peacock turned around in the front seat and announced that she had some work that needed doing.

"Go ahead," we told her. "We'll wait here."

"Like fun you will," she said.

We started outdoors, picking up turds deposited by the Doberman, whose name turned out to be Rascal. The front yard was mined with them, but the back, which Mrs. Peacock tended, was surprisingly normal, better than normal, really. There was a small lawn and, along its border, a narrow bed of low-lying flowers—pansies, I think. There were more flowers on the patio outside her door, most of them in plastic pots and kept company by little ceramic creatures: a squirrel with its tail broken off, a smiling toad.

I'd thought of Mrs. Peacock as a person for whom the word "cute" did not register, and so it was startling to enter her half of the house and find it filled with dolls. There must have been a hundred of them, all squeezed into a single room. There were dolls sitting on the television, dolls standing with their feet glued to the top of the electric fan, and tons more crowded onto floor-to-ceiling shelves. Strange to me was that she hadn't segregated them according to size or quality. Here was a fashion model in a stylish dress, dwarfed by a cheap bawling baby or a little girl who'd apparently come too close to the hot plate, her hair singed off, her face disfigured into a frown.

"First rule is that nobody touches nothing," Mrs. Peacock said. "Not nobody and not for no reason."

She obviously thought that her home was something special, a children's paradise, a land of enchantment, but to me it was just overcrowded.

"*And* dark," my sisters would later add. "*And* hot *and* smelly."

Mrs. Peacock had a Dixie cup dispenser mounted to the

wall above her dresser. She kept her bedroom slippers beside the bathroom door, and inside each one was a little troll doll, its hair blown back as if by a fierce wind. "See," she told us. "It's like they's riding in boats!"

"Right," we said. "That's really something."

She then pointed out a miniature kitchen set displayed on one of the lower shelves. "The refrigerator broke, so I made me another one out of a matchbox. Get up close, and y'all can look at it."

"You *made* this?" we said, though of course it was obvious. The strike pad gave it away.

Mrs. Peacock was clearly trying to be a good hostess, but I wished she would stop. My opinion of her had already been formed, was written on paper, even, and factoring in her small kindnesses would only muddy the report. Like any normal fifth grader, I preferred my villains to be evil and stay that way, to act like Dracula rather than Frankenstein's monster, who ruined everything by handing that peasant girl a flower. He sort of made up for it by drowning her a few minutes later, but, still, you couldn't look at him the same way again. My sisters and I didn't want to understand Mrs. Peacock. We just wanted to hate her, and so we were relieved when she reached into her closet and withdrew another backscratcher, the good one, apparently. It was no larger than the earlier model, but the hand was slimmer and more clearly defined, that of a lady rather than a monkey. The moment she had it, the hostess act melted away. Off came the man's shirt she'd worn over her slip, and she took up her position on the bed, surrounded by the baby dolls she referred to as "doll babies." Gretchen was given the first shift, and the rest of us were sent outside to pull weeds in the blistering sun.

"Thank God," I said to Lisa. "I was worried for a minute there that we'd have to feel sorry for her."

As children we suspected that Mrs. Peacock was crazy, a catchall term we used for anyone who did not recognize our charms. As adults, though, we narrow it down and wonder if she wasn't clinically depressed. The drastic mood swings, the hours of sleep, a gloom so heavy she was unable to get dressed or wash herself—thus the slip, thus the hair that grew greasier and greasier as the week progressed and left a permanent stain on our parents' gold bedspread.

"I wonder if she'd been institutionalized," Lisa will say. "Maybe she had shock treatments, which is what they did back then, the poor thing."

We'd like to have been that compassionate as children, but we already had our list, and it was unthinkable to disregard it on account of a lousy matchbox. Our parents returned from their vacation, and before they even stepped out of the car we were upon them, a mob, all of us talking at the same time. "She made us go to her shack and pick up turds." "She sent us to bed one night without supper." "She said the master bathroom was ugly, and that you were stupid to have air-conditioning."

"All right," our mother said. "Jesus, calm down."

"She made us scratch her back until our arms almost fell off." "She cooked sloppy joe every night, and when we ran out of buns she told us to eat it on crackers."

We were still at it when Mrs. Peacock stepped from the breakfast nook and out into the carport. She was dressed, for once, and even had shoes on, but it was too late to play normal. In the presence of my mother, who was tanned and pretty, she looked all the more unhealthy, sinister almost, her mouth twisted into a freaky smile.

"She spent the whole week in bed and didn't do laundry until last night."

I guess I expected a violent showdown. How else to explain my disappointment when, instead of slapping Mrs. Peacock across the face, my mother looked her in the eye, and said, "Oh, come on. I don't believe that for a minute." It was the phrase she used when she believed every word of it but was too tired to care.

"But she *abducted* us."

"Well, good for her." Our mother led Mrs. Peacock into the house and left my sisters and me standing in the carport. "Aren't they just horrible?" she said. "Honest to God, I don't know how you put up with them for an entire week."

"You don't know how *she* put up with *us?*"

*Slam!* went the door, right in our faces, and then our mom sat her guest down in the breakfast nook and offered her a drink.

Framed through the window, they looked like figures on a stage, two characters who seem like opposites and then discover they have a lot in common: a similarly hard upbringing, a fondness for the jugged Burgundies of California, and a mutual disregard for the rowdy matinee audience, pitching their catcalls from beyond the parted curtain.

# This Old House

When it came to decorating her home, my mother was nothing if not practical. She learned early on that children will destroy whatever you put in front of them, so for most of my youth our furniture was chosen for its durability rather than for its beauty. The one exception was the dining room set my parents bought shortly after they were married. Should a guest eye the buffet for longer than a second, my mother would jump in to prompt a compliment. "You like it?" she'd ask. "It's from Scandinavia!" This, we learned, was the name of a region, a cold and forsaken place where people stayed indoors and plotted the death of knobs.

The buffet, like the table, was an exercise in elegant simplicity. The set was made of teak and had been finished with tung oil. This brought out the character of the wood, allowing it, at certain times of day, to practically glow. Nothing was more beautiful than our dining room, especially after my father covered the walls with cork. It wasn't the kind you use on bulletin boards, but something coarse and dark, the color of damp pine mulch. Light the candles beneath the chafing dish, lay the table with the charcoal textured dinnerware we hardly ever used, and you had yourself a real picture.

This dining room, I liked to think, was what my family was all about. Throughout my childhood it brought me great pleasure, but then I turned sixteen and decided that I didn't like it anymore. What changed my mind was a television show, a weekly drama about a close-knit family in Depression-era Virginia. This family didn't have a blender or a country club membership, but they did have one another—that and a really great house, an old one, built in the twenties or something. All of their bedrooms had slanted clapboard walls and oil lamps that bathed everything in fragile golden light. I wouldn't have used the word "romantic," but that's how I thought of it.

"You think those prewar years were cozy?" my father once asked. "Try getting up at five a.m. to sell newspapers on the snow-covered streets. That's what I did, and it stunk to high heaven."

"Well," I told him, "I'm just sorry that you weren't able to appreciate it."

Like anyone nostalgic for a time he didn't live through, I chose to weed out the little inconveniences: polio, say, or the thought of eating stewed squirrel. The world was simply grander back then, somehow more civilized, and nicer to look at. And the history! Wasn't it crushing to live in a house no older than our cat?

"No," my father said. "Not at all."

My mother felt the same: "Boxed in by neighbors, having to walk through my parents' bedroom in order to reach the kitchen. If you think that was fun, you never saw your grandfather with his teeth out."

They were more than willing to leave their pasts behind them and reacted strongly when my sister Gretchen and I began dragging it home. "The *Andrews* Sisters?" My father groaned. "What the hell do you want to listen to them for?"

When I started buying clothes from Goodwill, he really went off, and for good reason, probably. The suspenders and knickers were bad enough, but when I added a top hat, he planted himself in the doorway and physically prevented me from leaving the house. "It doesn't make sense," I remember him saying. "That hat with those pants, worn with the damn platform shoes . . ." His speech temporarily left him, and he found himself waving his hands, no doubt wishing that they held magic wands. "You're just . . . a mess is what you are."

The way I saw it, the problem wasn't my outfit, but my context. Sure I looked out of place beside a Scandinavian buffet, but put me in the proper environment, and I'd undoubtedly fit right in.

"The environment you're looking for is called a psychiatric hospital," my father said. "Now give me the damn hat before I burn it off."

I longed for a home where history was respected, and four years later I finally found one. This was in Chapel Hill, North Carolina. I'd gone there to visit an old friend from high school, and because I was between jobs and had no real obligations I decided to stay for a while, and maybe look for some dishwashing work. The restaurant that hired me was a local institution, all dark wood and windowpanes the size of playing cards. The food was OK, but what the place was really known for was the classical music that the owner, a man named Byron, pumped into the dining room. Anyone else might have thrown in a compilation tape, but he took his responsibilities very seriously and planned each meal as if it were an evening at Tanglewood. I hoped that dishwashing might lead to a job in the dining room, busing tables and eventually waiting on them, but I kept these aspirations to myself. Dressed as I was, in jodhpurs and a smoking jacket, I should have been grateful that I was hired at all.

After getting my first paycheck, I scouted out a place to live. My two requirements were that it be cheap and close to where I worked, and on both counts I succeeded. I couldn't have dreamt that it would also be old and untouched, an actual boardinghouse. The owner was adjusting her Room for Rent sign as I passed, and our eyes locked in an expression that said, Hark, stranger, you are one of me! Both of us looked like figures from a scratchy newsreel, me the unemployed factory worker in tortoiseshell safety glasses and a tweed overcoat two sizes too large, and she, the feisty widow lady, taking in boarders in order to make ends meet. "Excuse me," I called, "but is that hat from the forties?"

The woman put her hands to her head and adjusted what looked like a fistful of cherries spilling from a velveteen saucer. "Why, yes it is," she said. "How canny of you to notice." I'll say her name was Rosemary Dowd, and as she introduced herself I tried to guess her age. What foxed me was her makeup, which was on the heavy side and involved a great deal of peach-colored powder. From a distance, her hair looked white, but now I could see that it was streaked with yellow, almost randomly, like snow that had been peed on. If she seemed somewhat mannish, it was the fault of her clothing rather than her features. Both her jacket and her blouse were kitted out with shoulder pads, and when worn together she could barely fit through the door. This might be a problem for others, but Rosemary didn't get out much. And why would she want to?

I hadn't even crossed the threshold when I agreed to take the room. What sold me was the look of the place. Some might have found it shabby—"a dump," my father would eventually call it—but, unless you ate them, a few thousand paint chips never hurt anyone. The same could be said for the groaning front porch and the occasional missing shingle. It was easy to imagine that the house, set as it was on the lip of a university parking lot, had dropped from the sky, like Dorothy's in *The Wizard of Oz,* but with a second story. Then there was the inside, which was even better. The front door opened onto a living room, or, as Rosemary called it, the "parlor." The word was old-fashioned but fitting. Velvet curtains framed the windows. The walls were papered in a faint, floral pattern, and doilies were everywhere, laid flat on tabletops and sagging like cobwebs from the backs of over-stuffed chairs. My eyes moved from one thing to another, and, like my mother with her dining room set, Rosemary took note of where they landed. "I see you like my daven-port," she said, and "You don't find lamps like that anymore. It's a genuine Stephanie."

It came as no surprise that she bought and sold antiques, or "dabbled" in them, as she said. Every available surface was crowded with objects: green glass candy dishes, framed photographs of movie stars, cigarette boxes with monogrammed lids. An umbrella leaned against an open steamer trunk, and, when I observed that its handle was Bakelite, my new land-lady unpinned her saucer of cherries and predicted that the two of us were going to get along famously.

And for many months, we did. Rosemary lived on the ground floor, in a set of closed-off rooms she referred to as her "chambers." The door that led to them opened onto the parlor, and when I stood outside I could sometimes hear her television. This seemed to me a kind of betrayal, like putting a pool table inside the Great Pyramid, but she assured me that the set was an old one—"My 'Model Tee Vee,'" she called it.

My room was upstairs, and in a letter home I described it as "hunky-dory." How else to capture my peeling, buckled wallpaper and the way that it brought everything together. The bed, the desk, the brass-plated floor lamp: it was all there waiting for me, and though certain pieces had seen better days—the guest chair, for instance, was missing its seat—at least everything was uniformly old. From my window I could see the parking lot, and beyond that the busy road leading to the restaurant. It pleased Rosemary that I worked in such a venerable place. "It suits you," she said. "And don't feel bad about washing dishes. I think even Gable did it for a while."

"Did he?"

I felt so clever, catching all her references. The other boarder didn't even know who Charlie Chan was, and the guy was half Korean! I'd see him in the hall from time to time—a chemistry major, I think he was. There was a third room as well, but because of some water damage Rosemary was having a hard time renting it. "Not that I care so much," she told me. "In my business, it's more about quality than quantity."

I moved in at the beginning of January, and throughout that winter my life felt like a beautiful dream. I'd come home at the end of the day and Rosemary would be sitting in the parlor, both of us fully costumed. "Aha!" she'd say. "Just the young man I was looking for." Then she'd pull out some new treasure she'd bought at an estate sale and explain what made it so valuable. "On most of the later Fire King loaf pans, the trademark helmet is etched rather than embossed."

The idea was that we were different, not like the rest of America, with its Fuzzbusters and shopping malls and rotating showerheads. "If it's not new and shiny, they don't want anything to do with it," Rosemary would complain. "Give them the Liberty Bell, and they'd bitch about the crack. That's how folks are nowadays. I've seen it."

There was a radio station in Raleigh that broadcast old programs, and sometimes at night, when the reception was good, we'd sit on the davenport and listen to Jack Benny or *Fibber McGee and Molly*. Rosemary might mend a worn WAC uniform with her old-timey sewing kit, while I'd stare into the fireplace and wish that it still worked. Maybe we'd leaf through some old *Look* magazines. Maybe the wind would rattle the windows, and we'd draw a quilt over our laps and savor the heady scent of mothballs.

I hoped our lives would continue this way forever, but inevitably the past came knocking. Not the good kind that was collectible but the bad kind that had arthritis. One afternoon in early April, I returned from work to find a lost-looking, white-haired woman sitting in the parlor. Her fingers were stiff and gnarled, so rather than shake hands I offered a little salute. "Sister Sykes" was how she introduced herself. I thought that was maybe what they called her in church, but then Rosemary walked out of her chambers and told me through gritted teeth that this was a professional name.

"Mother here was a psychic," she explained. "Had herself a tarot deck and a crystal ball and told people whatever stupid malarkey they wanted to hear."

"That I did." Sister Sykes chuckled.

You'd think that someone who occasionally wore a turban herself would like having a psychic as a mom, but Rosemary was over it. "If she'd forecast thirty years ago that I'd wind up having to take care of her, I would have put my head in the oven and killed myself," she told me.

When June rolled around, the chemistry student graduated, and his room was rented to a young man named Chaz, who worked on a road construction crew. "You know those guys that hold the flags?" he said. "Well, that's me. That's what I do."

His face, like his name, was chiseled and memorable and, after deciding that he was too handsome, I began to examine him for flaws. The split lower lip only added to his appeal, so I moved on to his hair, which had clearly been blow-dried, and to the strand of turquoise pebbles visible through his unbuttoned shirt.

"What are you looking at?" he asked, and before I had a chance to blush he started telling me about his ex-girlfriend. They'd lived together for six months, in a little apartment behind Fowlers grocery store, but then she cheated on him with someone named Robby, an asshole who went to UNC and majored in fucking up other people's lives. "You're not one of those college snobs, are you?" he asked.

I probably should have said "No" rather than "Not presently."

"What did you study?" he asked. "Bank robbing?"

"Excuse me?"

"Your clothes," he said. "You and that lady downstairs look like those people from *Bonnie and Clyde,* not the stars, but the other ones. The ones who fuck everything up."

"Yes, well, we're individuals."

"Individual freaks," he said, and then he laughed, suggesting that there were no hard feelings. "Anyway, I don't have time to stand around and jaw. A friend and me are hitting the bars."

He'd do this every time: start a conversation and end it abruptly, as if it had been me who was running his mouth. Before Chaz moved in, the upstairs was fairly quiet. Now I heard the sound of his radio through the wall, a rock station that made it all the harder to pretend I was living in gentler times. When he was bored, he'd knock on my door and demand that I give him a cigarette. Then he'd stand there and smoke it, complaining that my room was too clean, my sketches were too sketchy, my old-fashioned bathrobe was too old-fashioned. "Well, enough of this," he'd say. "I have my own life to lead." Three or four times a night this would happen.

As Chaz changed life on the second floor, Sister Sykes changed it on the first. I went to check my mail one morning and found Rosemary dressed just like anyone else her age: no hat or costume jewelry, just a pair of slacks and a ho-hum blouse with unpadded shoulders. She wasn't wearing makeup either and had neglected to curl her hair. "What can I tell you?" she said. "That kind of dazzle takes time, and I just don't seem to have any lately." The parlor, which had always been just so, had gone downhill as well. Now there were cans of iced tea mix sitting on the Victrola, and boxed pots and pans parked in the corner where the credenza used to be. There was no more listening to Jack Benny because that was Sister Sykes's bath time. "The queen bee," Rosemary called her.

Later that summer, just after the Fourth of July, I came downstairs and found a pair of scuffed white suitcases beside the front door. I hoped that someone was on his way out—Chaz, specifically—but it appeared that the luggage was coming rather than going. "Meet my daughter," Rosemary said, this with the same grudging tone she'd used to introduce her mother. The young woman—I'll call her Ava—took a rope of hair from the side of her head and stuck it in her mouth. She was a skinny thing and very pale, dressed in jeans and a Western-style shirt. "In her own little world," Sister Sykes observed.

Rosemary would tell me later that her daughter had just been released from a mental institution, and though I tried to act surprised I don't think I was very convincing. It was like she was on acid almost, the way she'd sit and examine something long after it lost its mystery: an ashtray, a dried-up moth, Chaz's blow-dryer in the upstairs bathroom. Everything got equal attention, including my room. There were no lockable doors on the second floor. The keys had been lost years earlier, so Ava just wandered in whenever she felt like it. I'd come home after a full day of work—my clothes smelling of wet garbage, my shoes squishy with dishwater—and find her sitting on my bed or standing like a zombie behind my door.

"You scared me," I'd say, and she'd stare into my face until I turned away.

The situation at Rosemary's sank to a new low when Chaz lost his job. "I was overqualified," he told me, but, as the days passed, his story became more elaborate, and he felt an ever-increasing urge to share it with me. He started knocking more often, not caring that it was 6:00 a.m. or well after midnight. "And another thing . . . ," he'd say, stringing together ten separate conversations. He got into a fight that left him with a black eye. He threw his radio out the window and then scattered the broken pieces throughout the parking lot.

Late one evening he came to my door, and when I opened it he grabbed me around the waist and lifted me off the floor. This might sound innocent, but his was not a cele-bratory gesture. We hadn't won a game or been granted a stay of execution, and carefree people don't call you a "hand puppet of the Dark Lord" when they pick you up without your consent. I knew then that there was something seri-ously wrong with the guy, but I couldn't put a name to it. I guess I thought that Chaz was too good-looking to be crazy.

When he started slipping notes under my door, I decided it was time to update my thinking. "Now I'm going to die and come back on the same day," one of them read. It wasn't just the messages, but the writing itself that spooked me, the letters all jittery and butting up against one another. Some of his notes included diagrams, and flames rendered in red ink. When he started leaving them for Rosemary, she called him down to the parlor and told him he had to leave. For a minute or two, he seemed to take it well, but then he thought better of it and threatened to return as a vapor.

"Did he say 'viper'?" Sister Sykes asked.

Chaz's parents came a week later and asked if any of us had seen him. "He's schizophrenic, you see, and sometimes he goes off his medication."

I'd thought that Rosemary would be sympathetic, but she was sick to death of mental illness, just as she was sick of old people, and of having to take in boarders to make ends meet. "If he was screwy, you should have told me before he moved in," she said to Chaz's father. "I can't have people like that running through my house. What with these antiques, it's just not safe." The man's eyes wandered around the parlor, and through them I saw what he did: a dirty room full of junk. It had never been anything more than that, but for some reason—the heat, maybe, or the couple's heavy, almost contagious sense of despair—every gouge and smudge jumped violently into focus. More depressing still was the thought that I belonged here, that I fit in.

For years the university had been trying to buy Rosemary's property. Representatives would come to the door, and her accounts of these meetings seemed torn from a late-night movie. "So I said to him, 'But don't you see? This isn't just a house. It's my home, sir. My home.'"

They didn't want the building, of course, but the land. With every passing semester, it became more valuable, and she was smart to hold out for as long as she did. I don't know what the final offer was, but Rosemary accepted it. She signed the papers with a vintage fountain pen and was still holding it when she came to give me the news. This was in August, and I was lying on my floor, making a sweat angel. A part of me was sad that the house was being sold, but another, bigger part—the part that loved air-conditioning— was more than ready to move on. It was pretty clear that as far as the restaurant was concerned, I was never going to advance beyond dishwashing. Then, too, it was hard to live in a college town and not go to college. The students I saw out my window were a constant reminder that I was just spinning my wheels, and I was beginning to imagine how I would feel in another ten years, when they started looking like kids to me.

A few days before I left, Ava and I sat together on the front porch. It had just begun to rain when she turned, and asked, "Did I ever tell you about my daddy?"

This was more than I'd ever heard her say, and before continuing she took off her shoes and socks and set them on the floor beside her. Then she drew a hank of hair into her mouth and told me that her father had died of a heart attack. "Said he didn't feel well, and an hour later he just plunked over."

I asked a few follow-up questions and learned that he had died on November 19, 1963. Three days after that, the funeral was held, and while riding from the church to the cemetery Ava looked out the window and noticed that everyone she passed was crying. "Old people, college students, even the colored men at the gas station—the soul brothers, or whatever we're supposed to call them now."

It was such an outmoded term, I just had to use it myself. "How did the soul brothers know your father?"

"That's just it," she said. "No one told us until after the burial that Kennedy had been shot. It happened when we were in the church, so that's what everyone was so upset about. The president, not my father."

She then put her socks back on and walked into the parlor, leaving both me and her shoes behind.

When I'd tell people about this later, they'd say, "Oh, come on," because it was all too much, really. An arthritic psychic, a ramshackle house, and either two or four crazy people, depending on your tolerance for hats. Harder to swallow is that each of us was such a cliché. It was as if you'd taken a Carson McCullers novel, mixed it with a Tennessee Williams play, and dumped all the sets and characters into a single box. I didn't add that Sister Sykes used to own a squirrel monkey, as it only amounted to overkill. Even the outside world seems suspect here: the leafy college town, the restaurant with its classical music.

I never presumed that Kennedy's death was responsible for Ava's breakdown. Plenty of people endure startling coincidences with no lasting aftereffects, so I imagine her troubles started years earlier. As for Chaz, I later learned that it was fairly common for schizophrenics to go off their medication. I'd think it strange that the boardinghouse attracted both him and me, but that's what cheap places do—draw in people with no money. An apartment of my own was unthinkable at that time of my life, and even if I'd found an affordable one it wouldn't have satisfied my fundamental need to live in a communal past, or what I imagined the past to be like: a world full of antiques. What I could never fathom, and still can't, really, is that at one point all those things were new. The wheezing Victrola, the hulking davenport—how were they any different from the eight-track tape player or my parents' Scandinavian dining room set? Given enough time, I guess anything can look good. All it has to do is survive.

# Buddy, Can You Spare a Tie?

When my older sister and I were young, our mother used to pick out our school clothes and hang them on our door-knobs before we went to bed. "How's that?" she'd ask, and we'd marvel at these stain-free, empty versions of ourselves. There's no denying that children were better dressed back then: no cutoffs, no T-shirts, and velveteen for everybody. The boys looked like effeminate homosexuals, and the girls like Bette Davis in *What Ever Happened to Baby Jane?* It was only at Halloween that we were allowed to choose our own outfits. One year I went as a pirate, but from then on I was always a hobo. It's a word you don't often hear anymore. Along with "tramp," it's been replaced by "homeless person," which isn't the same thing. Unlike someone who was evicted or lost his house in a fire, the hobo roughed it by choice. Being at liberty, unencumbered by bills and mortgages, better suited his drinking schedule, and so he found shelter wherever he could, never a bum, but something much less threatening, a figure of merriment, almost.

None of this had anything to do with my choice of Halloween costume. I went as a hobo because it was easy: a charcoal beard smudged on the cheeks, pants with holes in them, a hat, an oversized shirt, and a sport coat stained with food and cigarette ash. Take away the hat, and it's exactly how I've dressed since 1978. Throughout the eighties, the look had a certain wayfarer appeal, but now, accented by amber teeth and nicotine-stained fingers, the word I most often hear is "gnarly." If Hugh is asked directions to the nearest Citibank, I am asked directions to the nearest plasma bank.

This is not to say that I have no standards. The year I turned forty, I threw out all my denim, so instead of crummy jeans I walk around in crummy slacks. I don't own a pair of sunglasses, or anything with writing on it, and I wear shorts only in Normandy, which is basically West Virginia without the possums. It's not that I haven't bought nice clothes—it's just that I'm afraid to put them on, certain they'll get burned or stained.

The only expensive thing I actually wear is a navy blue cashmere sweater. It cost four hundred dollars and looks like it was wrestled from the mouth of a tiger. "What a shame," the dry cleaner said the first time I brought it in. The sweater had been folded into a loaf-sized bundle, and she stroked it, the way you might a freshly dead rabbit. "It's so soft," she whispered.

I didn't dare tell her that the damage was intentional. The lengthy run across the left shoulder, the dozens of holes in the arms and torso; each was specifically placed by the design team. Ordinarily I avoid things that have been distressed, but this sweater had been taken a step further and ruined. Having been destroyed, it is now indestructible, meaning I can wear it without worry. For half this price, I could have bought an intact sweater, thrown it to a tiger, and wrenched it back myself, but after a certain age, who has that kind of time?

My second most expensive purchase was a pair of shoes that look like they belong to a clown. They have what my sister Amy calls "a negative heel," meaning, I think, that I'm actually taller with just my socks on. While not the ideal choice for someone my size, they're the only shoes I have that don't leave me hobbling. My feet are completely flat, but for most of my life they were still shaped like feet. Now, thanks to bunions, they're shaped more like states, wide boring ones that nobody wants to drive through.

My only regret is that I didn't buy more clown shoes—a dozen pairs, two dozen, enough to last me for the rest of my life. The thought of the same footwear day after day might bother some people, but if I have one fashion rule, it's this: never change. That said, things change. I like to think I'm beyond the reach of trends, but my recent infatuation with the man-purse suggests otherwise. It seems I'm still susceptible to embarrassing, rashlike phases, and though I try my best to beat them down, I don't always succeed. In hopes of avoiding future humiliation, I've arranged some of my more glaring mistakes into short lessons I try to review whenever buying anything new. They are as follows:

## Guys Look Like Asses in Euro-style Glasses

High school taught me a valuable lesson about glasses: don't wear them. Contacts have always seemed like too much work, so instead I just squint, figuring that if something is more than six feet away I'll just deal with it when I get there. It might have been different in the eighteenth century when people wore nearly identical wire rims, but today's wide selection means that in choosing a pair of frames you're forced to declare yourself a certain type of person, or, in my case, a certain type of insect.

In 1976 my glasses were so big I could clean the lenses with a squeegee. Not only were they huge, they were also green with Playboy emblems embossed on the stems. Today these frames sound ridiculous, but back then they were actually quite stylish. Time is cruel to everything but seems to have singled out eyeglasses for special punishment. What looks good now is guaranteed to embarrass you twenty years down the line, which is, of course, the whole problem with fashion. Though design may reach an apex, it never settles back and calls it quits. Rather, it just keeps reaching, attempting to satisfy our insatiable need to buy new stuff. Squinting is timeless, but so, unfortunately, are the blinding headaches that often accompany it.

In the late 1990s, when I could no longer see my feet, I made an appointment with a Paris eye doctor who ran some tests and sent me off to buy some glasses. I'd like to blame my choice of frames on the fact that I couldn't see them clearly. I'd like to say they were forced upon me, but neither excuse is true. I made the selection of my own free will and chose them because I thought they made me look smart and international. The frames were made of dark plastic, with rectangular lenses not much larger than my eyes. There was something vaguely familiar about them, but I couldn't quite put my finger on it. After picking them up I spent a great deal of time in front of the mirror, pretending to share intelligent comments regarding the state of Europe. "Discount our neighbors to the east, and I think you'll find we've got a sleeping giant on our hands," I'd say.

I'd been wearing the glasses for close to a year when I finally realized who they rightfully belonged to. This person was not spotted on the cover of *Le Point* or *Foreign Affairs*—in fact, it wasn't even a real person. I was in New York, passing through a toy booth at the Chelsea flea market when I recognized my frames on the smug plastic face of Mrs. Beasley, a middle-aged doll featured on the 1960s television program *Family Affair*. This was the talking version, original, and in her box.

"Would you like me to pull the string?" the booth owner asked. I said no, and as I hurried away I could swear I heard a small whiny voice saying something about a sleeping giant.


## Better the Glasses Than Sweaty Fake Asses

Without a doubt, my best attributes are my calves. I don't know if they're earned or genetic, but they're almost comically muscular, the equivalent of Popeye's forearms. For years I was complimented on them. Strangers stopped me in the streets. But that all changed with the widespread availability of implants. Now when people look at my legs I sense them wondering why I didn't have my ass done at the same time.

It's how women with naturally shapely breasts must feel—robbed and full of rage.

In high school I bought a pair of platform shoes, partly because they were popular and partly because I wanted to be tall. I don't mean that I prayed for height—it never occurred to me that an extra three inches would solve any of my problems. I was just curious. It's like living on the ground floor and wondering what the view is like two stories up. The shoes I bought were red suede with a solid, slablike sole. I'd have looked less ridiculous with bricks tied to my feet, but of course I couldn't see it back then. Other guys could get away with platforms, but on me they read as desperation. I wore them to my high school graduation and made a little deal with myself: if I could cross the stage and make it home without falling, I'd learn to accept myself and be happy with what I had. In children's stories, such lessons are learned for life, but in the real world they usually need reinforcing every few years.

Which takes us to the mid-1990s: my biggest physical gripe is not my height or the arrangement of my facial features, but the fact that I don't have an ass. Others in my family fared pretty well in that department, but mine amounts to little more than a stunted peach. I'd pretty much resigned myself to long sport coats and untucked shirts when I came across an ad, the boldfaced headline reading, "Tired of Ill-Fitting Pants?" I don't recall the product's exact name, but it amounted to a fake padded butt, the shapely synthetic cheeks sewn into the lining of a generous brief. I put it on my Christmas list and was given a pair by my friend Jodi, who waited a few weeks before admitting she'd actually sent me a woman's ass—in essence, a fanny.

And so it was. But that didn't stop me from wearing it.

Though pear-shaped, my artificial bottom was not without its charms. It afforded me a confidence I hadn't felt in years and gave me an excuse to buy flattering slacks and waist-length jackets. While walking to the grocery store or post office, I'd invariably find myself passed by a stranger who'd clearly thought he was following somebody else: Little Miss January, or Pamela Anderson's stunt double.

My fanny kept me warm in the winter and early spring, but come hot weather it turned on me. The problem was the nylon padding, which, when coupled with a high tempera-ture, acted much like a heating pad, causing me to sweat away what little ass I'd had in the first place. Chafed and bony, by early June my natural bottom resembled a rusted coin slot.

It was fun while it lasted, but unless I tore myself away, I knew I'd be relying on prosthetics for the rest of my life. After one last walk around the block, I retired my fanny to its box in the hall closet. There it called to me, sirenlike, until a houseguest arrived, a tall, forlorn-looking woman who compared her ass, and not too favorably, to a cast-iron skillet. "I've got just the thing for you," I said. It wasn't my intention to give it to her, but after she tried it on, and I saw how happy it made her, how could I not? The woman stayed with us for a week, and while I hated for her to leave, I sort of loved watching her go.

## The Feminine Mistake

"Buy it." This is my sister Amy's advice in regard to every-thing, from a taxidermied horse head to a camouflage thong. "Just get it," she says. "You'll feel better."

Eye something closely or pick it up for further inspection, and she'll move in to justify the cost. "It's not really *that* expensive, and, besides, won't you be getting a tax refund? Go on. Treat yourself."

The object in question may be completely wrong for me, but still she'll push, effectively clouding my better instincts. She's not intentionally evil, my sister, she just loves to see that moment, the split second when doubt is replaced by complete conviction. *Yes,* I'll think. *I* have *worked hard, and buying this will bring me the happiness I truly deserve.* When handing over my money, I'm convinced that the purchase is not only right, but hard-won and necessary.

In the year 2000 I went on a diet and lost a little too much weight. Amy and I would go out shopping, and when nothing fit me in the men's department she'd slowly guide me toward the women's. "This is nice," she'd say. "Why don't you try it on?" Once it was a sweater with buttons running down the left side instead of the right. "Oh, come on," she said. "Do you honestly think people pay attention to things like that?" It did seem unlikely that someone would notice the placement of a button. But what about the shoulder pads?

"We can remove them," she said. "Go ahead. Get it. It'll look good on you."

Though she'd promised that no one would ever notice, you could always tell when I'd been clothes shopping with Amy. I was the guy at the crowded steak house, removing the jacket with a label reading Sassy Sport. That was me with the darts in his shirt, the fabric slack where it should be filled with breasts. I'd step up to the restroom urinal and remember that these particular pants zipped up the back. At this point, people noticed. Amy suggested that a calf-length vest would solve the problem, but I had a better idea. It was called the boy's department.

## With a Pal Like This, Who Needs Enemies

I've always liked the idea of accessories, those little pick-me-ups designed to invigorate what has come to feel drab and predictable. A woman might rejuvenate her outfit with a vintage Hermès scarf or jaunty rope belt, but the options for men aren't nearly so interesting. I have no use for cuff links or suspenders, and while I'll occasionally pick up a new tie it hardly leaves me feeling "kicky." Hidden accessories can do the trick, but again they're mainly the province of women. Garter belt and lingerie—yes. Sock garter and microbrief—no.

It was my search for something discreet, masculine, and practical that led me to the Stadium Pal, an external catheter currently being marketed to sports fans, truck drivers, and anyone else who's tired of searching for a bathroom. At first inspection, the device met all my criteria:

Was it masculine? Yes, and proudly so. Knowing that no sensible female would ever voluntarily choose to pee in her pants, the manufacturers went ahead and designed the product exclusively for men. Unlike a regular catheter, which is inserted directly into the penis, the Stadium Pal connects by way of a self-adhesive condom, which is then attached to a flexible rubber tube. Urine flows through the tube and collects in the "freedom leg bag," conveniently attached to the user's calf. The bag can be emptied and reused up to twelve times, making it both disgusting *and* cost effective. And what could be manlier?

Was it discreet? According to the brochure, unless you wore it with shorts, no one needed to know anything about it.

Was it practical? At the time, yes. I don't drive or attend football games, but I did have a book tour coming up, and the possibilities were endless. Five glasses of iced tea followed by a long public reading? *Thanks, Stadium Pal!* The window seat on an overbooked coast-to-coast flight? *Don't mind if I do!*

I ordered myself a Stadium Pal and realized that while it might make sense in a hospital, it really wasn't very practical for day-to-day use. In an open-air sporting arena, a piping hot thirty-two-ounce bag of urine might go unnoticed, but not so in a stuffy airplane or small, crowded bookstore. An hour after christening it, I smelled like a nursing home. On top of that, I found that it was hard to pee and do other things at the same time. Reading out loud, discussing my beverage options with the flight attendant, checking into a fine hotel: each activity required its own separate form of concentration, and while no one knew exactly what I was up to, it was pretty clear that something was going on. I think it was my face that gave me away. That and my oddly swollen calf.

What ultimately did me in was the self-adhesive condom. Putting it on was no problem, but its removal qualified as what, in certain cultures, is known as a *bris*. Wear it once, and you'll need a solid month to fully recover. It will likely be a month in which you'll weigh the relative freedom of peeing in your pants against the unsightly discomfort of a scab-covered penis, ultimately realizing that, in terms of a convenient accessory, you're better off with a new watchband.


## Never Listen to My Father

It was the weekend of my brother's wedding, and my father was trying to talk me into a bow tie. "Come on," he said. "Live a little!" Outside the window, waves pounded against the shore. Seabirds soared overhead screeching what sounded like "Queer, queer, queer."

When worn with a tuxedo, a bow tie makes a certain kind of sense, but with a suit I wasn't sure I trusted it. The model my father chose was red-and-white-striped, the size of a luna moth, and as he advanced I backed toward the door.

"It's just a strip of cloth," he said. "No different than a regular tie. Who the hell cares if it falls straight or swags from side to side?"

My inner hobo begged me not to do it, but I foolishly caved in, thinking it couldn't hurt to make an old man happy. Then again, maybe I was just tired and wanted to get through the evening saying as little as possible. The thing about a bow tie is that it does a lot of the talking for you. "Hey!" it shouts. "Look over here. I'm friendly, I'm interesting!" At least that's what I thought it was saying. It was a great evening, and at the end of it I thanked my father for his recommendation. "I knew you'd like it," he said. "A guy like you was made for a bow tie."

A short while after the wedding, while preparing for a monthlong cross-country trip, I bought one of my own and discovered that it said different things to different people. This bow tie was paisley, its dominant color a sort of midnight blue, and while a woman in Columbus thought it made me look scholarly, her neighbor in Cleveland suggested I might be happy selling popcorn.

"Like what's his name," she said. "The dead guy."

"Paul Newman is dead?"

"No," she said. "That other one. Orville Redenbacher."

Name association was big, as were my presumed interests in vaudeville and politics. In St. Louis the bow tie was characterized as "very Charlie McCarthy," while in Chicago a young man defined it as "the pierced eyebrow of the Republican party." This sent the bow tie back into my suitcase, where it begged forgiveness, evoking the names of Daniel Patrick Moynihan and Senator Paul Simon. "Oh come on," it said. "*They* were Democrats. Please let me out."

Political affiliation aside, I know what the young Chicagoan had meant. It's a pretty sorry world when wearing a bow tie amounts to being "out there." I'm just not sure which is worse, the people who consider it out there that someone's wearing a bow tie, or the person who thinks he's out there for wearing it.

I wore my bow tie to twenty-seven cities, and in each of them I found myself begging for affirmation. "Do you *really* think it looks OK? *Really?*" I simply could not tell whether it was right for me. Alone in an elevator I'd have moments of clarity, but just as I reached for the knot, I'd recall some compliment forced from a stranger. *"Oh, but it looks so adorable, so cute! I just want to take you home!"*

I'm told by my father that when I was an infant, people would peek into my carriage and turn to my mother saying,

"Goodness, what a . . . baby." I've never been described as cute, so why now? What was the bow tie saying behind my back? And how could I put it in contact with twenty-year-old marines rather than seventy-year-old women?

It was my friend Frank, a writer in San Francisco, who finally set me straight. When asked about my new look he put down his fork and stared at me for a few moments. "A bow tie announces to the world that you can no longer get an erection."

And that is *exactly* what a bow tie says. Not that you're powerless, but that you're impotent. People offer to take you home not because you're sexy but because you're sex*less,* a neutered cat in need of a good stiff cuddle. This doesn't mean that the bow tie is necessarily *wrong* for me, just that it's a bit premature. When I explained this to my father, he rolled his eyes. Then he said that I had no personality. "You're a lump."

He sees the bow tie, at least in my case, as a bright string wrapped around a run-of-the-mill gift. On opening the package, the receiver is bound to be disappointed, so why set yourself up? It's a question my father answers in the pained, repetitive voice of a parole officer. According to him, you set yourself up in order to *exceed* those expectations. "You dress to give a hundred percent, and then you give a hundred and twenty. Jesus," he says. "You're a grown man. Haven't we been through this?"

Grown or not, I still feel best—more true to myself—when dressed like a hobo. The die was cast for me on Halloween, and though it has certainly not been proven, I think it's this way for everyone. Look at my brother, who dressed as an ax murderer, and at my sister Amy, who went as a confused prostitute. As for the other kids in my neighborhood, the witches and ghosts, the vampires, robots, and, oh God, the mummies, I can only hope that, like me, they work at home.

# Road Trips

The house I grew up in is located in a subdivision, and when my family first arrived the front yards were, if not completely bare, then at least close to it. It was my father who rallied the neighbors and initiated a campaign to plant maples along the side of the road. Holes were dug, saplings were delivered, and my sisters and I remarked that, with the exception of birds, trees were the only things on earth that weren't cute when they were babies. They looked like branches stuck into the ground, and I remember thinking that by the time they were fully grown I would be old.

And that's pretty much what happened.

Throughout my teens and early twenties, I'd wonder if my father hadn't made a mistake and ordered pygmy maples, if such a thing exists. During my thirties, they grew maybe three feet, tops, but after that their development was astonishing. The last time I saw them, they were actual trees, so

tall that the upper branches on the left side of the road min-
gled with those on the right, forming a solid canopy of
shade. This was a few years ago. I was in Raleigh for the
night, and my father took me to a party hosted by one of his
neighbors. I used to know everyone on our street, but since
I'd left there had been a lot of turnover. People die, or move
into condominiums, and their homes are sold to young married couples who scrap the earth-toned carpets and build
islands in the kitchens. The interiors of these houses used to
look the same, and, eventually, as each is bought and remod-
eled, they'll look the same again, but in a different way.

The party was held at what I thought of as "the Rosens'
place," though that was two owners ago. The hostess was
one of the new people, as were her guests, and it surprised
me that my dad knew everyone's name. Here were Phil and
Becky, Ashley and Dave, and a high-spirited fifteen-year-old,
who threw himself onto the sofa with great flourish and
referred to my father as a she, as in "Lou Sedaris, who
invited *her?*"

"My son is gay!" the boy's mother announced, as if none
of us had figured this out yet. He may have attended one of
those magnet schools for the arts, but still it floored me that
a ninth grader in Raleigh, North Carolina—on the street
where I grew up—could comfortably identify himself as a
homosexual. I felt like someone in a ten-pound leg brace
meeting a beneficiary of the new polio vaccine. "*She* just
happens to be my father, young man, and I'd appreciate it if
you'd show her a little respect."

"Yes, ma'am."

When I was this kid's age, you'd be burned alive for such
talk. Being a homosexual was unthinkable, and so you

denied it, and found a girlfriend who was willing to settle for the sensitive type. On dates, you'd remind her that sex before marriage was just that, sex: what dogs did in the front yard. This as opposed to making love, which was more what you were about. A true union of souls could take anywhere from eight to ten years to properly establish, but you were willing to wait, and for this the mothers loved you. You sometimes discussed it with them over an iced tea, preferably on the back porch when your girlfriend's brother was mowing the lawn with his shirt off.

I kept my secret to myself until I was twenty years old, and I might have kept it even longer had a couple not picked me up when I was hitchhiking one night. It was 1:00 a.m., and the last thing I expected was a ride in a Cadillac. Stranger still was opening the back door and discovering that the people inside were old—my parents' age, at least. The car smelled of hair tonic. A CB radio crackled from its berth beside the steering wheel, and I wondered who they could be talking to at this time of night. Then I noticed that the woman was wearing a negligee. She leaned forward to press the cigarette lighter, and I could see a tag the size of an index card showing through the sheer fabric at the back of her neck. We drove in silence for a mile or two before the man turned in his seat and asked, as if he were inquiring about my health, "How'd you like to eat my wife's pussy?"

Then the woman turned as well, and it was to her that I made my confession: "I'm a homosexual." I'd been waiting to unload this for as long as I could remember, and, amid the screeching of tires and the violent swerve to the side of the road, I felt all the relief I'd imagined I would.

A few months later I said the same thing to my best

61

friend, Ronnie, who pretended to be surprised and then admitted that she'd known all along. "It's the way you run," she said. "You let your arms flop instead of holding them to your sides."

"Work on your run," I wrote in my diary the following morning.

At the age that many would consider their heyday, I had not had sex with anyone. My confessions did nothing to alter this situation, but for the first time in my life I felt that somebody actually knew me. Three somebodies, to be exact. Two were roaming the highway in a Cadillac, doing God knows what with a CB radio, but the other was as close to me as my own skin, and I could now feel the undiluted pleasure of her company.

Next on my list of people to tell was my former college roommate, Todd. I hitched from Raleigh to Kent, Ohio, but once I got there, the time didn't seem quite right. It was harder telling a guy than it was telling a girl, and harder still when you'd taken too much acid and were trying to keep the little people from sticking pins in your eyes.

After my failure in Ohio, I headed back south. It was early December, and I had forgotten how cold it could get in the Midwest.

Todd had suggested that I take his down jacket, but I thought it was unsightly, so here I was in a thrift-shop overcoat that didn't even button all the way up. He'd also offered a sweater that belted at the waist. It was thick and patterned in bright colors, the sort of thing a peasant might wear while herding llamas, but I'd said, "No, it might ruin my silhouette." That was the phrase I had used, and now I was paying for my vanity—because what difference would it have made? "Oh, goodness, I can't give *him* a ride. He looks too lumpy."

I'd left Kent at eight in the morning, and the next five hours had taken me less than fifty miles. Now it was lunchtime—not that there was anywhere to buy it, or anything much to buy it with. It began to rain, and, just as I thought of turning back, a tow truck pulled over and the driver motioned for me to get in. He told me that he wasn't going far—just thirty miles up the road—but I was grateful for the warmth and climbed into the passenger seat determined to soak up as much of it as I possibly could.

"So," the man said after I had settled in, "where you from?" I pegged him to be somewhere between old and ancient, midforties, maybe, with gray-tinged sideburns shaped like boots.

I told him I was from North Carolina, and he slapped his palm against the steering wheel. "North Carolina. Now, there's a state for you. My brother and me went down on vacation—Topsail Beach, I think it was—and we just had the time of our lives."

When the man turned to address me, I noticed that his ears stuck out and that his forehead was divided almost in two by a vertical dent that started at the intersection of his eyebrows and ran to within an inch of his hairline. It was the type of thing associated with heavy thought, but this was so deep and painful-looking that it might have been left by a hatchet.

"Yessiree, good old North Carolina," the man continued. "N.C., I guess you call it down there."

He went on about the state's climate and the friendliness of its people, and then he looked into his side mirror to monitor the progress of an advancing eighteen-wheeler. "All I know is that if anyone wanted to give me a blow job, or have me give him one, I'd do it."

This came out of nowhere, and what threw me was the way he'd attached it to his previous observation. North Carolina is temperate and populated with well-meaning people; therefore I will engage in oral sex with another man.

"Well," I said, "they're not *all* friendly. I remember one time I was walking down the street and a group of men grabbed me by the arms and spit in my face." The story was true, and, at its mention, I recalled the stench of their sour, phlegm-clotted saliva. I expected, and reasonably so, that the tow truck driver might ask for details: "Who were these men? Why did they spit in your face?"

But instead he picked up where he'd left off. "I mean to tell you that I would actually crouch down on this seat and perform fellatio," he said. "Either that or I'd sit up while someone performed it on me. I really would."

"Then, another time," I told him, "another time this guy threatened to knock my teeth down my throat. I was just standing there minding my own business, and all of a sudden there he was." This was a lie, or at least the last part was. The man had threatened to knock my teeth down my throat, but only because my friend and I had given him the finger and called him a crusty old redneck. "I was twelve years old at the time," I said. "In Ohio you'd never threaten a kid like that, but down in North Carolina it's par for the course."

*Par for the course.* I was sounding more idiotic by the minute—not that it mattered.

"I mean, why *not* give someone a blow job?" the driver

said. "It's just a penis, right? Probably no worse for you than smoking."

Outside the moving truck were flat, barren fields, some bordered by stands of trees and others stretching without interruption out to the horizon. One second they'd appear as a blur, and then the windshield wiper would make its shuddering pass and everything would leap back into focus. A station wagon pulled in front of us, and the children in the backseat signaled for my driver to blow his horn. He seemed not to notice them, and just as I thought to bring it to his attention I realized that the request included the word "blow." And so I let it drop and turned my attention back to the landscape.

Had I been able to address the real subject, I'd have told this man that I was saving myself for the right person. I wanted my first time to be special, meaning that I would know the other guy's name and, I hoped, his telephone number. After sex, we would lie in each other's arms and review the events that had brought us to this point. I could not predict exactly what this conversation would sound like, but I had not imagined it to include such lines as "I knew this would happen five minutes ago, the moment you climbed into my tow truck." Not that I minded this man's profession. It was the other stuff that bothered me: his dent, his forwardness, and his persistent refusal to turn the goddamn page. He sounded like me when I sensed that drugs were around: "All I know is that if someone wants to get high, or wants to watch while I smoke his dope, I'll do it. I really will."

I cringed to think of myself, skeeving pot off my friends and believing all the while that I was sounding casual. After dropping in uninvited and basically forcing someone to share his drugs, I'd pocket the roach and take my leave, saying, "That's the last time I let you fuck me up like this, I mean it."

"Yes, indeed," the tow truck driver said. "A little oral give-and-take would feel *pretty* good right about now."

I could have ended it so simply. "I don't think my girl-friend would like that too much," I might have said, but I wanted to put that particular lie behind me. There was my life *before* I told a strange woman in a negligee that I was a homosexual, and now there would be my life *after*, two chapters so dissimilar in style and content that they might have been written by different people. That's what I'd hoped, but of course it wouldn't work out that way. I needed a story that I could live with, and so I compromised and told the tow truck driver that I had an *ex*-girlfriend. "We just broke up a week ago, and now I'm going home to win her back."

"So?" he said. "I got an ex-*wife*. I got a current one, too, but that doesn't mean it wouldn't feel good to give someone a blow job, or to have somebody give you one while you laid back and enjoyed it a little."

Mine was the lie that got you nowhere, and, as I berated myself for wasting it, the driver took his right hand off the steering wheel and laid it on the seat between us. For a moment it was idle, and then it began to lumber in my direction, its movement as hesitant and blocky as a turtle's. "Yessiree," its owner said.

There would come times in later years when I would have sex against my wishes. No one forced me, exactly—it wasn't that. I just wasn't sure how to say "Go. Get out. I don't want this." Often, I'd feel sorry for the guy: he was deformed through no fault of his own, he bought all his clothes at Sears, he said he loved me on the first date. Once or twice I'd be too scared to say no, but this particular man didn't frighten me. I looked at him in much the same way that the fifteen-year-old, my father's neighbor, must have looked at me: as a relic of an earlier era, when trees were stubs, women could be deceived, and everything inside your home was the color of rust or dirt.

When the shambling hand at last reached my coat, I thought of how I'd assert myself and tell the driver that this was an excellent place for me to get out.

"What?" he'd say? "Here? Are you sure?"

The man would pull over, and I would take my place by the side of the road, a virgin with three dollars in his pocket, and his whole life ahead of him.

# What I Learned

It's been interesting to walk around campus this afternoon, as when *I* went to Princeton things were completely different. This chapel, for instance—I remember when it was just a clearing, cordoned off with sharp sticks. Prayer was compulsory back then, and you couldn't just fake it by moving your lips; you had to know the words, and really mean them. I'm dating myself, but this was before Jesus Christ. We worshipped a God named Sashatiba, who had five eyes, including one on the Adam's apple. None of us ever met him, but word had it that he might appear at any moment, so we were always at the ready. *Whatever you do, don't look at his neck,* I used to tell myself.

It's funny now, but I thought about it a lot. Some people thought about it a little too much, and it really affected their academic performance. Again, I date myself, but back then we were on a pass-fail system. If you passed, you got to live, and if you failed you were burned alive on a pyre that's now the Transgender Studies Building. Following the first grading period, the air was so thick with smoke you could barely find your way across campus. There were those who said that it smelled like meat, no different from a barbecue, but I could tell the difference. I mean, really. Since when do you grill hair? Or sweaters? Or those dumb, chunky shoes we all used to wear?

It kept you on your toes, though, I'll say that much. If I'd been burned alive because of bad grades, my parents would have killed me, especially my father, who meant well but was just a little too gung ho for my taste. He had the whole outfit: Princeton breastplate, Princeton nightcap; he even got the velvet cape with the tiger head hanging like a rucksack from between the shoulder blades. In those days, the mascot was a saber-tooth, so you can imagine how silly it looked, and how painful it was to lean back in your chair. Then, there was his wagon, completely covered with decals and bumper stickers: "I Hold My Horses for Ivy League Schools," "My Son Was Accepted at the Best University in the United States, and All I Got Was a Bill for $168,000." On and on, which was just so . . . *wrong*.

One of the things they did back then was start you off with a modesty seminar, an eight-hour session that all the freshmen had to sit through. It might be different today, but in my time it took the form of a role-playing exercise, my classmates and I pretending to be graduates, and the teacher assuming the part of an average citizen: the soldier, the bloodletter, the whore with a heart of gold.

"Tell me, young man. Did you attend a university of higher learning?"

To anyone holding a tool or a weapon, we were trained to respond, "What? Me go to college? Whoever gave you that idea?" If, on the other hand, the character held a degree, you were allowed to say, "Sort of," or, sometimes, "I think so."

And it was the next bit that you had to get just right. Inflection was everything, and it took the foreign students forever to master it.

"So where do you sort of think you went?"

And we'd say, "Umm, Princeton?"—as if it were an oral exam, and we weren't quite sure that this was the correct answer.

"Princeton! My goodness," the teacher would say. "That must have been quite something!"

You had to let him get it out, but once he started in on how brilliant and committed you must be it was time to hold up your hands, saying, "Oh, it isn't that hard to get into."

Then he'd say, "Really? But I heard—"

"Wrong," you'd tell him. "You heard wrong. It's not that great of a school."

This was the way it had to be done. You had to play it down, which wasn't easy when your dad was out there, reading your acceptance letter into a bullhorn.

I needed to temper his enthusiasm a bit, and so I announced that I would be majoring in patricide. The Princeton program was very strong back then, the best in the country, but it wasn't the sort of thing your father could get too worked up about. Or at least, most fathers wouldn't. Mine was over the moon. "Killed by a Princeton graduate!" he said. "And my own son, no less."

My mom was actually jealous. "So what's wrong with

71

matricide?" she asked. "What, I'm not good enough to murder? You too high and mighty to take out your only mother?"

They started bickering, so in order to make peace, I promised to consider a double major.

"And how much more is *that* going to cost us?" they said.

Those last few months at home were pretty tough, but then I started my freshman year and got caught up in the life of the mind. My idol-worship class was the best, but my dad didn't get it at all. "What the hell does that have to do with patricide?" he asked.

And I said, "Umm. *Everything.*"

He didn't understand that it's all connected, that one subject leads to another and forms a kind of chain that raises its head and nods like a cobra when you're sucking on a bong after three days of no sleep. On acid, it's even wilder and appears to eat things. But not having gone to college, my dad had no concept of a well-rounded liberal arts education. He thought that all my classes should be murder-related, with no lunch breaks or anything. Fortunately, though, it doesn't work that way.

I'd told my parents I'd major in killing them, but that was just to get them off my back. In truth, I had no idea what I wanted to study, so for the first few years I took everything that came my way. History was interesting, but I have no head for dates and tend to get my eras confused. I enjoyed pillaging and astrology, but the thing that ultimately stuck was comparative literature. There wasn't much of it to compare back then, no more than a handful of epic poems and one novel about a lady detective, but that's part of what I liked about it. The field was new and full of possibilities.

A well-versed graduate might go *anywhere,* but try telling that to my parents.

"You mean you *won't* be killing us?" my mother said. "But I told everyone you were going for that double major."

Dad followed his "I'm-so-disappointed" speech with a lecture on career opportunities. "You're going to study literature and get a job doing what?" he said. *"Literaturizing?"*

We spent my entire vacation arguing; then, just before I went back to school, my father approached me in my bedroom. "Promise me you'll keep an open mind," he said. And as he left, he slipped an engraved dagger into my book bag.

I had many fine teachers during my years at Princeton, but the one I think of most often was my fortune-telling professor, a complete hag with wild gray hair, warts the size of new potatoes, the whole nine yards. She taught us to forecast the weather up to two weeks in advance, but ask for anything weightier, and you were likely to be disappointed.

The alchemy majors all wanted to know how much money they'd be making after graduation. "Just give us an approximate figure," they'd say, and the professor would shake her head and cover her crystal ball with a little cozy given to her by one of her previous classes. When it came to our futures, she drew the line, no matter how hard we begged—and, I mean, we really tried. I was as let down as the next guy, but, in retrospect, I can see that she acted in our best interest. Look at yourself on the day that you graduated from college, then look at yourself today. I did that recently, and it was like, "Yikes! What the hell happened?"

The answer, of course, is life. What the hag chose not to

foretell—and what we, in our certainty, could not have fath-omed—is that stuff comes up. Weird doors open. People fall into things. Maybe the engineering whiz will wind up brewing cider, not because he has to, but because he finds it challeng-ing. Who knows? Maybe the athlete will bring peace to all nations, or the class moron will go on to become the president of the United States—though that's more likely to happen at Harvard or Yale, schools that will pretty much let in anybody.

There were those who left Princeton and soared like arrows into the bosoms of power and finance, but I was not one of them. My path was a winding one, with plenty of obstacles along the way. When school was finished, I went back home, an Ivy League graduate with four years' worth of dirty laundry and his whole life ahead of him. "What are you going to do now?" my parents asked.

And I said, "Well, I was thinking of washing some of these underpants."

That took six months. Then I moved on to the shirts.

"Now what?" my parents asked.

And when I told them I didn't know, they lost what little patience they had left. "What kind of a community-college answer is that?" my mother said. "You went to the best school there is. How can you *not* know something?"

And I said, "I don't know."

In time my father stopped wearing his Princeton gear. My mother stopped talking about my "potential," and she and my dad got themselves a brown and white puppy. In terms of intelligence, it was just average, but they couldn't see that at all. "Aren't you just the smartest dog in the world?" they'd ask, and the puppy would lick their fingers in a way that was disturbingly familiar.

My first alumni weekend cheered me up a bit. It was nice to know that I wasn't the only unemployed graduate in the world, but the warm feeling evaporated when I got back home and saw that my parents had given the dog my bedroom. Above the dresser, in place of the Princeton pennant they'd bought me for my first birthday, was a banner reading "Westminster or Bust."

I could see which way the wind was blowing, and so I left and moved to the city, where a former classmate, a philosophy major, got me a job on his ragpicking crew. When the industry moved overseas—the doing of *another* former classmate—I stayed put and eventually found work skinning hides for a rat catcher, a thin, serious man with the longest beard I had ever seen.

. At night, I read and reread the handful of books I'd taken with me when I left home, and eventually, out of boredom as much as anything else, I started to write myself. It wasn't much, at first: character sketches, accounts of my day, parodies of articles in the alumni newsletter. Then, in time, I became more ambitious and began crafting little stories about my family. I read one of them out loud to the rat catcher, who'd never laughed at anything, but roared at the description of my mother and her puppy. "My mom was just the same," he said. "I graduated from Brown, and two weeks later she was raising falcons on my top bunk!" The story about my dad defecating in his neighbor's well pleased my boss so much that he asked for a copy and sent it to his own father.

This gave me the confidence to continue, and in time I completed an entire book, which was subsequently published. I presented a first edition to my parents, who started with the story about our neighbor's well, and then got up to close the drapes. Fifty pages later, they were boarding up the door and looking for ways to disguise themselves.

Other people had loved my writing, but these two didn't get it at all. "What's wrong?" I asked.

My father adjusted his makeshift turban and sketched a mustache on my mother's upper lip. "What's wrong?" he said. "I'll tell you what's wrong: you're killing us."

"But I thought that's what you wanted?"

"We did," my mother wept, "but not this way."

It hadn't occurred to me until that moment, but I seemed to have come full circle. What started as a dodge had inadvertently become my life's work, an irony I never could have appreciated had my extraordinary parents not put me through Princeton.

# That's Amore

Beside our apartment building in New York, there was a narrow gangway, and every evening, just after dark, rats would emerge from it and flock to the trash cans lining the curb. The first time I saw them, I started and screamed, but after that I made it a point to walk on the other side of the street, pausing and squinting to take them all in. It was like moving to Alaska and seeing a congregation of bears—I knew to expect them, but still I could never quite believe my eyes. Every now and then, one of them would get flattened by a cab, and I'd bend over the body, captivated by the foulness of it. Twenty, maybe thirty seconds of reverie, and then the spell would be broken, sometimes by the traffic, but more often by my neighbor Helen, who'd shout at me from her window.

Like the rats that spilled from the gangway, she was exactly the type of creature I'd expected to find living in New

York. Arrogant, pushy, proudly, almost fascistically opinionated, she was the person you found yourself quoting at dinner parties, especially if your hosts were on the delicate side and you didn't much care about being invited back. Helen on politics, Helen on sex, Helen on race relations: the response at the table was almost always the same. "Oh, that's horrible. And *where* did you know this person from?"

It was Hugh who first met her. This was in New York, on Thompson Street, in the fall of 1991. There was a combination butcher shop and café there, and he mentioned to the owner that he was looking to rent an apartment. While talking, he noticed a woman standing near the door, seventy at least, and no taller than a ten-year-old girl. She wore a sweat suit, tight through the stomach and hips. It wasn't the pastel-colored, ladylike kind, but just plain gray, like a boxer's. Her glasses were wing-shaped, and at their center, just over her nose, was a thick padding of duct tape. Helen, she said her name was. Hugh nodded hello, and as he turned to leave, she pointed to some bags lying at her feet. "Carry my groceries upstairs." She sounded like a man, or, rather, a hit man, her voice coarse and low, like heavy footsteps on gravel.

"Now?" Hugh asked.

She said, "What? You got something better to do?"

They walked into the building next door, a tenement, and were on the second floor, slowly climbing to the fifth, when she told him of a vacant apartment. The former tenant had died a month earlier, and his place would be available in a week or so. Helen was not the super or the manager. She had no official title but was friendly with the landlord, and thus had a key. "I can let you have a look, but that doesn't mean you're going to get it."

As one-bedrooms went, this was on the small side, narrow too, and as low-ceilinged as a trailer. The walls were covered with cheap dark paneling, but that could be gotten rid of easily enough. What sold Hugh was the ferocity of the sunlight, that and the location. He got the address of the landlord, and before leaving to fill out an application he gave this Helen woman seventy-five dollars. "Just for showing me the place," he told her. She stuffed the money down the front of her sweatshirt, and then she made sure we got the apartment.

I first saw it a few days later. Hugh was in the living room taking down the paneling while I sat on a paint bucket and tried to come to terms with my disappointment. For starters, there was the kitchen floor. The tiles there were brown and tan and ocher, the colors seemingly crocheted as they would be on an afghan. Then there was the size. I was wondering how two people could possibly live in such a tight space, when there was a knock at the unlocked door, and this woman I didn't know stepped uninvited onto the horrible tiles. Her hair was dyed the color of a new penny, and she wore it pulled back into a thumb-sized ponytail. This put the focus on her taped-up glasses, and on her lower jaw, which stuck out slightly, like a drawer that hadn't quite been closed. "Can I help you?" I asked, and her hand went to a whistle that hung from a string around her neck.

"Mess with me, and I'll stick my foot so far up your ass I'll lose my shoe."

Someone says this, and you naturally look down, or at least I do. The woman's feet were tiny, no longer than hot dog buns. She had on puffy sneakers, cheap ones made of air and some sort of plastic, and, considering them, I frowned.

"They might be small, but they'll still do the job, don't you worry," she said.

Right about then, Hugh stepped out of the living room with a scrap of paneling in his hand. "Have you met Helen?" he asked.

The woman unfurled a few thick fingers, the way you might when working an equation: 2 young men + 1 bedroom – ugly paneling = fags. "Yeah, we met." Her voice was heavy with disdain. "We met, all right."

For the first few weeks that we lived in the apartment, Helen clearly preferred Hugh over me. "My boyfriend," she called him. Then the two of them got to talking, and she switched her allegiance. I knew I'd won her favor when she invited me into her kitchen. Owing to her Sicilian blood, Helen had an innate gift for cooking. This she boasted as she jammed meatballs into a frozen store-bought pie crust. Then she drowned them in a mixture of beaten eggs and skim milk. "My Famous Italian Quiche," she called it. Other dishes included "My Famous Eggplant Parmesan with the Veal in It," "My Famous Tomato Gravy with Rice and Canned Peas," and "My Famous Spaghetti and Baked Bean Casserole." If Helen's food was truly famous, it was so in the way of sun poisoning and growling dogs with foam on their lips: things you avoided if you knew what was good for you. If I was superstoned I might wash the sauce off a bit of veal and eat it atop a cracker, but, for the most part, her food went straight into the trash can.

Throughout the seven years Hugh and I lived on

Thompson Street, our lives followed a simple pattern. He would get up early and leave the house no later than 8:00. I was working for a housecleaning company, and though my schedule varied from day to day, I usually didn't start until 10:00. My only real constant was Helen, who would watch Hugh leave the building, and then cross the hall to lean on our doorbell. I would wake up, and just as I was belting my robe, the ringing would be replaced by a pounding, frantic and relentless, the way you might rail against a coffin lid if you'd accidentally been buried alive.

"All right, all right."

"What were you, asleep?" Helen would say as I opened the door. "I've been up since five." In her hand would be an aluminum tray covered with foil, either that or a saucepan with a lid on it.

"Well," I'd tell her, "I didn't go to bed until three."

"I didn't go to bed until three thirty."

This was how it was with her: If you got fifteen minutes of sleep, she got only ten. If you had a cold, she had a flu. If you'd dodged one bullet, she'd dodged five. Blindfolded. After my mother's funeral, I remember her greeting me with "So what? My mother died when I was half your age."

"Gosh," I said. "Think of everything she missed."

To Helen, a gift was not something you gave to person number one, but something you *didn't* give to person number two. This was how we wound up with a Singer sewing machine, the kind built into a table. A woman on the third floor made her own clothes and, in her own quiet way, had asked if she could have it.

"So you want my sewing machine, do you?" Helen said. "Let me think about it." Then she picked up the phone and gave Hugh and me a call. "I got something for you," she told us. "The only deal is that you can't give it to nobody else, especially nobody who lives in this building on the third floor."

"But we don't need a sewing machine," I said.

"What, are you saying you already have one?"

"Well, no—"

"All right then, so shut up. Everybody needs a sewing machine, especially this one—top of the line. I can't tell you all the outfits I made over the years."

"Yes, but—"

"But nothing. It's a present from me to you."

As Hugh manhandled it through our door, I tried to block him. "But there's hardly enough room for us," I said. "Where are we supposed to put a full-sized sewing machine? I mean, really, why not just give us a tugboat? It would take up the same amount of space."

Hugh, though, you really have to hand it to him. He sat on the horrid little bench that came with the machine, and five minutes later he was teaching himself to sew. That's the kind of person he is—capable of anything.

"Can you make a body bag?" I asked.

Every day for the next six months, Helen mentioned her gift. "So how's that Singer? You made any pants yet? You made any jeans?"

It was the same with the food she gave us. "So did you like the turkey meat loaf with Italian seasoning?"

"Very much."

"Nobody makes it like me, you know."

"You won't get any argument there."

The food Helen brought was presented as a slight to the

couple next door. "The sons of bitches, if they knew that I was making this for you, they'd die."

The common areas of our building were covered in small ceramic tiles, giving the impression that you were in an empty pool. Even the slightest noises were amplified, so with very little effort, your voice could be deafening. Standing in the hallway outside my door, Helen would shout so loud that the overhead lights would dim. "All week they've been trying to beg food off of me. 'What's that that smells so delicious?' they want to know. 'You got any extras that need a good home? We're practically dying of hunger over here.'"

In real life the couple next door were pleasant and soft-spoken. At the time we moved in, the wife had already developed Alzheimer's, and her husband, an eighty-five-year-old man named Joe, was doing his best to care for her. I never heard him whine or grovel, so that, I suspected, was just wishful thinking on Helen's part. None of her impersonations were very good, but there was no denying her showmanship. She was a dynamic person, and even Joe, whom she was crueler to than anyone, was quick to acknowledge her weird star power. "A real pistol," he'd call her. "A peach of a girl."

"Begging off of me when he's got his railroad pension, that plus the social security. The both of them can go fuck themselves," Helen would shout.

Hugh is the type who'd hear this sort of thing, and say, "Oh, come on, now. That's no way to talk about your neighbors."

This was why Helen waited until he left for work every morning—he was a downer. "Living with someone like that,

I'd go crazy," she'd say. "Jesus Christ, I don't know how you can stand it."

Before moving to New York I spent six years in Chicago. During most of that time, I lived with my then boyfriend and, between the two of us, we seemed to know a fair number of people. There were wild dinners, wild parties— always something fun and druggy going on. Never again would I have so many friends, and such good ones, though I'm not exactly sure why. Perhaps I've grown less likable over the years, or maybe I've just forgotten how to meet people. The initial introduction—the shaking-hands part—I can still manage. It's the follow-up that throws me. Who calls whom, and how often? What if you decide after the second or third meeting that you don't really like this person? Up to what point are you allowed to back out? I used to know these things, but now they're a mystery.

Had I met Helen when I was in my twenties, we wouldn't have spent nearly so much time together. I'd have been off with people my own age, either taking drugs or looking for them, this as opposed to drinking instant coffee and listening to someone talk about her colitis. When Helen said "oil," it sounded like "earl." Subsequently, "toilet" came out as "terlet," as in "I was up and back to the fucking terlet six times last night. Shit so hard I think I sprained my asshole."

That we both found this fascinating was, I suppose, proof that we had at least one thing in common. Another thing we could always agree on was a soap opera called *One Life to Live*. It aired in the early afternoon, and, often, when I wasn't working, I'd go across the hall and watch it at her place.

Helen had lived in the same apartment for close to fifty

years, though you'd never know to look at it. I had stuff everywhere—the sewing machine, for example—but her living room, much like her kitchen, was spartan. On one wall was a framed photograph of herself, but no pictures of her daughters, or any of her seven grandchildren. There were no chairs, either, just a sofa and a coffee table. These faced the room's only extravagance: a tower of three televisions stacked one atop another. I don't know why she kept them. The black-and-white model on the bottom had died years earlier, and the one above it had no volume control. This left the TV at the top of the pile. It blathered away, all but ignored in favor of the window, which afforded a view of the entire block and was Helen's preferred source of entertainment. When in the living room, she usually sat on the radiator, her lower half indoors and her head and shoulders as far out as they could go. The waitress on the second floor coming home at 2:00 a.m., the shopkeeper across the street accepting a package from the UPS man, a woman in a convertible applying lipstick: nothing escaped her attention.

During the years I knew her, I'd guess that Helen spent a good ten hours a day at her window. Midmornings you could find her in the kitchen, but at 11:00, when the soap operas began, she'd switch off the radio and return to her perch. It hurt her neck to turn from the street to the screen, so most programs were listened to rather than watched. Exceptions were made for Friday episodes of *One Life to Live,* and, occasionally, for Oprah, who was one of the few black people Helen had any regard for. Perhaps in the past she had been more open-minded, but getting mugged in the foyer of our building convinced her that they were all crooks and sex maniacs. "Even the light-skinned ones."

Talk show hosts were scumbags as well, but Oprah; anyone could see that she was different. While the rest of the pack accentuated the negative, she encouraged people to feel good about themselves, be they single mothers—a group that had included Helen—or horribly disfigured children. "I never would have thought about it, but I guess that girl does have a pretty eye," she once said, referring to the young Cyclops fidgeting on the screen.

One afternoon Oprah interviewed a group of women who had overcome seemingly insurmountable obstacles. Susan fell overboard while sailing and managed to survive for six days by clinging to a cooler. Colleen taught herself to read and got a job as an executive secretary. The third guest, a poet, had recently published a memoir about her cancer and the many operations performed in an effort to reconstruct her jaw. The poet and I had met and spoken on several occasions. Now here she was on *Oprah,* and nothing would do until I ran across the hall to tell Helen. She'd been half watching from her spot on the radiator and didn't seem terribly impressed with my news.

"You don't get it," I said, and I pointed to the screen. "I *know* that person. She's my friend." It was too strong a word for what was, at best, a nodding relationship, but Helen didn't need to know that.

"So what?" she said.

"So I have a friend on *Oprah.*"

"Big deal. You think that makes you special?"

If Helen had known someone who'd appeared on *Oprah,* she'd have had T-shirts made up, but of course that was different. She was allowed to brag and name-drop, but no one else was. Announce an accomplishment—signing a book contract, getting your play reviewed in the *Times*—and her hackles would go up. "You think your shit smells better than mine? Is that what you're trying to say?"

"But you're *old*," I once told her. "Your job is to be happy for me."

"Stick it up your ass," she said. "I'm not your goddamn mother."

With the exception of my immediate family, no one could provoke me quite like Helen could. One perfectly aimed word, and within an instant I was eight years old and unable to control my temper. I often left her apartment swearing I'd never return. Once I slammed her door so hard, her clock fell off the wall, but still I went back—"crawled back," she would say—and apologized. It seemed wrong to yell at a grand-mother, but more than that I found that I missed her, or at least missed someone I could so easily drop in on. The beauty of Helen was that she was always there, practically begging to be disturbed. Was that a friend, or had I chosen the wrong word? What was the name for this thing we had?

When I told Hugh about the Oprah business, he said, "Well, of course she acted that way. You were being pretentious."

The word threw me. "'Pretentious' is knowing someone who met Pina Bausch, not someone who met Oprah."

"It depends on what circles you're running in," he said, and I supposed he was right, not that it gave Helen anything to be snippy about. I'd lost count of all the times she'd men-tioned her friendship with John Gotti, head of the Gambino crime family. "He's a very good-looking man," she'd say. "Pictures don't do him justice." After pressing, I learned that by "friend" she meant they had been introduced at a party thirty years earlier and had danced for two minutes before someone cut in. "John is very light on his feet," she told me. "That's something most people don't know about him."

"Maybe they'll bring it up at his murder trial," I said.

Helen fell in the tub and sprained her wrist. "That's it for the cooking," she told us. "You're not getting any more free meals out of me."

Hugh and I shuffled back across the hall and shut the door behind us. No more "Famous Veal Cutlet"! No more "Famous Sausage Casserole"! No more "Famous Chicken with the Oriental Vegetables"! We could hardly believe our luck.

While Helen was laid up, I went to the store for her. Hugh took down her trash and delivered her mail. Joe, a widower now, offered to help as well. "Anything that needs doing around the house, you just let me know," he told her. He meant that he'd change lightbulbs or run a mop across her floor, but Helen took it the wrong way and threw him out of her apartment. "He wants to give me a bath," she told me. "He wants to see my twat."

It was shocking to hear this word from a seventy-three-year-old woman, and in response I winced.

"What?" she said. "You think I ain't got one?"

Three months after Hugh joined the scenic union, the membership voted to go on strike. This is the group that paints backdrops for movies and plays. I wanted to be supportive, and so I tried coming up with slogans that might sound good on a picket sign: "Broadway Gives 829 the Brush-off" was my idea, as was "Scenic Painters Find New Contract Unpaletteable."

On the first morning of the strike, Hugh left the house at 7:00 a.m. A short while later, Helen called. I normally wouldn't pick up at that hour, but her voice on the machine was slurred and frantic, and so I answered. Since I had known her, Helen had, in her words, "taken" three strokes. They were, she'd admit, little ones, but still it worried me that she might have had another, and so I got dressed and headed across the hall to her apartment. The door jerked open before I could knock, and she stood in the frame, her lower jaw sunken, the lip invisible. It seemed that she had been at her window, surveying the scene below, and when the super in the building across the street threw a lit cigarette into our trash can, she yelled at him with such force that she blew her lower plate right out of her mouth. "Itch in da schwubs," she said. "Go giddit."

A minute later I was downstairs searching the planter in front of our building. There I found a beer bottle, a slice of pizza with ants on it, and, finally, the dentures, incredibly unbroken by their five-story fall. It is not unpleasant to hold someone else's warm teeth in your hand, and before returning upstairs, I paused, studying the damp plastic horseshoe that served as Helen's gum. What made it all look so fake was its perfection. No single tooth protruded or towered above its neighbor. Even in shape and color, they resembled a row of ceramic tiles.

Back upstairs, I found Helen waiting on the landing. She slid the dentures, unwashed, back into her mouth, and it was like popping the batteries into a particularly foul toy. "Rat bastard motherfucker could have set our whole building on fire."

*

In the mornings Helen listened to the radio, an oldies station I referred to as "K-WOP." All the singers seemed to be Italian, and all were backed by swollen string arrangements. Whenever a favorite song came on, she'd crank up the volume, subjecting us to countless versions of "Volare" and "That's Amore."

Radio meant a lot to Helen, but only *her* station. When I was invited to record a series of commentaries for NPR, she took no interest whatsoever. The morning my first story was broadcast, she pounded on our door. I was in the bedroom with a pillow over my head, so Hugh answered, and gestured to the air around him. "Listen," he whispered. "David is on the radio."

"So what?" Helen said. "A lot of people are on the radio." Then she handed him an envelope and asked if we'd mail in her stool sample. "It's not the whole thing, just a smear," she told him. When the broadcast was over and I finally got out of bed, I noticed that she'd posted her stool sample with Christmas stamps and included the spidery handwritten message "Happy Holidays."

Our building was full of people who, for one reason or another, had found their way onto Helen's shit list. Some were doomed right from the start: she didn't like their looks or the sounds of their voices. They were stuck up. They were foreign. Our landlord had a small office just off Bleecker Street, and Helen used to call him at least three times a day. She was like the secret police, always watching, always taking notes.

Then the landlord died, and the building was sold to a real estate conglomerate located somewhere in New Jersey. The new owners didn't care that the woman on the second floor had found a black boyfriend, or that the super was composing electronic music instead of improving his English. Overnight Helen became powerless, and those who had lived in fear of her grew progressively more defiant. You'd think she would hate being called a tattletale or, even worse, "a nosy old bitch," but, strangely, such names seemed only to invigorate her.

"You think I can't kick your ass?" I'd hear her yell. "Ya mutt, I'll mop the fucking floor with you."

The first few times I heard this, I laughed. Then it was me she was threatening to mop the floor with, and it suddenly didn't seem so funny. This was another of those arguments that came out of nowhere: a word here, a word there, and the next thing I knew we were at each other's throats. Ironically, the fight started over a blown fuse. My electricity had gone out, and I needed a key to the basement. Helen had one, and when she refused to loan it to me, I told her she was being an asshole.

"That's better than being a drunk," she said, and she waited a moment for the word to settle in. "That's right. You think I don't see you with the empty cans and bottles every morning. You think I can't see it in your swollen face?"

Had I not been so loaded that I could barely stand, my denial might have carried a bit more weight. As it was, I sounded pathetic. "You don' know. Anything about . . . what. Goes on with. Me."

We were in her doorway when she put her hands on my chest and pushed. "You think you're tough? You think I can't kick your ass?"

Hugh came up the stairs just then, his ears ringing from all the noise. "You're like children, the both of you," he told us.

Following our little scene, Helen and I didn't talk for a month. I'd hear her in the hall sometimes, most often in the morning, giving food to Joe. "It's my Famous Pasta Fagioli, and that one next door, the Greek bastard, would die if he knew I was giving it to you."

It was a stranger who brought us back together. In the ten or so years before she retired, Helen cleaned house for a group of priests in Murray Hill. "They were Jesuits," she told me. "That means they believe in God but not in terlet paper. You should have seen their underwear. Disgusting."

In her opinion, a person who hired a housekeeper was a person who thought himself better than everyone else. She loved a story in which a snob got his comeuppance, but the people I worked for were generally pretty thoughtful. I felt like a bore, telling her how unobtrusive and generous every-one was, and so it came as a pleasant surprise when I was sent to clean an apartment near the Museum of Modern Art. The woman who lived there was in her late sixties and had hair the color of a newly hatched chick. Mrs. Oakley, I'll say her name was. She wore a denim skirt with a matching blouse and had knotted a red bandana around her throat. With some people this might be it, their look, but on her it seemed like a costume, like she was going to a party with a cattle-rustling theme.

Most often a homeowner would take my jacket, or direct me toward the closet. Mrs. Oakley did neither, and when I made for the brass rack that she herself clearly used, she said, "Not there," her voice a bark. "You can put your things in the guest bathroom. Not on the countertop, but on the toilet." She pointed to a door at one end of the foyer. "Put the lid down first," she told me. "Then put your coat and scarf on top of the lid."

I wondered who would be stupid enough not to have understood that, and I imagined a simpleton with a puzzled expression on his face. "Hey," he might say. "How come my jacket's all wet? And while we're at it, who put this turd in my pocket?!"

"Something amuses you, does it?" Mrs. Oakley asked.

I said, "No. Not at all." Then I jotted down the time in my portable notebook.

She saw me writing and put her hands on her hips. "I am not paying you to practice your English," she told me.

"Excuse me?"

She pointed to my notebook. "This is not a language institute. You are here to work, not to learn new words."

"But I'm an American," I told her. "I spoke English before I got here. Like at home, growing up and stuff."

Mrs. Oakley sniffed but did not apologize. I think she wanted a foreigner so badly that she heard an accent where there was none. How else to explain it? Being a desperate, godforsaken immigrant, it went without saying that I coveted everything before me: the white wall-to-wall carpet, the framed reproduction of Renoir's *Brat with Watering Can,* the gold-plated towel rack in the marble master bathroom.

"I have very nice things," she announced. "And I expect to *still* have them after you've left."

Was this the moment I decided to make up with Helen, or was it later, when Mrs. Oakley screamed at me for opening the medicine cabinet? "When I told you to clean the master bathroom, I meant everything *but that.* What are you, an idiot?"

At the end of the day I caught the subway home. Helen was staring down from her window as I approached our building, and when I waved at her, she waved back. Three minutes later I was sitting at her kitchen table. "So then she told me, 'I have very nice things and I expect to still have them after you've left.'"

"Oh, she was asking for it, that one," Helen said. "What did she say when you slapped her?"

"I didn't slap her."

She looked disappointed. "OK, then, what did you break on your way out?"

"Nothing. I mean, I didn't walk out."

"Are you telling me you stayed and took that shit?"

"Well . . . sure."

"Then what the fuck?" She lit a fresh cigarette and tucked her disposable lighter back into her pack. "What the fuck are you good for?"

The first time I went to Normandy I stayed for three weeks. After returning, I went straight to Helen's, but she refused to hear about it. "The French are faggots," she said. As evidence, she brought up Bernard, who was born in Nice and lived on the fourth floor.

"Bernard's not a homosexual," I told her.

"Maybe not, but he's filthy. Did you ever see his apartment?"

"No."

"OK then, so shut up." This was her way of saying that the argument was over and that she had won. "I bet you're glad to be back, though. You couldn't pay me to go overseas. I like it where's it's civilized and you can drink the water without running to the terlet every five minutes."

While in France, I'd bought Helen some presents, nothing big or expensive, just little things a person could use and then throw away. I placed the bag of gifts on her kitchen table and she halfheartedly pawed through it, holding the objects upside down and sideways, the way a monkey might. A miniature roll of paper towels, disposable napkins with *H*'s printed on them, kitchen sponges tailored to fit the shape of the hand: "I don't have any use for this crap," she said. "Take it away. I don't want it."

I put the gifts back into the bag, ashamed at how deeply my feelings were hurt. "Most people, most humans, receive a present and say thank you," I told her.

"Not when they get garbage like that, they don't," she said.

In fact these things were perfect for her, but Helen wouldn't accept them for the same reason she wouldn't accept anything: the other person had to owe and be beholden. Forever.

I picked up the bag and headed for the door. "You know what you have?" I said. "You have a gift disorder."

"A what?"

"It's like an eating disorder, only with presents."

"Take that back," she said.

"My point exactly." And then I left, slamming the door behind me.


Helen knocked on January 1, just as I was leaving for a cleaning job. "Work on New Year's Day, and you'll work every day of the year," she told me. "It's the truth. You can ask anybody."

I wondered for a moment if she was right, and then I considered the last little truism she had passed my way: you won't get a hangover if you sleep with the TV on. She also claimed you could prevent crib death by making the sign of the cross three times with a steak knife.

"If you're camping, could you use a Swiss Army knife instead?" I asked.

She looked at me and shook her head. "Who the fuck goes camping with a baby?"

Helen was shaking out her pills: the ones for her heart and her high blood pressure, the pain in her side and the new one in her right leg. Trips to the doctor were her only ticket out of the apartment, and after each visit she'd spend hours on the phone, haranguing the people at Medicare. When that got old, she'd phone McKay's drugstore and have a go at the pharmacist. "I'd like to cut his balls off and stuff them down his throat," she told me.

Now there were new pills she needed to take. I offered to pick them up for her, and along with the prescription she handed me a receipt. It seemed her enemy at McKay's had overcharged her for her last order, so after getting this new one I was to tell the hook-nosed Jew bastard that he owed my neighbor four cents. I was then to suggest that he shove his delivery charge up his fat ass.

"Got that?" Helen asked.

I was happy to pick up the medicine, but when it came to the disputed bill—and toward the end there was always a dispute—I'd make it up out of my own pocket and lie when she prodded me for details. "The pharmacist said he was very sorry and that it won't happen again," I'd tell her.

"Did you tell him what he can do with his delivery charge?"

"I sure did."

"And what did he say?"

"Pardon?"

"When you told him to shove it up his ass, what did he say?"

"He said, um, 'I bet that's going to hurt.'"

"You're damn right it will," she'd say.

Back when she could still get up and down the stairs, Helen had all the run-ins she could handle: on the bus, at the post office, wherever peace reigned, she shattered it. Now she had to import her prey, deliverymen, most of them. The ones from the Grand Union, the supermarket we favored, tended to be African, recent immigrants from Chad and Ghana. "You black bastards," I'd hear her yell. "You think I don't know what you're up to?"

She hit bottom when she physically attacked a deaf-mute. This was a boy of fourteen, a beloved neighborhood figure who delivered for the nearby deli. "How could you?" Hugh scolded.

"What do you expect me to do when somebody's stealing my things?" she asked. "What, am I just supposed to stand there and do nothing?" It eventually came out that by "stealing" she meant that he had borrowed her pen. After using it to tally the bill, he stuck it in his shirt pocket, absentmindedly, most likely. Helen reacted by pulling his hair and digging her nails into his neck. "But not hard," she said. "There was barely any blood at all."

When asked why the boy would steal a thirty-cent pen, a pen he could surely get for free at his father's store, Helen sighed, exhausted at having to explain the obvious. "He's

*Portuguese,*" she said. "You know what those bastards are like. You've seen them." But there was a hint of desperation in her voice, the fear that maybe this time she had gone too far.

The following morning she called our apartment and asked, almost sheepishly, if I'd rub in some Tiger Balm for her. I crossed the hall and, after letting me in, she took a seat and pointed out her sore shoulder. "I think I sprained it smacking that little freak," she said.

It was February 14, Valentine's Day, and after a few more words about the delivery boy, Helen's thoughts turned to love, or, more specifically, to my father. He'd visited me the previous autumn, and she'd been talking about him ever since. "That Lou is a very good-looking man. Too bad you didn't get any of his genes."

"Well, I'm sure I got some of them," I told her.

"No, you didn't. You must take after your mother. And she's dead, right?"

"Yes, she's dead."

"You know we're the same age, me and Lou. Is he dating anybody?"

The thought of my father and Helen together made the bottoms of my feet sweat. "No, he's not dating anyone, and he's not going to, either."

"No need to get so sensitive," she said. "Jesus, I was only asking." And then she lowered her shirt a little and asked me to do her back.

I'd just returned from another trip to the pharmacy when Helen asked me to dab some white shoe polish on her kitchen ceiling. A slight stain had formed, and she insisted that it was dog urine, leaking down from the apartment above her. "The sons of bitches, they think that if they ruin my ceiling, it'll drive me into a nursing home."

I don't remember why I didn't do it. Maybe I had someone waiting for me, or perhaps I'd just had enough for one day. "I'll do it tomorrow," I told her, and as I shut the door, I heard her say, "Right. You and your 'tomorrows.'"

It was Joe who found her. Helen kept a sawed-off two-by-four in her kitchen, a weapon against possible intruders, and he awoke to hear her banging it against the inside of her door. He had a key in case of emergency and entered the apartment to find her on the floor. Beside her was the overturned step stool, and beneath the kitchen table, lying just out of reach, was the bottle of white shoe polish.

On *One Life to Live,* and all soap operas, really, the characters are forever blaming themselves. The male lead is nearly killed in a car accident, and as the surgeons do what they can to save him, the family gathers in the waiting room to accept responsibility. "It was my fault," the ex-wife says. "I never should have upset him with the news about the baby." She starts to bang her head against the wall and is stopped by the lead's father. "Don't be stupid. If anyone's to blame, it's me." Then the girlfriend horns in and decides that it was all *her* fault. In the end, the only one who won't feel guilty is the driver of the other car.

"Why the heck would she stand on a chair to polish her shoes?" Joe asked as the ambulance headed off toward St. Vincent's. "That's what I can't figure out."

"Me neither," I said.

*

99

During the next few months Hugh and I visited Helen in the hospital. The problem wasn't her broken hip, but the series of strokes that followed her operation. It was as if she had been struck by lightning, that's how fried and out of it she was. Unable to put a sentence together, she'd also been literally defanged. No teeth, no glasses, and when the last of the henna had faded, her hair, like her face, was the color of old cement.

The hospital room was small and hot. Near the door was a second bed, and in it lay a Dominican woman who had recently lost a leg. Each time I was there, she pointed to Helen's food tray and begged. "Is she going to eat that applesauce? Do you think she wants those crackers? If not, I'll take them."

Had Helen been her old self, this woman would have been missing a lot more than a leg. As it was, the roommate left no more of an impression than the wall-mounted TV, which was permanently tuned to the Bullshit station, and was on all the time.

At the funeral home were people I had heard about but never met. Helen once told me that as a young woman her nickname had been Rocky, as in Graziano, the fighter, but according to her sister, she was called any number of things. "To me she was always Baby Hippo, on account of her great big behind," she told me. "I'd call her that and, oh, she used to get so mad."

Most everyone I met had a good anger story: Helen cursing, Helen smacking, Helen slamming down the phone. In the months after she died, these were the moments I'd recall as well. Gradually, though, the focus shifted, and instead of

Helen attacking a deaf-mute, I'd picture her the following morning, sitting in her kitchen as I applied the Tiger Balm. It was such a strange thing for her to have, let alone say. "It's Oriental," she told me. "I think the Chinese invented it."

I am not a terribly physical person. Helen wasn't either. We'd never hugged or even shaken hands, so it was odd to find myself rubbing her bare shoulder and then her back. It was, I thought, like stroking some sort of a sea creature, the flesh slick and fatty beneath my palms. In my memory, there was something on the stove, a cauldron of tomato gravy, and the smell of it mixed with the camphor of the Tiger Balm. The windows were steamed, Tony Bennett was on the radio, and saying, "Please," her voice catching on the newness of the word, Helen asked me to turn it up.

# The Monster Mash

The thing about dead people is that they look really dead, fake almost, like models made of wax. This I learned at the medical examiner's office I visited in the fall of 1997. While the bodies seemed unreal, the tools used to pick them apart were disturbingly familiar. It might be different in places with better funding, but here the pathologists used hedge clippers to snip through rib cages. Chest cavities were emptied of blood with cheap metal soup ladles, the kind you'd see in cafeterias, and the autopsy tables were lubricated with whatever dish detergent happened to be on sale. Also familiar were the songs, oldies mainly, that issued from the blood-spattered radio and formed a kind of sound track. When I was young, I associated Three Dog Night with my seventh-grade shop teacher, who proudly identified himself as the group's biggest fan. Now, though, whenever I hear "Joy to the World," I think of a fibroid tumor positioned upon a Styrofoam plate. Funny how that happens.

While at the medical examiner's office, I dressed in a protective suit, complete with a bonnet and a pair of Tyvek booties. Citizens were disemboweled, one right after another, and on the surface I'm sure I seemed fine with it. Then at night I'd return to my hotel, double-lock the door, and stand under the shower until all the soap and shampoo were used up. The people in the next room must have wondered what was going on. An hour of running water, and then this blubbery voice: "I do believe in spooks, I do believe in spooks, I do, I do, I do, I do, I do."

It's not as if I'd walked into this completely unprepared. Even as a child I was fascinated by death, not in a spiritual sense, but in an aesthetic one. A hamster or guinea pig would pass away, and, after burying the body, I'd dig it back up: over and over, until all that remained was a shoddy pelt. It earned me a certain reputation, especially when I moved on to other people's pets. "Igor," they called me. "Wicked, spooky." But I think my interest was actually fairly common, at least among adolescent boys. At that age, death is something that happens only to animals and grandparents, and studying it is like a science project, the good kind that doesn't involve homework. Most kids grow out of it, but the passing of time only heightened my curiosity.

As a young man, I saved up my dishwashing money and bought a seventy-five-dollar copy of *Medicolegal Investigations of Death,* a sort of bible for forensic pathologists. It shows what you might look like if you bit an extension cord while standing in a shallow pool of water, if you were crushed by a tractor, struck by lightning, strangled with a spiral or nonspiral telephone cord, hit with a claw hammer, burned, shot, drowned, stabbed, or feasted upon by wild or domestic animals. The captions read like really great poem titles, my favorite being "Extensive Mildew on the Face of a Recluse." I stared at that picture for hours on end, hoping it might inspire me, but I know nothing about poetry, and the best I came up with was pretty lame:

> *Behold the recluse looking pensive!*
> *Mildew, though, is quite extensive*
> *On his head, both aft and fore.*
> *He maybe shoulda got out more.*

I know nothing about biology either. The pathologists tried to educate me, but I was too distracted by the grotesque: my discovery, for instance, that if you jump from a tall building and land on your back, your eyes will pop out of your head and hang by bloody cables. "Like those joke glasses!" I said to the chief medical examiner. The man was nothing if not professional, and his response to my observations was always the same: "Well." He'd sigh. "Not really."

After a week in the autopsy suite, I still couldn't open a Denny's menu without wanting to throw up. At night I'd close my eyes and see the buckets of withered hands stored in the office's secondary cooler. The cooler contained brains too, a whole wall of them shelved like preserves in a general store. Then there were the bits and pieces: a forsaken torso, a pretty blond scalp, a pair of eyes floating in a baby food jar. Put them all together, and you had an incredibly bright secretary who could type like the wind but never answer the telephone. I'd lie awake thinking of things like this, but then my mind would return to the freshly dead, who were most often whole, or at least whole-*ish*.

Most of the them were delivered naked, zipped up in identical body bags. Family members were not allowed inside the building, and so the corpses had no context. Unconnected to the living, they were like these strange creatures, related only to one another. A police report would explain that Mrs. Daniels had been killed when a truck lost control and drove through the front window of a hamburger stand, where she had been waiting in line for her order. But that was it in terms of a narrative. Did the victim have children? Was there a Mr. Daniels? How was it that she found herself at this particular hamburger stand on this particular afternoon? In cases like hers, I needed more than a standard report. There had to be a reason this woman was run down, as, without one, the same thing might happen to me. Three men are shot to death while attending a child's christening, and you tell yourself, *Sure. They were hanging out with the wrong crowd.* But buying a hamburger? *I* buy hamburgers. Or I used to, anyway.

This medical examiner's office was in the western United States, in a city where guns are readily available and drivers are known to shoot each other over parking spaces. The building was low-slung and mean-looking, set on the far edge of the downtown area, between the railroad tracks and a rubber stamp manufacturer. In the lobby was a potted plant and a receptionist who kept a can of Mountain Glen air freshener in her desk drawer. "For decomps," she explained, meaning those who had died alone and rotted awhile before being found. We had such a case on Halloween, an eighty-year-old man who had tumbled from a ladder while replacing a lightbulb. Four and a half days on the floor of his un-air-conditioned home, and as the bag was unzipped the room filled with what the attending patholo-gist termed "the smell of job security." The autopsy took place in the morning and was the best argument for the buddy system I had ever seen. *Never live alone,* I told myself. *Before you change a lightbulb, call someone from the other room and have him watch until you are finished.*

By this point in my stay, my list of don'ts covered three pages and included such reminders as: never fall asleep in a Dumpster, never underestimate a bee, never drive a con-vertible behind a flatbed truck, never get old, never get drunk near a train, and never, under any circumstances, cut off your air supply while masturbating. This last one is a nationwide epidemic, and it's surprising the number of men who do it while dressed in their wife's clothing, most often while she is out of town. To anyone with similar inclina-tions, a word of warning: after you're discovered, the police will take snapshots of your dead, costumed body, which will then be slid into photo albums and pored over by people like me, who can't take the stench of an incoming decomp, so hole themselves up in the records room, moaning, "Oh, my God. Oh, my God. Oh, my God," not sure if they're refer-ring to your plum-colored face or to the squash blossom necklace you've chosen to go with that blouse.

I hadn't timed my visit to coincide with Halloween, but that's the way it worked out. You'd think that most of the casualties would involve children, trick-or-treaters hit by cars or done in by tainted candy, but actually the day was just like any other. In the morning we had our decomposed senior, and after lunch I accompanied a female pathologist to a murder trial. She had performed the victim's autopsy and was testifying on behalf of the prosecution. There were plenty of things that should have concerned me—the blood-spatter evidence, the trajectory of the bullets—but all I could concentrate on was the defendant's mother, who'd come to court wearing cutoff jeans and a *Ghostbusters* T-shirt. It couldn't have been easy for her, but still you had to wonder: what *would* she consider a dress-up occasion?

After the trial, I watched as another female pathologist collected maggots from a spinal column found in the desert. There was a decomposed head, too, and before leaving work she planned to simmer it and study the exposed cranium for contusions. I was asked to pass this information along to the chief medical examiner, and, looking back, I perhaps should have chosen my words more carefully. "Fire up the kettle," I told him. "Ol'-fashioned skull boil at five p.m."

It was, of course, the fear talking, that and a pathetic desire to appear casual, one of the gang. That evening, instead of returning to my hotel, I sat around with the trans-porters, one of whom had recently been ticketed for using the car pool lane and had argued, unsuccessfully, that the dead body he was carrying in the back constituted a second passenger. I'd thought these guys would be morose and scary-looking, the type who live in basements and have no social skills, but they were actually just the opposite. Several of them had worked for undertakers, and told me that gypsy funerals were the worst. "They set up in the parking lot, tap into the electricity, and grill chicken until, like, forever." They recalled finding the eye of a suicide victim stuck to the bottom of a bedroom door, and then they turned on the TV and started watching a horror movie, which I can't believe had any real effect on them.

It was just the four of us until around midnight, when a tipsy man in a Daytona Beach sweatshirt came to the front gate and asked for a tour. When the transporters refused him, he gestured toward an idling car and got his girlfriend to ask. The young woman was lovely and flirtatious, and as she pressed herself against the gate I imagined her lying upon an autopsy table, her organs piled in a glistening heap beside her. I now looked at everyone this way, and it worried me that I'd never be able to stop. This was the consequence of seeing too much and understanding the horrible truth: No one is safe. The world is not manageable. The trick-or-treater may not be struck down on Halloween, but sooner or later he is going to get it, as am I, and everyone I have ever cared about.

It goes without saying that for the next few weeks I was not much fun to live with. In early November, I returned home and repelled every single person I came into contact with. Gradually, though, my gloominess wore off. By Thanksgiving I was imagining people naked rather than dead and naked, which was an improvement. A week later, I was back to smoking in bed, and, just as I thought that I'd put it all behind me, I went to my neighborhood grocery store and saw an elderly woman slip on a grape. She fell hard, and after running to her side I took her by the arm. "You really have to watch yourself in this produce aisle."

"I know it," she said. "I could have broken my leg."

"Actually," I told her, "you could have been killed."

The woman attempted to stand, but I wouldn't let her. "I'm serious. People die this way. I've seen it."

109

Her expression changed then, becoming fearful rather than merely pained. It was the look you get when facing a sudden and insurmountable danger: the errant truck, the shaky ladder, the crazy person who pins you to the linoleum and insists, with increasing urgency, that everything you know and love can be undone by a grape.

# In the Waiting Room

Six months after moving to Paris, I gave up on French school and decided to take the easy way out. All I ever said was "Could you repeat that?" And for what? I rarely understood things the second time around, and when I did it was usually something banal, the speaker wondering how I felt about toast, or telling me that the store would close in twenty minutes. All that work for something that didn't really matter, and so I began saying *"D'accord,"* which translates to "I am in agreement," and means, basically, "OK." The word was a key to a magic door, and every time I said it I felt the thrill of possibility.

*"D'accord,"* I told the concierge, and the next thing I knew I was sewing the eye onto a stuffed animal belonging to her granddaughter. *"D'accord,"* I said to the dentist, and she sent me to a periodontist, who took some X-rays and called me into his conference room for a little talk. *"D'accord,"* I said,

and a week later I returned to his office, where he sliced my gums from top to bottom and scraped great deposits of plaque from the roots of my teeth. If I'd had any idea that this was going to happen, I'd never have said *d'accord* to my French publisher, who'd scheduled me the following evening for a television appearance. It was a weekly cultural program, and very popular. I followed the pop star Robbie Williams, and as the producer settled me into my chair I ran my tongue over my stitches. It was like having a mouthful of spiders—spooky, but it gave me something to talk about on TV, and for that I was grateful.

I said *d'accord* to a waiter and received a pig's nose standing erect on a bed of tender greens. I said it to a woman in a department store and walked away drenched in cologne. Every day was an adventure.

When I got a kidney stone, I took the Métro to a hospital and said *"D'accord"* to a cheerful redheaded nurse, who led me to a private room and hooked me up to a Demerol drip. That was undoubtedly the best that *d'accord* got me, and it was followed by the worst. After the stone had passed, I spoke to a doctor, who filled out an appointment card and told me to return the following Monday, when we would do whatever it was I'd just agreed to. *"D'accord,"* I said, and then I supersized it with *"génial,"* which means "great!"

On the day of my appointment, I returned to the hospital, where I signed the register and was led by a slightly less cheerful nurse to a large dressing room. "Strip to your underwear," she told me, and I said, *"D'accord."* As the woman turned to leave, she said something else, and, looking back, I really should have asked her to repeat it, to draw a picture if that's what it took, because once you take your pants off, *d'accord* isn't really OK anymore.

There were three doors in the dressing room, and after removing my clothes I put my ear against each one, trying to determine which was the safest for someone in my condition. The first was loud, with lots of ringing telephones, so that was out. The second didn't sound much different, and so I chose the third and entered a brightly painted waiting room set with plastic chairs and a glass-topped coffee table stacked high with magazines. A potted plant stood in the corner, and beside it was a second door, which was open and led into a hallway.

I took a seat and had been there for a minute or so when a couple came in and filled two of the unoccupied chairs. The first thing I noticed was that they were fully dressed, and nicely, too—no sneakers or sweat suits for them. The woman wore a nubby gray skirt that fell to her knees and matched the fabric of her husband's sport coat. Their black hair, which was obviously dyed, formed another match, but looked better on her than it did on him—less vain, I supposed.

*"Bonjour,"* I said, and it occurred to me that possibly the nurse had mentioned something about a robe, perhaps the one that had been hanging in the dressing room. I wanted more than anything to go back and get it, but if I did the couple would see my mistake. They'd think I was stupid, so to prove them wrong I decided to remain where I was and pretend that everything was normal. *La la la.*

It's funny the things that run through your mind when you're sitting in your underpants in front of a pair of strangers. Suicide comes up, but just as you embrace it as a

113

viable option you remember that you don't have the proper tools: no belt to wrap around your neck, no pen to drive through your nose or ear and up into your brain. I thought briefly of swallowing my watch, but there was no guarantee I'd choke on it. It's embarrassing, but, given the way I normally eat, it would probably go down fairly easily, strap and all. A clock might be a challenge, but a Timex the size of a fifty-cent piece—no problem.

The man with the dyed black hair pulled a pair of glasses from his jacket pocket, and as he unfolded them I recalled a summer evening in my parents' backyard. This was ages ago, a dinner for my sister Gretchen's tenth birthday. My father grilled steaks. My mother set the picnic table with insect-repelling candles, and just as we started to eat she caught me chewing a hunk of beef the size of a coin purse. Gorging always set her off, but on this occasion it bothered her more than usual.

"I hope you choke to death," she said.

I was twelve years old, and paused, thinking, *Did I hear her correctly?*

"That's right, piggy, suffocate."

In that moment, I hoped that I *would* choke to death. The knot of beef would lodge itself in my throat, and for the rest of her life my mother would feel haunted and responsible. Every time she passed a steak house or browsed the meat counter of a grocery store, she would think of me and reflect upon what she had said, the words "hope" and "death" in the same sentence. But, of course, I hadn't choked. Instead, I had lived and grown to adulthood, so that I could sit in this waiting room dressed in nothing but my underpants. *La la la.*

It was around this time that two more people entered. The woman looked to be in her midfifties, and accompanied an elderly man who was, if anything, overdressed: a suit, a sweater, a scarf, *and* an overcoat, which he removed with great difficulty, every button a challenge. *Give it to me,* I thought. *Over here.* But he was deaf to my telepathy and handed his coat to the woman, who folded it over the back of her chair. Our eyes met for a moment—hers widening as they moved from my face to my chest—and then she picked a magazine off the table and handed it to the elderly man, who I now took to be her father. She then selected a magazine of her own, and as she turned the pages I allowed myself to relax a little. She was just a woman reading a copy of *Paris Match,* and I was just the person sitting across from her. True, I had no clothes on, but maybe she wouldn't dwell on that, maybe none of these people would. The old man, the couple with their matching hair: "How was the hospital?" their friends might ask, and they'd answer, "Fine," or "Oh, you know, the same."

"Did you see anything fucked-up?"

"No, not that I can think of."

It sometimes helps to remind myself that not everyone is like me. Not everyone writes things down in a notebook and then transcribes them into a diary. Fewer still will take that diary, clean it up a bit, and read it in front of an audience:

"March 14. Paris. Went with Dad to the hospital, where we sat across from a man in his underpants. They were briefs, not boxers, a little on the gray side, the elastic slack from too many washings. I later said to Father, 'Other people have to use those chairs, too, you know,' and he agreed that it was unsanitary.

"Odd little guy, creepy. Hair on his shoulders. Big idiot smile plastered on his face, just sitting there, mumbling to himself."

How conceited I am to think I might be remembered, especially in a busy hospital where human misery is a matter of course. If any of these people *did* keep a diary, their day's entry would likely have to do with a diagnosis, some piece of news either inconvenient, or life-altering: the liver's not a match, the cancer has spread to the spinal column. Compared with that, a man in his underpants is no more remarkable than a dust-covered plant, or the magazine subscription card lying on the floor beside the table. Then, too, good news or bad, these people would eventually leave the hospital and return to the street, where any number of things might wipe me from their memory.

Perhaps on their way home they'll see a dog with a wooden leg, which I saw myself one afternoon. It was a German shepherd, and his prosthesis looked as though it had been fashioned from a billy club. The network of straps holding the thing in place was a real eye-opener, but stranger still was the noise it made against the floor of the subway car, a dull thud that managed to sound both plaintive and forceful at the same time. Then there was the dog's owner, who looked at the homemade leg and then at me, with an expression reading, Not bad, huh?

Or maybe they'll run into something comparatively small yet no less astonishing. I was walking to the bus stop one morning and came upon a well-dressed woman lying on the sidewalk in front of an office-supply store. A small crowd had formed, and just as I joined it a fire truck pulled up. In America, if someone dropped to the ground, you'd call an ambulance, but in France it's the firemen who do most of the rescuing. There were four of them, and, after checking to see that the woman was OK, one of them returned to the truck and opened the door. I thought he was looking for an aluminum blanket, the type they use for people in shock, but instead he pulled out a goblet. Anywhere else it would have been a cup, made of paper or plastic, but this was glass and had a stem. I guess they carry it around in the front seat, next to the axes or whatever.

The fireman filled the goblet with bottled water, and then he handed it to the woman, who was sitting up now and running her hand over her hair, the way one might when waking from a nap. It was the lead story in my diary that night, but no matter how hard I fiddled with it I felt that something was missing. Had I mentioned that it was autumn? Did the leaves on the sidewalk contribute to my sense of utter delight, or was it just the goblet and the dignity it bespoke: "Yes, you may be on the ground; yes, this drink may be your last—but let's do it right, shall we?"

Everyone has his own standards, but in my opinion a sight like that is at least fifty times better than what I was providing. A goblet will keep you going for years, while a man in his underpants is good for maybe two days, a week at the most. Unless, of course, you *are* the man in his underpants, in which case it will probably stay with you for the rest of your life—not floating on the exact edge of your consciousness, not handy like a phone number, but still within easy reach, like a mouthful of steak, or a dog with a wooden leg. How often you'll think of the cold plastic chair, and of the nurse's face as she passes the room and discovers you with your hands between your knees. Such surprise, such amusement, as she proposes some new adventure, then stands there, waiting for your *"d'accord."*

# Solution to Saturday's Puzzle

On the flight to Raleigh, I sneezed, and the cough drop I'd been sucking on shot from my mouth, ricocheted off my folded tray table, and landed, as I remember it, on the lap of the woman beside me, who was asleep and had her arms folded across her chest. I'm surprised the force didn't wake her—that's how hard it hit—but all she did was flutter her eyelids and let out a tiny sigh, the kind you might hear from a baby.

Under normal circumstances, I'd have had three choices, the first being to do nothing. The woman would wake in her own time and notice what looked like a shiny new button sewn to the crotch of her jeans. This was a small plane, with one seat per row on aisle A, and two seats per row on aisle B. We were on B, so should she go searching for answers I would be the first person on her list. "Is this yours?" she'd ask, and I'd look dumbly into her lap.

"Is what mine?"

Option number two was to reach over and pluck it from her pants, and number three was to wake her up and turn the tables, saying, "I'm sorry, but I think you have something that belongs to me." Then she'd hand the lozenge back and maybe even apologize, confused into thinking that she'd somehow stolen it.

These circumstances, however, were *not* normal, as before she'd fallen asleep the woman and I had had a fight. I'd known her for only an hour, yet I felt her hatred just as strongly as I felt the stream of cold air blowing into my face—this after she'd repositioned the nozzle above her head, a final fuck-you before settling down for her nap.

The odd thing was that she hadn't looked like trouble. I'd stood behind her while boarding and she was just this woman, forty at most, wearing a T-shirt and cutoff jeans. Her hair was brown and fell to her shoulders, and as we waited she gathered it into a ponytail and fastened it with an elastic band. There was a man beside her who was around the same age and was also wearing shorts, though his were hemmed. He was skimming through a golf magazine, and I guessed correctly that the two of them were embarking on a vacation. While on the gangway, the woman mentioned a rental car and wondered if the beach cottage was far from a grocery store. She was clearly looking forward to her trip, and I found myself hoping that, whichever beach they were going to, the grocery store wouldn't be too far away. It was just one of those things that go through your mind. *Best of luck,* I thought.

Once on board, I realized that the woman and I would be sitting next to each other, which was fine. I took my place on the aisle, and within a minute she excused herself and walked a few rows up to talk to the man with the golf magazine. He was at the front of the cabin, in a single bulkhead seat, and I recall feeling sorry for him, because I hate the bulkhead. Tall people covet it, but I prefer as little leg room as possible. When I'm on a plane or in a movie theater, I like to slouch down as low as I can and rest my knees on the seat back in front of me. In the bulkhead, there is no seat in front of you, just a wall a good three feet away, and I never know what to do with my legs. Another drawback is that you have to put all of your belongings in the overhead compartment, and these are usually full by the time I board. All in all, I'd rather hang from one of the wheels than have to sit up front.

When our departure was announced, the woman returned to her seat but hovered a half foot off the cushion so she could continue her conversation with the man she'd been talking to earlier. I wasn't paying attention to what they were saying, but I believe I heard him refer to her as Becky, a wholesome name that matched her contagious, almost childlike enthusiasm.

The plane took off, and everything was as it should have been until the woman touched my arm and pointed to the man she'd been talking to. "Hey," she said, "see that guy up there?" Then she called out his name—Eric, I think—and the man turned and waved. "That's my husband, see, and I'm wondering if you could maybe swap seats so that me and him can sit together."

"Well, actually—," I said, and, before I could finish, her face hardened, and she interrupted me, saying, "What? You have a *problem* with that?"

"Well," I said, "ordinarily I'd be happy to move, but he's in the bulkhead, and I just hate that seat."

"He's in the *what?*"

"The bulkhead," I explained. "That's what you call that front row."

"Listen," she said, "I'm not asking you to switch because it's a bad seat. I'm asking you to switch because we're married." She pointed to her wedding ring, and when I leaned in closer to get a better look at it she drew back her hand, saying, "Oh, never mind. Just forget it."

It was as if she had slammed a door in my face, and quite unfairly it seemed to me. I should have left well enough alone, but instead I tried to reason with her. "It's only a ninety-minute flight," I said, suggesting that in the great scheme of things it wasn't that long to be separated from your husband. "I mean, what, is he going to prison the moment we land in Raleigh?"

"No, he's not going to *prison*," she said, and on the last word she lifted her voice, mocking me.

"Look," I told her, "if he was a child I'd do it." And she cut me off, saying, "Whatever." Then she rolled her eyes and glared out the window.

The woman had decided that I was a hard-ass, one of those guys who refuse under any circumstances to do anyone a favor. But it's not true. I just prefer that the favor be *my* idea, and that it leaves me feeling kind rather than bullied and uncomfortable. *So no. Let her sulk,* I decided.

Eric had stopped waving, and signaled for me to get Becky's attention. "My wife," he mouthed. "Get my wife."

There was no way out, and so I tapped the woman on the shoulder.

"Don't touch me," she said, all dramatic, as if I had thrown a punch.

"Your husband wants you."

"Well, that doesn't give you the right to *touch* me." Becky unbuckled her seat belt, raised herself off the cushion, and spoke to Eric in a loud stage whisper: "I asked him to swap seats, but he won't do it."

He cocked his head, sign language for "How come?" and she said, much louder than she needed to, "'Cause he's an *asshole,* that's why."

An elderly woman in aisle A turned to look at me, and I pulled a *Times* crossword puzzle from the bag beneath my seat. That always makes you look reasonable, especially on a Saturday, when the words are long and the clues are exceptionally tough. The problem is that you have to concentrate, and all I could think of was this Becky person.

Seventeen across: a fifteen-letter word for enlightenment. "I am not an asshole," I wrote, and it fit.

Five down: six-letter Indian tribe. "You are."

Look at the smart man, breezing through the puzzle, I imagined everyone thinking. He must be a genius. That's why he wouldn't swap seats for that poor married woman. He knows something we don't.

It's pathetic how much significance I attach to the *Times* puzzle, which is easy on Monday and gets progressively harder as the week advances. I'll spend fourteen hours finishing the Friday, and then I'll wave it in someone's face and demand that he acknowledge my superior intelligence. I think it means that I'm smarter than the next guy, but all it really means is that I don't have a life.

As I turned to my puzzle, Becky reached for a paperback novel, the kind with an embossed cover. I strained to see what the title was, and she jerked it closer to the window. Strange how that happens, how you can feel someone's eyes on your book or magazine as surely as you can feel a touch. It only works for the written word, though. I stared at her feet for a good five minutes, and she never jerked those away. After our fight, she'd removed her sneakers, and I saw that her toenails were painted white and that each one was perfectly sculpted.

Eighteen across: "Not impressed."

Eleven down: "Whore."

I wasn't even looking at the clues anymore.

When the drink cart came, we fought through the flight attendant.

"What can I offer you folks?" she asked, and Becky threw down her book, saying, "We're not together." It killed her that we might be mistaken for a couple, or even friends, for that matter. "I'm traveling with my husband," she continued. "He's sitting up there. In *the bulkhead.*"

*You learned that word from me,* I thought.

"Well, can I offer—"

"I'll have a Coke," Becky said. "Not much ice."

I was thirsty, too, but more than a drink I wanted the flight attendant to like me. And who would you prefer, the finicky baby who cuts you off and gets all specific about her ice cubes, or the thoughtful, nondemanding gentleman who smiles up from his difficult puzzle, saying, "Nothing for me, thank you"?

Were the plane to lose altitude and the only way to stay aloft was to push one person out the emergency exit, I now felt certain that the flight attendant would select Becky rather than me. I pictured her clinging to the doorframe, her hair blown so hard it was starting to fall out. "But my husband—," she'd cry. Then I would step forward, saying, "Hey, I've been to Raleigh before. Take me instead." Becky would see that I am not the asshole she mistook me for, and in that instant she would lose her grip and be sucked into space.

Two down: "Take that!"

It's always so satisfying when you can twist someone's hatred into guilt—make her realize that she was wrong, too quick to judge, too unwilling to look beyond her own petty concerns. The problem is that it works both ways. I'd taken this woman as the type who arrives late at a movie, then asks me to move behind the tallest person in the theater so that she and her husband can sit together. Everyone has to suffer just because she's sleeping with someone. But what if I was wrong? I pictured her in a dimly lit room, trembling before a portfolio of glowing X-rays. "I give you two weeks at the most," the doctor says. "Why don't you get your toenails done, buy yourself a nice pair of cutoffs, and spend some quality time with your husband. I hear the beaches of North Carolina are pretty this time of year."

I looked at her then, and thought, *No.* If she'd had so much as a stomachache, she would have mentioned it. Or would she? I kept telling myself that I was within my rights, but I knew it wasn't working when I turned back to my puzzle and started listing the various reasons why I was not an asshole.

Forty across: "I give money to p—"

Forty-six down: "—ublic radio."

While groping for Reason number two, I noticed that Becky was not making a list of her own. She was the one who called me a name, who went out of her way to stir up trouble, but it didn't seem to bother her in the least. After finishing her Coke, she folded up the tray table, summoned the flight attendant to take her empty can, and settled back for a nap. It was shortly afterward that I put the throat lozenge in my mouth, and shortly after that that I sneezed, and it shot like a bullet onto the crotch of her shorts.

Nine across: "Fuck!"

Thirteen down: "Now what?"

It was then that another option occurred to me. *You know,* I thought. *Maybe I* will *swap places with her husband.* But I'd waited too long, and now he was asleep as well. My only way out was to nudge this woman awake and make the same offer I sometimes make to Hugh. We'll be arguing, and I'll stop in midsentence and ask if we can just start over. "I'll go outside and when I come back in we'll just pretend this never happened, OK?"

If the fight is huge, he'll wait until I'm in the hall, then bolt the door behind me, but if it's minor he'll go along, and I'll reenter the apartment, saying, "What are you doing home?" Or "Gee, it smells good in here. What's cooking?"— an easy question as he's always got something on the stove.

For a while, it feels goofy, but eventually the self-consciousness wears off, and we ease into the roles of two decent people, trapped in a rather dull play. "Is there anything I can do to help?"

"You can set the table if you want."

"All-righty, then!"

I don't know how many times I've set the table in the

middle of the afternoon, long before we sit down to eat. But the play would be all the duller without action, and I don't want to do anything really hard, like paint a room. I'm just so grateful that he goes along with it. Other people's lives can be full of screaming and flying plates, but I prefer that my own remains as civil as possible, even if it means faking it every once in a while.

I'd gladly have started over with Becky, but something told me she wouldn't go for it. Even asleep, she broadcast her hostility, each gentle snore sounding like an accusation. *Asshole. Ass-ho-ole.* The landing announcement failed to wake her, and when the flight attendant asked her to fasten her seat belt she did it in a drowse, without looking. The lozenge disappeared beneath the buckle, and this bought me an extra ten minutes, time spent gathering my things, so that I could make for the door the moment we arrived at our gate. I just didn't count on the man in front of me being a little bit quicker and holding me up as he wrestled his duffel bag from the overhead bin. Had it not been for him, I might have been gone by the time Becky unfastened her seat belt, but as it was I was only four rows away, standing, it turned out, right beside the bulkhead.

The name she called me was nothing I hadn't heard before, and nothing that I won't hear again, probably. Eight letters, and the clue might read, "Above the shoulders, he's nothing but crap." Of course, they'd don't put words like that in the *Times* crossword puzzle. If they did, anyone could finish it.

# Adult Figures Charging Toward
## a Concrete Toadstool

Before it was moved out near the fairground, the North Carolina Museum of Art was located in downtown Raleigh, and often, when we were young, my sister Gretchen and I would cut out of church and spend an hour looking at the paintings. The collection was not magnificent, but it was enough to give you a general overview, and to remind you that you pretty much sucked. Both Gretchen and I thought of ourselves as artists. She the kind that could actually draw and paint, and me the kind that pretended I could actually draw and paint. When my sister looked at a picture, she would stand at a distance, and then slowly, almost imperceptibly, drift forward, until her nose was right up against the canvas. She examined all of the painting, and then parts of it, her fingers dabbing in sympathy as she studied the brushstrokes.

"What are you thinking about?" I once asked.

And she said, "Oh, you know, the composition, the

surfaces, the way things look realistic when you're far away but weird when you're up close."

"Me too," I said, but what I was really thinking was how grand it would be to own a legitimate piece of art and display it in my bedroom. Even with my babysitting income, paintings were out of the question, so instead I invested in postcards, which could be bought for a quarter in the museum shop and matted with shirt cardboard. This made them look more presentable.

I was looking for framing ideas one afternoon when I wandered into a little art gallery called the Little Art Gallery. It was a relatively new place, located in the North Hills Mall and owned by a woman named Ruth, who was about my mom's age, and introduced me to the word "fabulous," as in: "If you're interested, I've got a fabulous new Matisse that just came in yesterday."

This was a poster rather than a painting, but still I regarded it the way I thought a connoisseur might, removing my glasses and sucking on the stem as I tilted my head. "I'm just not sure how it will fit in with the rest of my collection," I said, meaning my Gustav Klimt calendar and the cover of the King Crimson LP tacked above my dresser.

Ruth treated me as an adult, which must have been a task, given the way I carried on. "I don't know if you realize it," I once told her, "but it seems that Picasso is actually Spanish."

"Is he?" she said.

"I had a few of his postcards on my French wall, the one where my desk is, but now I've moved them next to my bed, beside the Miró."

She closed her eyes, pretending to imagine this new configuration. "Good move," she said.

The Little Art Gallery was not far from my junior high, and I used to stop by after class and hang out. Hours later I'd return home, and when my mother asked where I had been, I'd say, "Oh, at my dealer's."

In 1970, the only artwork in my parents' house was a family tree and an unframed charcoal portrait of my brother, my four sisters, and me done by a guy at a street fair. Both hung in the dining room, and I thought they were pretty good until I started spending time with Ruth and decided that they weren't challenging enough.

"What more do you want from a group picture of six spoiled children?" my mother asked, and rather than trying to explain I took her to see Ruth. I knew that the two of them would get along. I just didn't think they would get along so well. At first the topic of conversation was me—Ruth doing the cheerleading and Mom just sort of agreeing. "Oh, yes," she said. "His bedroom is lovely. Everything in its place."

Then my mother started hanging out at the gallery as well, and began buying things. Her first purchase was an elongated statue of a man made from what looked like twisted paper but was actually metal pressed into thin sheets. He stood maybe two feet tall and held three rusted wires, each attached to a blown-glass balloon that floated above his head. *Mr. Balloon Man,* she called it.

"I'm just not certain he needs that top hat," I told her.

And my mother said, "Oh, really?" in a way that meant: If I want your opinion, I'll ask for it.

It bothered me that she'd bought something without seeking my advice, and so I continued to offer my thoughtful criticism, hoping it might teach her a lesson.

\*

Her next piece was a grandfather clock with a body made of walnut and a human face pounded from what appeared to be a Chinese gong. The face wasn't realistic but what my mother called "semiabstract," a word she had picked up from Ruth. A word that was supposed to be mine. I didn't know exactly how much the clock had cost, but I knew it was expensive. She called it *Mr. Creech,* in honor of the artist, and when I tried to explain that art was not a pet you gave a little name to, she told me she could call it whatever the hell she wanted to.

"Should I put *Mr. Creech* next to *Mr. Balloon Man,* or does that make the dining room too busy?"

"Don't ask me," I told her. "You're the expert."

Then my father was introduced to Ruth, and he became an expert as well. Art brought my parents together in a way that nothing else had, and because their interest was new they were able to share it without being competitive. Suddenly they were a team, the Walter and Louise Arensberg of Raleigh, North Carolina.

"Your mother's got a real eye," my father boasted—this in regard to *Cracked Man,* a semiabstract face made by the same potter who had crafted our new coffee table. Dad wasn't in the habit of throwing money around, but this, he explained, was an investment, something that, like stocks and bonds, would steadily appreciate in value, ultimately going "right through the roof."

"And in the meantime, we all get to enjoy it," my mother said. "All of us except Mr. Crabby," by which she meant me.

The allure of art had always been that my parents knew nothing about it. It had been a private interest, something between me and Gretchen. Now, though, everyone was in on it. Even my Greek grandmother had an opinion, that being that unless Jesus was in the picture it wasn't worth looking at. *Yiayia* was not discriminating—a Giotto or a Rouault, it made no difference so long as the subject was either nailed to a cross or raising his arms before a multitude. She liked her art to tell a story, and, though that particular story didn't interest me, I liked the same thing. It's why I preferred the museum's *Market Scene on a Quay* to its Kenneth Noland. When it came to *making* art, however, I tended toward the Noland, as measuring out triangles was a lot easier than painting a realistic-looking haddock.

Before my parents started hanging out at the gallery, they thought I was a trailblazer. Now they saw me for what I was: not just a copycat, but a lazy one. Looking at my square of green imposed atop a pumpkin-colored background, my father stepped back, saying, "That's just like what's-his-name, that guy who lives on the Outer Banks."

"Actually, it's more like Ellsworth Kelly," I said.

"Well, he must have gotten his ideas from the guy on the Outer Banks."

At the age of fifteen, I was maybe not the expert I made myself out to be, but I did own a copy of *The History of Art* and knew that eastern North Carolina was no hotbed of artistic expression. I was also fairly certain that no serious painter would devote half the canvas to his signature, or stick an exclamation point at the end of his name.

"That shows what *you* know," my mother said. "Art isn't about following the rules. It's about breaking them. Right, Lou?"

And my father said, "You got it."

The next thing they bought was a portrait done by a man I'll call Bradlington.

"He's an alcoholic," my mother announced, this as if his drinking somehow made him more authentic.

With the exception of my grandmother, everyone liked the Bradlington, especially me. It brought to mind a few of the Goyas I'd seen in my art history book—the paintings he did toward the end, when the faces were just sort of slashed on. "It's very moody," I pronounced. "Very . . . invocative."

A few months later, they bought another Bradlington, a portrait of a boy lying on his back in a ditch. "He's stargazing," my mother said, but to me the eyes seemed blank, like a dead person's. I thought my parents were on a roll, and was disappointed when, instead of buying a third Bradlington, they came home with an Edna Hibel. This was a lithograph rather than a painting, and it pictured a young woman collecting flowers in a basket. The yellow of the blossoms matched the new wallpaper in the breakfast nook, and so it was hung above the table. The idea of matching artwork to decor was, to me, an abomination, but anything that resulted in new stuff was just fine by my mother. She bought a sofa the salesman referred to as "the Navajo," and then she bought a piece of pottery that complemented the pattern of the upholstery. It was a vase that stood four feet high and was used to hold the dried sea oats that matched the frame of an adjacent landscape.

My mother's sister, Joyce, saw a photo of our new living room and explained that the American Indians were a lot more than sofa cushions. "Do you have any idea how those people live?" she asked. Joyce did charity work with the tribes in New Mexico, and, through her, my mother learned about desperate poverty and kachina dolls.

My father preferred the tribes of the Pacific Northwest, and began collecting masks, which smirked and glowered from the wall above the staircase. I'd hoped that the Indian stuff might lead my parents to weed out some of their earlier choices, but no such luck. "I can't get rid of *Mr. Creech,*" my mother said. "He hasn't appreciated yet."

I was in my second year of college by then and was just starting to realize that the names my parents so casually tossed around were not nationally known and never would be. Mention Bradlington to your Kent State art history teacher, and she'd take the pencil out of her mouth and say, "Who?"

"He's an alcoholic? Lives in North Carolina?"

"I'm sorry, but I've never heard of him."

As for the others, the Edna Hibels and Stephen Whites, they were the sort whose work was advertised in *ARTnews* rather than *Artforum,* their paintings and lithographs "proudly shown" alongside wind chimes at places with names like the Screeching Gull, or Desert Sunsets, galleries almost always located in a vacation spot. I tried pointing this out to my parents, but they wouldn't listen. Maybe *today* my art history teacher drew a blank on Bradlington, but after his liver gave out she'd sure as hell know who he was. "That's the way it works sometimes," my father said. "The artist is only appreciated after he's dead. Look at Van Gogh!"

"So will *every* artist be appreciated after his death?" I asked. "If I'm hit by a bus tomorrow afternoon, will the painting I did last week be worth a fortune?"

"In a word, no," my father said. "I mean, it's not enough

to just be dead. You've got to have some talent. Bradlington's got it out the ass, and so does Hibel. The gal who made the coffee table is going to last for an eternity, but as for you, I wouldn't bank on it."

"What's that supposed to mean?" I asked.

My father settled down on the Navajo. "It means that your artwork doesn't look like art."

"And you're the expert on that?"

"I'd say so, yes."

"Well, you can just go to hell," I told him.

I'd never have admitted it, but I knew exactly what my father was talking about. At its best, my art looked like homework. This was to be expected with painting and drawing—things requiring actual skill—but even my later conceptual pieces were unconvincing. The airmail envelope full of toenail clippings, the model of the Lincoln Memorial made of fudge—in someone else's hands, such objects might provoke discussion, but in my own they seemed only desperate and pretentious. Not just homework but bad homework.

I quit making homework when I turned thirty, and I started collecting paintings some ten years later, shortly after moving to Europe. A few of my canvases are French or English, portraits mainly, dating from the 1800s, but the ones I most care about are Dutch, and were done in the seventeenth century. *Monkey Eating Peaches, Man Fleeing a Burning Village, Figures Tormented by Devils in Hell*—how can you go wrong with such straightforward titles? The artists are minor—sons, most often, of infinitely more talented fathers—but if I say their names with a certain authority I can almost always provoke a response. ("Did you say Van der Pol? Oh, right, I think I saw something of his at the Louvre.")

People hush up when they stand before my paintings. They clasp their hands behind their backs and lean forward, wondering, most likely, how much I paid. I want to tell them that each cost less than the average person spends on car insurance, that and general upkeep—oil changes and break pads and such. I, myself, don't have a car, so why not take that money and put it toward something I like? Then, too, the paintings will appreciate, maybe not a lot, but given time I can surely get my money back, so in a way I'm just guarding them. Explaining, though, would ruin the illusion that I am wealthy and tasteful. A connoisseur. A collector.

The sham falls apart only when I'm visited by a real collector, or, even worse, by my father, who came in the winter of 2006 and spent a week questioning my judgment. One of my paintings shows a group of cats playing musical instruments. It sounds hokey on paper—cute, even—but in real life it's pleasantly revolting, the musicians looking more like monsters than anything you'd keep as a pet. I have it in my living room, and, after asking the price, my father shook his head the way you might when witnessing an accident. "Boy," he said. "They sure saw *you* coming."

Whether I'm buying a painting or a bedspread, his premise is always the same—namely, that I am retarded, and people take advantage of me.

"Why would something that's survived three hundred years *not* cost that much?" I asked, but he'd moved to another evident eyesore, this one Dutch, showing a man undergoing a painful and primitive foot surgery. "I wouldn't spend two minutes looking at this one," he told me.

"That's OK," I said.

"Even if I were in prison, and this was the only thing on my wall, I wouldn't waste my time with it. I'd look at my feet or at my mattress or whatever, but not this, no way."

I tried my best not to sound too hopeful. "Is someone sending you to prison?"

"No," he said. "But whoever sold this to you should be there. I don't know what you paid, but if it was more than ten dollars I think you could probably sue the guy for fraud." He looked it over one last time and then rubbed his eyes as if they'd been gassed. "God Almighty. What were you thinking?"

"If art is a matter of personal taste, why are you being so aggressive?" I asked.

"Because your taste stinks," he told me. This led him to reflect upon *Cracked Man,* which still hangs in the foyer beside his living room. "It's three slabs of clay cemented to a board, and not a day goes by when I don't sit down and look at that thing," he said. "I don't mean glancing, but full-fledged staring. Contemplating, if you catch my drift."

"I do," I said.

He then described the piece to Hugh, who had just returned from the grocery store. "It was done by a gal named Proctor. I'm sure you've heard of her."

"Actually, no," Hugh said.

My father repeated the name in his normal tone of voice. Then he began yelling it, and Hugh interrupted, saying, "Oh, right. I think I've read something about her."

"You're damn right you have," my father said.

Before they started collecting art, my parents bought some pretty great things, the best being a concrete lawn ornament

138

they picked up in the early 1960s. It's a toadstool, maybe three feet tall, with a red spotted cap and a benevolent little troll relaxing at its base. My father placed it just beyond the patio in our backyard, and what struck my sisters and me then, and still does, is the troll's expression of complete acceptance. Others might cry or get bent out of shape when their personal tastes are denounced and ridiculed, but not him. Icicles hang off his beard, slugs cleave to the tops of his pointed shoes: "Oh, well," he seems to say. "These things happen."

Even when we reached our teens and developed a sense of irony, it never occurred to us to think of the troll as tacky. No one ever stuck a lit cigarette in his mouth, or disgraced him with sexual organs, the way we did with *Mr. Balloon Man* or my mother's kitchen witch. One by one, my sisters and I left home, and the backyard became a dumping ground. Snakes nested beneath broken bicycles and piles of unused building supplies, but on return visits we would each screw up our courage and step onto the patio for an audience with Mr. Toadstool. "You and that lawn ornament," my mom would say. "Honest to God, you'd think you'd been raised in a trailer."

Standing in her living room, surrounded by her art collection, our mother frequently warned us that death brought out the worst in people. "You kids might think you're close, but just wait until your father and I are gone, and you're left to divide up our property. Then you'll see what savages you really are."

My sisters and I had always imagined that when the time came we would calmly move through the house, putting our names on this or that. Lisa would get the dessert plates;

Amy, the mixer; and so on, without dissent. It was distressing, then, to discover that the one thing we all want is that toadstool. It's a symbol of the people our parents used to be, and, more than anything in the house itself, it looks like art to us.

When my father dies, I envision a mad dash through the front door, past the Hibel and the Bradlingtons, past *Cracked Man* and *Mr. Balloon Man,* and into Indian territory, where we'll push one another down the stairs, six connoisseurs, all with gray hair, charging toward a concrete toadstool.

# Memento Mori

For the past fifteen years or so, I've made it a habit to carry a small notebook in my front pocket. The model I currently favor is called the Europa, and I pull it out an average of ten times a day, jotting down grocery lists, observations, and little thoughts on how to make money, or torment people. The last page is always reserved for phone numbers, and the second to last I use for gift ideas. These are not things I might give to other people, but things that they might give to me: a shoehorn, for instance—always wanted one. The same goes for a pencil case, which, on the low end, probably costs no more than a doughnut.

I've also got ideas in the five-hundred-to-two-thousand-dollar range, though those tend to be more specific. This nineteenth-century portrait of a dog, for example. I'm not what you'd call a dog person, far from it, but this particular one—a whippet, I think—had alarmingly big nipples, huge, like bolts screwed halfway into her belly. More interesting was that she seemed aware of it. You could see it in her eyes as she turned to face the painter. "Oh, not now," she appeared to be saying. "Have you no decency?"

I saw the portrait at the Portobello Road market in London, and though I petitioned hard for months, nobody bought it for me. I even tried initiating a pool and offered to throw in a few hundred dollars of my own money, but still no one bit. In the end I gave the money to Hugh and had him buy it. Then I had him wrap it up and offer it to me.

"What's this for?" I asked.

And, following the script, he said, "Do I need a reason to give you a present?"

Then I said, "Awwwww."

It never works the other way around, though. Ask Hugh what he wants for Christmas or his birthday, and he'll answer, "You tell me."

"Well, isn't there something you've had your eye on?"

"Maybe. Maybe not."

Hugh thinks that lists are the easy way out and says that if I *really* knew him I wouldn't have to ask what he wanted. It's not enough to search the shops; I have to search his soul as well. He turns gift-giving into a test, which I don't think is fair at all. Were I the type to run out at the last minute, he might have a valid complaint, but I start my shopping months in advance. Plus I pay attention. If, say, in the middle of the summer, Hugh should mention that he'd like an electric fan, I'll buy it that very day and hide it in my gift cupboard. Come Christmas morning, he'll open his present and frown at it for a while, before I say, "Don't you remember? You said you were burning up and would give anything for a little relief."

That's just a practical gift, though, a stocking stuffer. His main present is what I'm really after, and, knowing this, he offers no help whatsoever. Or, rather, he *used* to offer no help. It wasn't until this year that he finally dropped a hint, and even then it was fairly cryptic. "Go out the front door and turn right," he said. "Then take a left and keep walking."

He did not say "Stop before you reach the boulevard" or "When you come to the Czech border you'll know you've gone too far," but he didn't need to. I knew what he was talking about the moment I saw it. It was a human skeleton, the genuine article, hanging in the window of a medical bookstore. Hugh's old drawing teacher used to have one, and though it had been ten years since he'd taken the woman's class, I could suddenly recall him talking about it. "If I had a skeleton like Minerva's . . .," he used to say. I don't remember the rest of the sentence, as I'd always been sidetracked by the teacher's name, Minerva. Sounds like a witch.

There are things that one enjoys buying and things that one doesn't. Electronic equipment, for example. I hate shopping for stuff like that, no matter how happy it will make the recipient. I feel the same about gift certificates, and books about golf or investment strategies or how to lose twelve pounds by being yourself. I thought I would enjoy buying a human skeleton, but looking through the shop window I felt a familiar tug of disappointment. This had nothing to do with any moral considerations. I was fine with buying someone who'd been dead for a while; I just didn't want to wrap him. Finding a box would be a pain, and then there'd be the paper, which would have to be attached in strips because no one sells rolls that wide. Between one thing and another, I was almost relieved when told that the skeleton was not for sale. "He's our mascot," the store manager said. "We couldn't possibly get rid of him."

In America this translates to "Make me an offer," but in France they really mean it. There are shops in Paris where nothing is for sale, no matter how hard you beg. I think people get lonely. Their apartments become full, and, rather than rent a storage space, they take over a boutique. Then they sit there in the middle of it, gloating over their fine taste.

Being told that I couldn't buy a skeleton was just what I needed to make me really want one. Maybe that was the problem all along. It was too easy: "Take a right, take a left, and keep walking." It took the hunt out of it.

"Do you know anyone who *will* sell me a skeleton?" I asked, and the manager thought for a while. "Well," she said, "I guess you could try looking on bulletin boards."

I don't know what circles this woman runs in, but I have never in my life seen a skeleton advertised on a bulletin board. Used bicycles, yes, but no human bones, or even cartilage for that matter.

"Thank you for your help," I said.

Because I have nothing better to do with my time than shop, I tend to get excited when someone wants something obscure: an out-of-print novel, a replacement for a shattered teacup. I thought that finding another skeleton would prove difficult, but I came across two more that very afternoon— one a full-grown male and the other a newborn baby. Both were at the flea market, offered by a man who specializes in what he calls "the sorts of things that are not for everyone."

The baby was tempting because of its size—I could have wrapped it in a shoe box—but ultimately I went for the adult, which is three hundred years old and held together by a network of fine wires. There's a latch in the center of the forehead, and removing the linchpin allows you to open the skull and either root around or hide things—drugs, say, or small pieces of jewelry. It's not what one hopes for when thinking about an afterlife ("I'd like for my head to be used as a stash box"), but I didn't let that bother me. I bought the skeleton the same way I buy most everything. It was just an arrangement of parts to me, no different from a lamp or a chest of drawers.

I didn't think of it as a former person until Christmas Day, when Hugh opened the cardboard coffin. "If you don't like the color, we can bleach it," I said. "Either that or exchange it for the baby."

I always like to offer a few alternatives, though in this case they were completely unnecessary. Hugh was beside himself, couldn't have been happier. I assumed he'd be using the skeleton as a model and was a little put off when, instead of taking it to his studio, he carried it into the bedroom and hung it from the ceiling.

"Are you sure about this?" I asked.

The following morning, I reached under the bed for a discarded sock and found what I thought was a three-tiered earring. It looked like something you'd get at a craft fair, not pretty, but definitely handmade, fashioned from what looked like petrified wood. I was just holding it to the side of my head when I thought, *Hang on, this is an index finger.*

It must have fallen off while Hugh was carrying in the skeleton. Then he or I or possibly his mother, who was in town for the holidays, accidentally kicked it under the bed.

I don't think of myself as overly prissy, but it bothered me to find a finger on my bedroom floor. "If this thing is going to start shedding parts, you really *should* put it in your studio," I said to Hugh, who told me that it was his present and he'd keep it wherever the hell he wanted to. Then he got out some wire and reattached the missing finger.

It's the things you *don't* buy that stay with you the longest. This portrait of an unknown woman, for instance. I saw it a few years ago in Rotterdam, and rather than following my instincts I told the dealer that I'd think about it. The next day, I returned, and it was gone, sold, which is maybe for the best. Had I bought it myself, the painting would have gone on my office wall. I'd have admired it for a week or two, and then, little by little, it would have become invisible, just like the portrait of the dog. I wanted it, I wanted it, I wanted it, but the moment it was mine, it ceased to interest me. I no longer see the shame-filled eyes or the oversized nipples, but I do see the unknown woman, her ruddy, pious face, and the lace collar that hugged her neck like an air filter.

As the days pass, I keep hoping that the skeleton will become invisible, but he hasn't. Dangling between the dresser and the bedroom door, he is the last thing I see before falling asleep, and the first thing I see when opening my eyes in the morning.

It's funny how certain objects convey a message—my washer and dryer, for example. They can't speak, of course, but whenever I pass them they remind me that I'm doing fairly well. "No more laundromat for you," they hum. My stove, a downer, tells me every day that I can't cook, and before I can defend myself my scale jumps in, shouting from the bathroom, "Well, he must be doing *something*. My numbers are off the charts." The skeleton has a much more limited vocabulary and says only one thing: "You are going to die."

I'd always thought that I understood this, but lately I realize that what I call "understanding" is basically just fantasizing. I think about death all the time, but only in a romantic, self-serving way, beginning, most often, with my tragic illness and ending with my funeral. I see my brother squatting beside my grave, so racked by guilt that he's unable to stand. "If only I'd paid him back that twenty-five thousand dollars I borrowed," he says. I see Hugh, drying his eyes on the sleeve of his suit jacket, then crying even harder when he remembers I bought it for him. What I *didn't* see were all the people who might celebrate my death, but that's all changed with the skeleton, who assumes features at will.

One moment he's an elderly Frenchwoman, the one I didn't give my seat to on the bus. In my book, if you want to be treated like an old person, you have to look like one. That means no face-lift, no blond hair, and definitely no fishnet stockings. I think it's a perfectly valid rule, but it wouldn't have killed me to take her crutches into consideration.

"I'm sorry," I say, but before the words are out of my mouth the skeleton has morphed into a guy named Stew, who I once slighted in a drug deal.

Stew and the Frenchwoman will be happy to see me go, and there are hundreds more in line behind them, some I can name, and others I'd managed to hurt and insult without a formal introduction. I hadn't thought of these people in years, but that's the skeleton's cleverness. He gets into my head when I'm asleep and picks through the muck at the bottom of my skull. "Why me?" I ask. "Hugh is lying in the very same bed. How come you don't go after him?"

And the skeleton says, "You are going to die."

"But I'm the one who found your finger."

"You are going to die."

I say to Hugh, "Are you *sure* you wouldn't be happier with the baby?"

For the first few weeks, I heard the voice only when I was in the bedroom. Then it spread and took over the entire apartment. I'd be sitting in my office, gossiping on the telephone, and the skeleton would cut in, sounding like an international operator. "You are going to die."

I stretched out in the bathtub, soaking in fragrant oils, while outside my window beggars were gathered like kittens upon the heating grates.

"You are going to die."

In the kitchen I threw away a perfectly good egg. In the closet I put on a sweater some half-blind child was paid ten sesame seeds to make. In the living room I took out my notebook and added a bust of Satan to the list of gifts I'd like to receive.

"You are going to die. You are going to die. You are going to die."

"Do you think you could alter that just a little?" I asked. But he wouldn't.

Having been dead for three hundred years, there's a lot the skeleton doesn't understand: TV, for instance. "See," I told him, "you just push this button, and entertainment comes into your home." He seemed impressed, and so I took it a step further. "I invented it myself, to bring comfort to the old and sick."

"You are going to die."

He had the same reaction to the vacuum cleaner, even after I used the nozzle attachment to dust his skull. "You are going to die."

And that's when I broke down. "I'll do anything you like," I said. "I'll make amends to the people I've hurt, I'll bathe in rainwater, you name it, just please say something, anything, else."

The skeleton hesitated a moment. "You are going to be dead . . . some day," he told me.

And I put away the vacuum cleaner, thinking, *Well, that's a start.*

# All the Beauty You Will Ever Need

In Paris they warn you before cutting off the water, but out in Normandy you're just supposed to know. You're also supposed to be prepared, and it's this last part that gets me every time. Still, though, I manage to get by. A saucepan of chicken broth will do for shaving, and in a pinch I can always find something to pour into the toilet tank: orange juice, milk, a lesser champagne. If I really get hard up, I suppose I could hike through the woods and bathe in the river, though it's never quite come to that.

Most often, our water is shut off because of some reconstruction project, either in our village or in the next one over. A hole is dug, a pipe is replaced, and within a few hours things are back to normal. The mystery is that it's so perfectly timed to my schedule. This is to say that the tap dries up at the exact moment I roll out of bed, which is usually between 10:00 and 10:30. For me this is early, but for

Hugh and most of our neighbors it's something closer to midday. What they do at 6:00 a.m. is anyone's guess. I only know that they're incredibly self-righteous about it and talk about the dawn as if it's a personal reward, bestowed on account of their great virtue.

The last time our water was cut, it was early summer. I got up at my regular hour and saw that Hugh was off somewhere, doing whatever it is he does. This left me alone to solve the coffee problem—a sort of catch-22, as in order to think straight I need caffeine, and in order to make that happen I need to think straight. Once, in a half sleep, I made it with Perrier, which sounds plausible but really isn't. On another occasion, I heated up some leftover tea and poured that over the grounds. Had the tea been black rather than green, the coffee might have worked out, but, as it was, the result was vile. It wasn't the sort of thing you'd try more than once, so this time I skipped the teapot and headed straight for a vase of wildflowers sitting by the phone on one of the living room tables.

Hugh had picked them the previous day, and it broke my heart to think of him marching across a muddy field with a bouquet in his hand. He does these things that are somehow *beyond* faggy and seem better suited to some hardscrabble pioneer wife: making jam, say, or sewing bedroom curtains out of burlap. Once I caught him down at the riverbank, beating our dirty clothes against a rock. This was before we got a washing machine, but still, he could have laundered things in the tub. "Who *are* you?" I'd said, and, as he turned, I half expected to see a baby at his breast, not nestled in one of those comfortable supports but hanging, red-faced, by its gums.

When Hugh beats underpants against river rocks or decides that it might be fun to grind his own flour, I think of a couple I once met. This was years ago, in the early nineties. I was living in New York and had returned to North Carolina for Christmas, my first priority being to get high and stay that way. My brother, Paul, knew of a guy who possibly had some pot to sell, so a phone call was made, and, in the way that these things happen, we found ourselves in a trailer twenty-odd miles outside of Raleigh.

The dealer was named Little Mike, and he addressed both Paul and me as "Bromine." He looked like a high school student, or, closer still, like one of those kids who dropped out and then spent all day hanging around the parking lot: tracksuit, rattail, a wisp of thread looped through his freshly pierced ear. After a few words regarding my brother's car, Little Mike ushered us inside and introduced us to his wife, who was sitting on their sofa, watching a Christmas special. The girl's stockinged feet were resting on the coffee table, and settled between her legs, just south of her lap, was a flat-faced Persian. Both she and the cat had wide-set eyes, and ginger-colored hair, though hers was partially hidden beneath a woolen cap. Common too was the way they stuck their noses in the air when my brother and I entered the room. A little hostility was to be expected from the Persian, and I guessed I couldn't blame the wife either. Here she was trying to watch TV, and these two guys show up—people she didn't even know.

"Don't mind Beth," Little Mike said, and he smacked the underside of the girl's foot.

"Owww, asshole."

He advanced upon the other foot, and I pretended to

admire the Christmas tree, which was miniature and artificial, and stood upon a barstool beside the front door. "This is nice," I announced, and Beth shot me a withering look. *Liar,* it said. *You're just saying that because my stupid husband sells reefer.*

She really wanted us out of there, but Little Mike seemed to welcome our company. "Sit down," he told me. "Have a libation." He and Paul went to the refrigerator to get us some beers, and the girl called after them to bring her a rum and Coke. Then she turned back to the TV and glared at the screen, saying, "This show's boring. Hand me the nigger."

I smiled at the cat, as if this would somehow fix things, and when Beth pointed to the far end of the coffee table, I saw that she was referring to the remote control. Under other circumstances, I might have listed the various differences between black people, who had been forced to work for no money, and black, battery-operated channel changers, which had neither thoughts nor feelings and didn't mind doing stuff for free. But the deal hadn't started yet, and, more than anything, I wanted my drugs. Thus the remote was handed over, and I watched as the pot dealer's wife flicked from one station to the next, looking for something that might satisfy her.

She had just settled on a situation comedy when Paul and Little Mike returned with the drinks. Beth was dissatisfied with her ice-cube count, and, after suggesting that she could just go fuck herself, our host reached into the waistband of his track pants and pulled out a bag of marijuana. It was eight ounces at least, a small cushion, and as I feasted my eyes upon it Little Mike pushed his wife's feet off the coffee table, saying, "Bitch, go get me my scale."

"I'm watching TV. Get it your own self."

"Whore," he said.

"Asshole."

"See the kind of shit I have to live with?" Little Mike sighed and retreated to the rear of the trailer—the bedroom, I guessed—returning a minute later with a scale and some rolling papers. The pot was sticky with lots of buds, and its smell reminded me of a Christmas tree, though not the one perched atop the barstool. After weighing my ounce and counting out my money, Little Mike rolled a joint, which he lit, drew upon, and handed to my brother. It then went to me, and just as I was passing it back to our host, his wife piped up: "Hey, what about *me?*"

"Now look who wants to play," her husband said. "Women. They'll suck the fucking paper off a joint, but when old Papa Bear needs a little b.j. action they've always got a sore throat."

Beth tried to speak and hold in the smoke at the same time: "Hut hup, hasshole."

"Either of you guys married?" Little Mike asked, and Paul shook his head no. "I got pre-engaged one time, but David here hasn't never come close, his being a faggot and all."

Little Mike laughed, and then he looked at me. "For real?" he said. "Is Bromine telling me the truth?"

"Oh, he's all up inside that shit," Paul said. "Has hisself a cocksucker—I mean a boyfriend—and everything."

I could have done my own talking, but it was sort of nice listening to my brother, who sounded almost boastful, as if I were a pet that had learned to do math.

"Well, what do you know," Little Mike said.

His wife stirred to action then and became almost

sociable. "So this boyfriend," she said. "Let me ask. Which one of you is the woman?"

"Well, neither of us," I told her. "That's what makes us a homosexual couple. We're both guys."

"But no," she said. "I mean, like, in prison or whatnot. One of you has to be in for murder and the other for child molesting or something like that, right? I mean, one is more like a normal man."

I wanted to ask if that would be the murderer or the child molester, but instead I just accepted the joint, saying, "Oh, we live in New York," as if that answered the question.

We stayed in the trailer for another half hour, and during the ride back to Raleigh I thought about what the drug dealer's wife had said. Her examples were a little skewed, but I knew what she was getting at. People I know, people who live in houses and do not call their remote control "the nigger," have often asked the same question, though usually in regard to lesbians, who are always either absent or safely out of earshot. "Which one's the man?"

It's astonishing the amount of time that certain straight people devote to gay sex—trying to determine what goes where and how often. They can't imagine any system outside their own, and seem obsessed with the idea of roles, both in bed and out of it. Who calls whom a bitch? Who cries harder when the cat dies? Which one spends the most time in the bathroom? I guess they think that it's that cut-and-dried, though of course it's not. Hugh might do the cooking, and actually wear an apron while he's at it, but he also chops the firewood, repairs the hot-water heater, and could tear off my arm with no more effort than it takes to uproot a dandelion. Does that make him the murderer, or do the homemade curtains reduce him to the level of the child molester?

I considered these things as I looked at the wildflowers he'd collected the day before the water was shut off. Some were the color I associate with yield signs, and others a sort of muted lavender, their stems as thin as wire. I pictured Hugh stooping, or maybe even kneeling, as he went about picking them, and then I grabbed the entire bunch and tossed it out the window. That done, I carried the vase into the kitchen and emptied the yellow water into a pan. I then boiled it and used it to make coffee. There'd be hell to pay when my man got home, but at least by then I would be awake and able to argue, perhaps convincingly, that I am all the beauty he will ever need.

# Town and Country

They looked like people who had just attended a horse show: a stately couple in their late sixties, he in a cashmere blazer and she in a gray tweed jacket, a gem-encrusted shamrock glittering against the rich felt of her lapel. They were my seatmates on the flight from Denver to New York, and as I stood in the aisle to let them in, I felt the shame of the tragically outclassed. The sport coat I had prided myself on now looked clownish, as did my shoes, and the fistful of pine straw I refer to as my hair. "Excuse me," I said, apologizing, basically, for my very existence.

The couple took their seats and, just as I settled in beside them, the man turned to the woman, saying, "I don't want to hear this shit."

I assumed he was continuing an earlier argument, but it turned out he was referring to the Gershwin number the airline had adopted as its theme song. "I can't believe the fucking crap they make you listen to on planes nowadays."

The woman patted her silver hair and agreed, saying that whoever had programmed the music was an asshole.

"A cocksucker," the man corrected her. "A goddamn cock-sucking asshole." They weren't loud people and didn't even sound all that angry, really. This was just the way they spoke, the verbal equivalent of their everyday china. Among company, the wife might remark that she felt a slight chill, but here that translated to "I am fucking freezing."

"Me too," her husband said. "It's cold as shit in here." *Shit* is the tofu of cursing and can be molded to whichever condition the speaker desires. Hot as shit. Windy as shit. I myself was confounded as shit, for how had I so misjudged these people? Why, after all these years, do I still believe that expensive clothing signifies anything more than a disposable income, that tweed and cashmere actually bespeak refinement?

When our boxed bistro meals were handed out, the couple really went off. "What is this garbage?" the man asked.

"It's shit," his wife said. "A box of absolute fuck-ing shit."

The man took out his reading glasses and briefly examined his plastic-wrapped cookie before tossing it back into the box. "First they make you listen to shit, and then they make you eat it!"

"Well, I'm not fucking eating it," the woman said. "We'll just have to grab something at the airport."

"And pay some son of a bitch fifteen bucks for a sandwich?"

The woman sighed and threw up her hands. "What

choice do we have? It's either that or eat what we've got, which is shit."

"Aww, it's all shit," her husband said.

It was as if they'd kidnapped the grandparents from a Ralph Lauren ad and forced them into a David Mamet play—and that, in part, is why the couple so appealed to me: there was something ridiculous and unexpected about them. They made a good team, and I wished that I could spend a week or two invisibly following behind them and seeing the world through their eyes. "Thanksgiving dinner, my ass," I imagined them saying.

It was late afternoon by the time we arrived at LaGuardia. I caught a cab outside the baggage claim and stepped into what smelled like a bad tropical cocktail, this the result of a coconut air freshener that dangled from the rearview mirror. One hates to be a baby about this kind of thing, and so I cracked the window a bit and gave the driver my sister's address in the West Village.

"Yes, sir."

The man was foreign, but I have no idea where he was from. One of those tragic countries, I supposed, a land beset by cobras and typhoons. But that's half the world, really. He had dark skin, more brown than olive, and thick black hair he had treated with oil. The teeth of his comb had left deep troughs that ran down the back of his head and disappeared beneath the frayed collar of his shirt. The cab left the curb, and as he merged into traffic the driver opened the window between the front and back seats and asked me my name. I told him, and he looked at me in the rearview mirror, saying, "You are a good man, David, is that right? Are you good?"

I said I was OK, and he continued. "David is a good name, and New York is a good town. Do you think so?"

"I guess," I said.

The driver smiled shyly, as if I had paid him a compliment, and I wondered what his life was like. One reads things, newspaper profiles and so forth, and gets an idea of the tireless, hardworking immigrant who hits the ground running—or, more often, driving. The man couldn't have been older than thirty-five, and after his shift I imagined that he probably went to school and studied until he couldn't keep his eyes open. A few hours at home with his wife and children, and then it was back to the front seat, and on and on until he earned a diploma and resumed his career as a radiologist. The only thing holding him up was his accent, but that would likely disappear with time and diligence.

I thought of my first few months in Paris and of how frustrating it had been when people spoke quickly or used improper French, and then I answered his question again, speaking as clearly as possible. "I have no opinion on the name David," I said. "But I agree with you regarding the city of New York. It is a very satisfactory place."

He then said something I didn't quite catch, and when I asked him to repeat it, he became agitated and turned in his seat, saying, "What is the problem, David? You cannot hear when a person is talking?"

I told him my ears were stopped up from the plane, though it wasn't true. I could hear him perfectly. I just couldn't understand him.

"I ask you what you do for a profession," he said. "Do you make a lot of moneys? I know by your jacket that you do, David. I know that you are rich."

Suddenly my sport coat looked a lot better. "I get by," I said. "That is to say that I am able to support myself, which is not the same as being rich."

He then asked if I had a girlfriend, and when I told him no he gathered his thick eyebrows and made a little *tsk*ing sound. "Oh, David, you need a woman. Not for love, but for the pussy, which is a necessary thing for a man. Like me, for example. I fuck daily."

"Oh," I said. "And this is . . . Tuesday, right?" I'd hoped I might steer him onto another track—the days of the week, maybe—but he was tired of English 101.

"How is it that you do not need pussy?" he asked. "Does not your dick stand up?"

"Excuse me?"

"Sex," he said. "Has no one never told you about it?"

I took the *New York Times* from my carry-on bag and pretended to read, an act that apparently explained it all.

"Ohhh," the driver said. "I understand. You do not like pussy. You like the dick. Is that it?" I brought the paper close to my face, and he stuck his arm through the little window and slapped the back of his seat. "David," he said. "David, listen to me when I am talking to you. I asked do you like the dick?"

"I just work," I told him. "I work, and then I go home, and then I work some more." I was trying to set a good example, trying to be the person I'd imagined him to be, but it was a lost cause.

"I fucky-fuck every day," he boasted. "Two women. I have a wife and another girl for the weekend. Two kind of pussy. Are you sure you no like to fucky-fuck?"

If forced to, I can live with the word "pussy, "but "fucky-fuck" was making me carsick. "That is not a real word,"

163

I told him. "You can say that you *fuck,* but *fucky-fuck* is just nonsense. Nobody talks that way. You will never get ahead with that kind of language."

Traffic thickened because of an accident and, as we slowed to a stop, the driver ran his tongue over his lips. "Fucky-fuck," he repeated. "I fucky-fucky-fucky-fuck."

Had we been in Manhattan, I might have gotten out and found myself another taxi, but we were still on the expressway, so what choice did I have but to stay put and look with envy at the approaching rescue vehicles? Eventually the traffic began moving, and I resigned myself to another twenty minutes of torture.

"So you go to West Village," the driver said. "Very good place for you to live. Lots of boys and boys together. Girls and girls together."

"It is not where I live," I said. "It is the apartment of my sister."

"Tell me how those lesbians have sex? How do they do it?"

I said I didn't know, and he looked at me with the same sad expression he had worn earlier when told that I didn't have a girlfriend. "David." He sighed. "You have never seen a lesbian movie? You should, you know. You need to go home, drink whiskey, and watch one just to see how it is done. See how they get their pussy. See how they fucky-fuck."

And then I snapped, which is unlike me, really. "You know," I said, "I do not think that I am going to take you up on that. In fact, I *know* that I am not going to take you up on that."

"Oh, but you should."

"Why?" I said. "So I can be more like *you?* That's a worth-while goal, isn't it? I will just get myself a coconut air freshener and drive about town impressing people with the beautiful language I have picked up from pornographic movies. 'Hello, sir, does not your dick stand up?' 'Good afternoon, madam, do you like to fucky-fuck?' It sounds enchanting, but I don't know that I could stand to have such a rewarding existence. I am not worthy, OK, so if it is all right with you, I will not watch any lesbian movies tonight or tomorrow night or any other night, for that matter. Instead I will just work and leave people alone."

I waited for a response, and when none came I settled back in my seat, completely ashamed of myself. The driver's familiarity had been maddening, but what I'd said had been cruel and uncalled for. Mocking him, bringing up his air freshener: I felt as though I had just kicked a kitten—a filthy one, to be sure—but still something small and powerless. Sex is what you boast about when you have no exterior signs of wealth. It's a way of saying, "Look, I might not own a fancy sport coat, or even a carry-on bag, but I do have two women and all the intercourse I can handle." And would it have hurt me to acknowledge his success?

"I think it is wonderful that you are so fulfilled," I said, but rather than responding the driver turned on the radio, which was of course tuned to NPR.

By the time I got to my sister's, it was dark. I poured myself a Scotch and then, like always, Amy brought out a few things she thought I might find interesting. The first was a copy of *The Joy of Sex,* which she'd found at a flea market and planned to leave on the coffee table the next time our

165

father visited. "What do you think he'll say?" she asked. It was the last thing a man would want to find in his daughter's apartment—that was my thought anyway—but then she handed me a magazine called *New Animal Orgy*, which was *truly* the last thing a man would want to find in his daughter's apartment. This was an old issue, dated 1974, and it smelled as if it had spent the past few decades in the dark, not just hidden but locked in a chest and buried underground.

"Isn't that the filthiest thing you've ever seen in your life?" Amy asked, but I found myself too stunned to answer. The magazine was devoted to two major stories—photo essays, I guess you could call them. The first involved a female cyclist who stops to rest beside an abandoned windmill and seduces what the captions refer to as "a stray collie."

"He's not a stray," Amy said. "Look at that coat. You can practically smell the shampoo."

The second story was even sadder and concerned a couple of women named Inga and Bodil, who stimulate a white stallion using first their hands and later their tongues. It was supposedly the luckiest day of the horse's life, but if the sex was really that good you'd think he would stop eating or at least do something different with his eyes. Instead he just went about his business, acting as if the women were not there. On the next page, he's led into the bedroom, where he stands on the carpet and stares dumbly at the objects on the women's dresser: a hairbrush, an aerosol can turned on its side, a framed photo of a girl holding a baby. Above the dresser was a curtainless window, and through it could be seen a field leading to a forest of tall pines.

Amy leaned closer and pointed to the bottom of the

picture. "Look at the mud on that carpet," she said, but I was way ahead of her.

"Number one reason *not* to blow a horse in your bedroom," I told her, though it was actually much further down on the list. Number four maybe, the top slots being reserved for the loss of dignity, the invitation to disease, and the off chance that your parents might drop by.

Once again the women stimulate the horse to an erection, and then they begin to pleasure each other—assuming, I guess, that he will enjoy watching. This doesn't mean they were necessarily lesbians—not any more than the collie was a stray—but it gave me pause and forced me to think of the cabdriver. "I am not like you," I had told him. Then, half an hour later, here I was: a glass in one hand and in the other a magazine showing two naked women making out in front of a stallion. Of course, the circumstances were a bit different. I was drinking Scotch instead of whiskey. This was a periodical rather than a video. I was with my sister, and we were just two decent people having a laugh. Weren't we?

# Aerial

The latest Kate Bush CD includes a song called "Aerial," and one spring afternoon Hugh sat down to listen to it. In the city, I'm forever nagging him about the volume. "The neighbors!" I say. But out in Normandy, I lose my excuse and have to admit that it's me who's being disturbed. The music I can usually live with. It's the lyrics I find irritating, especially when I'm at my desk and am looking for a reason to feel distracted. If one line ends with, say, the word "stranger," I'll try to second-guess the corresponding rhyme. *Danger,* I'll think. Then, *No, wait, this is a Christmas album. Manger. The word will be "manger."*

If I guess correctly, the songwriter will be cursed for his predictability. If I guess incorrectly, he's being "willfully obtuse," a phrase I learned from my publisher, who applied it to the title of my last book. It's a no-win situation that's made even worse when the lyrics are unintelligible, the voice a shriek embedded in noise. This makes me feel both cranky *and* old, the type of pill who says things like, "You and that rock!"

There are singers Hugh's not allowed to listen to while I'm in the house, but Kate Bush isn't one of them, or at least she wasn't until recently. The song I mentioned, "Aerial," opens with the trilling of birds. This might be startling if you lived in the city, but out in Normandy it's all we ever hear: a constant din of chirps and whistles that may grow faint at certain times of year but never goes away. It's like living in an aviary. Added to the calls of larks and swallows are the geese and chickens that live across the road. After they've all gone to bed, the owls come out and raise hell until dawn, when the whole thing starts over again.

The Kate Bush song had been playing for all of thirty seconds when we heard an odd noise and turned to see a bird rapping its beak against the windowpane. A moment later, its identical twin appeared at the adjacent window and began to do the same thing. Had they knocked once or twice, I'd have chalked it up to an accident, but these two were really going at it, like woodpeckers, almost. "What's gotten into them?" I asked.

Hugh turned to the liner notes, hoping to find some sort of an explanation. "Maybe the recorded birds are saying something about free food," he suggested, but to me the message seemed much darker: a call to anarchy, or possibly even murder. Some might think this was crazy, but I'd been keeping my ear to the ground and had learned that birds are not as carefree as they're cracked up to be. Take the crows that descend each winter on the surrounding fields and pluck the eyes out of newborn lambs. Are they so hard up for a snack that they have to blind an international symbol of youth and innocence, or are they simply evil, a quality they possibly share with these two things at the window?

"What do you *want* from us?" I asked, and the birds stepped back into the flower box, getting a little traction before hurling themselves against the glass.

"They'll wear themselves out sooner or later," Hugh said. But they didn't, not even after the clouds moved in and it began to rain. By late afternoon, they were still at it, soaking wet, but no less determined. I was lying on the daybed, working a crossword puzzle and listening to the distinct sound of feathers against glass. Every two minutes, I'd put aside my paper and walk across the room. "You think it's so great in here?" I'd ask. "You think we've got something you can't live without?" At my approach, the birds would fly away, returning the moment I'd settled back down. Then I'd say, "All right, if you really want to come in that much . . ."

But the two lost interest as soon as the windows were open. And so I'd close them up again and return to my puzzle, at which point the birds would reappear and continue their assault. Then I'd say, "All right, if you really want to come in that much . . ."

Einstein wrote that insanity is doing the same thing over and over and expecting a different result each time. That said, is it crazier to repeatedly throw yourself against a window, or to repeatedly *open* that window, believing the things that are throwing themselves against it might come into your house, take a look around, and leave with no hard feelings?

I considered this as I leafed through *Birds of the World,* an illustrated guidebook as thick as a dictionary. After learning about the Philippine eagle—a heartless predator whose diet consists mainly of monkeys—I identified the things at the window as chaffinches. The size was about right, six inches from head to tail, with longish legs, pink breasts, and crooked white bands running along the wings. The book explained that they eat fruit, seeds, and insects. It stated that some chaffinches prefer to winter in India or North Africa, but it did not explain why they were trying to get into my house.

"Could it be something they picked up in Africa?" I wondered. And Hugh, who had lived there until his late teens, said, "Why are you asking me?"

When the sun finally set, the birds went away, but they were at it again the following morning. Between their running starts and their pitiful back-assed tumbles, the flowers in the window box had been trashed, petals and bits of stem scattered everywhere. There were scratch marks on the windowpanes, along with what I'm guessing was saliva, the thick, bubbly kind that forms when you're enraged.

"What do we do now?" I asked.

And Hugh told me to ignore them. "They just want attention." This is his explanation for everything from rowdy children to low-flying planes. "Turn the other way and they'll leave," he told me. But how could I turn away?

The solution, it seemed, was to make some kind of a scarecrow, which is not a bad project if you're in the proper mood. My first attempt involved an upside-down broom and a paper bag, which I placed over the bristles and drew an angry face on. For hair, I used a knot of steel wool. This made the figure look old and powerless, an overly tanned grandma mad because she had no arms. The birds thought it was funny, and after chuckling for a moment or two they took a step back and charged against the window.

Plan B was much easier, involving nothing more than a climb to the attic, which Hugh uses as his studio. A few years earlier, bored, and in the middle of several projects, he started copying head shots he'd clipped from the newspaper. The resulting portraits were done in different styles, but the ones that best suited my purposes looked Mesopotamian and pictured the hijackers of American Airlines Flight 11. Mohammed Atta fit perfectly into the windowpane, and his effect was immediate. The birds flew up, saw a terrorist staring back at them, and took off screaming.

I was feeling very satisfied with myself when I heard a thud coming from behind a closed curtain next to the bookcase. Another trip upstairs, another hijacker, and so on, until all four living room windows were secured. It was then that the birds focused their attention on the bedroom, and I had no choice but to return to the attic.

Aside from CDs, which Hugh buys like candy, his record collection is also pretty big. Most are albums he bought in his youth and shipped to Normandy against my wishes: *Led Zeppelin II,* Pink Floyd's *Dark Side of the Moon.* If it played nonstop in a skanky-smelling dorm room, he's got it. I come home from my 5:00 walk, and here's Toto or Bad Company blaring from the attic. "Turn that crap off," I yell, but of course Hugh can't hear me. So I go up, and there he is, positioned before his easel, one foot rigid on the floor and the other keeping time with some guy in a spandex jumpsuit.

"Do you mind?" I say.

I never thought I would appreciate his music collection,

but the chaffinches changed all that. What I needed were record jackets featuring life-sized heads, so I started with the *A*'s and worked my way through the stack of boxes. The surprise was that some of Hugh's albums weren't so bad. "I didn't know he had this," I said to myself, and I raced downstairs to prop Roberta Flack in the bedroom window. This was the cover of *Chapter Two,* and while, to me, the singer looked welcoming, the birds thought differently, and moved on to a room that once functioned as a milking parlor. There I filled the windows with Bob Dylan, Bruce Springsteen, Joan Armatrading, and Donna Summer, who has her minuses but can really put the fear of God into a chaffinch.

The pair then moved upstairs to my office, where Janis Joplin and I were waiting for them. Bonnie Raitt and Rodney Crowell were standing by in case there was trouble with the skylights, but, strangely, the birds had no interest in them. Horizontal surfaces were not their thing, and so they flew on to the bathroom.

By late afternoon, every window was filled. The storm clouds that had appeared the previous day finally blew off, and I was able to walk to the neighboring village. The route I normally take is circular and leads past a stucco house occupied by a frail elderly couple. For years they raised rabbits in their front yard, but last summer they either ate them, which is normal in this area, or turned them loose, which is unheard of. Then they got rid of the pen and built in its place a clumsy wooden shed. A few months later a cage appeared on its doorstep. It was the type you might keep a rodent in, but instead of a guinea pig they use it to hold a pair of full-grown magpies. They're good-sized birds— almost as tall as crows—and their quarters are much too small for them. Unlike parakeets, which will eventually settle down, the magpies are constantly searching for a way out, and move as if they're on fire, darting from one end of the cage to another and banging their heads against the wire ceiling.

Their desperation is contagious, and watching them causes my pulse to quicken. Being locked up is one thing, but to have no concept of confinement, to be ignorant of its terms and never understand that struggle is useless—that's what hell must be like. The magpies leave me feeling so depressed and anxious that I wonder how I can possibly make it the rest of the way home. I always do, though, and it's always a welcome sight, especially lately. At around 7:00 the light settles on the western wall of our house, just catching two of the hijackers and a half-dozen singer-songwriters, who look out from the windows, some smiling, as if they are happy to see me, and others just staring into space, the way one might when listening to music, or waiting, halfheartedly, for something to happen.

# The Man in the Hut

A single road runs through our village in Normandy, and, depending on which direction you come from, either the first or the last thing you pass is a one-story house—a virtual Quonset hut—made of concrete blocks. The roof is covered with metal, and large sheets of corrugated plastic, some green and others milk-colored, have been joined together to form an awning that sags above the front door. It's so ugly that the No Trespassing sign reads as an insult. *"As if,"* people say. "I mean, *really.*"

The hut was built by a man I'll call Jackie, who used to live there with his wife and his wife's adult daughter, Clothilde, who was retarded. On summer evenings after their dinner, the wife would dress her daughter in pajamas and a bathrobe and walk her either through the village or in the opposite direction, where the road steepens and winds in a series of blind curves. Depending upon the weather,

Clothilde wore plaid bedroom slippers or a pair of rubber boots that came to above her knees and changed her walk to a kind of goose step. I'd heard from neighbors that she attended a special school, but I think it was more of a sheltered workshop, the type at which the students perform simple tasks—putting bolts into bags, say. Though I never heard her speak, she did make noises. It's a contradiction in terms, but, if forced to describe what came out of her mouth, I'd call it an "upbeat moan," not unpleasant but joyful. I can't say that Clothilde was a friend, but it made me happy to know that she was around. The same was true of her mother and her stepfather: the whole family.

Jackie had some sort of problem with his leg and usually walked no farther than he had to. He drove a truck so small and quiet it seemed like a toy, and every so often, as I was walking into town, he'd pull over and offer me a ride. On one of these trips, he attempted to explain that he had a metal plate in his head. My French comprehension wasn't very good at the time, and his pointing back and forth between his temple and the door of the glove compartment only confused me. "You invented glove compartments? Your glove compartment has ideas of its own? I'm sorry . . . I don't . . . I don't understand."

I later learned that when he was a boy Jackie had found an unexploded grenade in one of the nearby fields. He pulled the pin and threw it, but not quite far enough; thus the metal plate and his messed-up leg. His hearing had been affected as well, and his eyes were deeply shadowed and encircled by spidery scars. Crew cut, dented brow, lower jaw jutting just slightly forward: had he been tall, his appearance might have startled you, but, as it was, he was pint-sized, five

178

feet two, maybe five-four, tops. When the villagers spoke of Jackie, they used the words "slow" and "gentle," and so it seemed outrageous when the police stormed the ugly cinder-block hut and took him off to jail. Someone or other spoke to the local councilor, and within an hour everyone knew that Jackie was suspected of sexually molesting his wife's grandchildren, who were aged six and eight and occasionally visited from their home, an hour or so away. It was speculated that he also molested Clothilde, but I couldn't bring myself to believe it. Hugh says I just don't want to believe it, and I tell him he's right—I don't. She and her mother left our village shortly after Jackie was taken away, and I never saw either of them again.

With no one to maintain it, the house that was ugly became even uglier. Our neighbors across the road would often comment on what an eyesore it was, and, while agreeing, I'd lament the sorry state of my French. Oh, my comprehension had improved—I could understand just about everything that was said to me—but when it came to speaking I tended (and still do) to freeze up. It wouldn't hurt me to be more social, but I don't see that happening anytime soon. The phone rings and I avoid it. Neighbors knock and I duck into the bedroom or crouch behind the daybed until they've left. How different things might be, I think, if, like Jackie, I had no more hiding places. Though harsh in other respects, prison would be an excellent place to learn a foreign language—total immersion, and you'd have the new slang before it even hit the streets. Unlike the French school that I actually attended, this one, when it came to verbs, would likely start with the imperative: "Bend over." "Take it." That

179

kind of thing. Still, though, you'd have your little conversations. In the cafeteria, in the recreation room or crafts center,
if they have them in a French prison, and I imagine they do.
"Tell me, Jean-Claude, do you like the glaze I've applied to
my shapely jug?"

Of the above, I can say, "Tell me, Jean-Claude, do you
like the . . . jug?"

"Glaze" is one of those words that shouldn't be too difficult to learn, and the same goes for "shapely." I'm pretty
good when it comes to retaining nouns and adjectives, but
the bit about applying the glaze to the shapely jug—that's
where I tend to stumble. In English, it's easy enough—"I
put this on that"—but in French, such things have a way of
biting you in the ass. I might have to say, "Do you like the
glaze the shapely jug accepted from me?" or "Do you like the
shapely jug in the glaze of which I earlier applied?"

For safety's sake, perhaps I'd be better off breaking the one
sentence into three:

"Look at the shapely jug."

"Do you like the glaze?"

"I did that."

If I spent as much time speaking to my neighbors as I do
practicing imaginary conversations in the prison crafts
center, I'd be fluent by now and could quit making excuses
for myself. As it is, whenever someone asks how long I've
been in France I wonder if it's possible to literally die of
shame. "I'm away a lot," I always say. "Two and a half
months a year in America, and at least two in England,
sometimes more."

"Yes, but how long ago did you come to France?"

"What?"

"I asked, 'How. Long. Have. You. Been. In. France?'"

Then I might say, "I love chicken," or "Big bees can be dangerous," anything to change the subject.

What I needed was an acquaintance, and what I wound up with was Jackie. This was after his release, obviously. He'd been gone for close to three years when I walked past the hut one day and noticed a pair of little black socks hanging on the clothesline.

"Who do you suppose those belong to?" I asked the woman across the road, and she pulled an unusually sour face, and said, "Who do you think?"

I'd imagined that, like his wife and stepdaughter, Jackie would move away and start over, but it seemed he had no place to go and no money to go there with. After hanging out his socks, he picked up his rake and hoe and started getting his lawn in shape. It was strange. Were an American sex offender to return home, there'd be a big to-do. Here, though, it was all very quiet. No meeting was held that I was aware of, but somehow or other it was agreed that no one would look at or speak to this man. He would be treated as if he were invisible, and, with luck, the isolation would drive him away.

He'd been back in his hut for a week or so when I walked by and saw him inside his front gate, worrying something with the tip of his cane. Jackie had always been kind to me, so when he looked up and said hello I employed one of the formalities I'd learned years earlier in French class. "I am content to see you again," I said. Then I shook his hand.

"What did you do that for?" Hugh asked later, and I said, "Well, what *could* I do? Someone says hello and sticks his hand out, and you're just supposed to walk away?"

181

"If he's a child molester, yes," he said. But I'd like to see what he would have done in the same situation.

A few years later, after Jackie died of cancer, and the garden he so carefully tended had turned to weeds, I gave the baccalaureate address at a certain American university. When the speech was finished, I joined a procession of deans and distinguished fellows back to the president's house, and it was there that a well-known politician approached and extended his hand, saying, "I just want you to know how much I enjoyed that." Now, this politician—it's not that I simply disagree with him. I despise him. I loathe him. My friends and I, the way we throw his name around, you'd think we were talking about the Devil himself. Spittle forms in the corners of our mouth as we denounce him, his party, and the people we refer to as his henchmen and cronies.

I hadn't known that this politician was going to be in the procession that day; rather, I turned around and there he was, the two of us dressed in flowing robes, like wizards.

"I just want you to know how much I enjoyed that." So did I place a pox upon him? Did I spit in his face, or even turn my back?

Of course not. With everyone watching, I looked up, and said, "Oh. Thank you." And because he had held out his hand I took it, just as I had taken Jackie's after his release from prison.

I said to Hugh after the graduation, "But I wasn't enthusiastic about it. Sure, I said, 'Oh' and 'Thank you,' but anyone who knows me would know that I was faking it, that I didn't really mean the 'thank you' part."

"Well," Hugh said, "I guess you showed him."

Had the politician been my neighbor, I might have moved. That's how disgusted I would have felt, but Jackie, because of the metal plate in his head, because you could put a magnet to his temple and it would stay there, aroused pity rather than anger, or at least he did in me. I didn't go out of my way to pass his hut, but neither did I go out of my way to avoid passing it. If he was in the yard, he'd say hello and I would say hello back, or "Yes, it certainly is warm," or whatever answer seemed called for. And in this way—a word here, a wave there—little by little the summer advanced, and Jackie came to see the two of us as friends. One afternoon he invited me inside his front gate to show me the tomatoes he'd planted.

"Well," and I looked to see if any of our neighbors were watching. No one was, so I opened the latch, saying, "OK, sure."

During the years that he had been away, Jackie's hair had gone from brown to gray. His eyes were flat and more heavily shadowed, and what had once been a pronounced limp had grown more subtle. It seemed that while in prison he had had a hip replaced, and the way he walked now was miles better than it had been before the operation. "Hey," he said, and he gestured behind him in the direction of his open front door. "Do you . . . want to come in and look at my X-rays?"

As I later said to Hugh, "Do you tell a person, 'No. I *don't* want to see pictures of your insides'? Of course not. How can you?"

The hut was a lot cozier than I'd imagined it. In the kitchen were the same sorts of things you'd find in the homes of any of our neighbors: a postal calendar picturing a kitten, a hanging copper saucepan turned into a clock, sou-venir salt and pepper shakers in the shapes of castles and peasants and wooden shoes. The room was tight and clean and smelled of watermelon-scented dish detergent. From the kitchen, I could see the bedroom, and rows of medications neatly arranged on the dresser. Little radio. Little TV. Little easy chair. It was like a troll's house.

Jackie's X-rays were as large as bath mats, and he washed and dried his hands before removing them from their sepa-rate envelopes and presenting them to me. When handed a photograph of someone's wife or children, I know how to form the appropriate compliment. "How pretty!" I can say. Or "How like you." "What nice eyes." "What a pleasant smile." Hip replacement presented more of a challenge, and I alternated between "I like the pin" and, simply, "Ouch." On or about the fifth X-ray, I looked through a clear patch of plastic, past the front yard, and into the hills on the oppo-site side of the road, where another of our neighbors grazes his sheep. The flock had been shorn earlier that day, and those in view seemed oddly aware of how dumpy and vul-nerable they looked.

"I have to go," I said, and in the way of good neighbors the world over, Jackie said, "Stay, why don't you? I was just going to make some coffee."

A few weeks after that, he invited me in to look at his gov-ernment-issued ID card.

"Oh, I don't want to put you out."

"Not at all," he said, and two minutes later I found myself back at his kitchen table. The ID was in a bright plastic folder, the sort of thing that a young girl might carry. On the cover was a cartoon pony having his mane braided by a troop of friendly ladybugs.

I think I said, "All right, then." Jackie opened the folder and withdrew his identity card, a small color photograph attached by grommets to a stiff piece of paper. As when looking at the X-rays, I didn't know quite what to say. His birth date, his height, the color of his eyes. He was obviously proud of something, but I couldn't tell what it was.

"See," he said. "Right here. Look." He pointed to the corner, and I saw that the government had classified him as a "grand mutilated" person. The "grand" business was new to me, but the other part was familiar from riding the Paris buses. "These seats are reserved for the elderly and for those who have been mutilated in the war," the signs used to read. It's a much stronger word than "wounded" or "handi-capped," and I imagine that, if we used it in the United States, enlistment in the volunteer army would fall by at least half.

As a grand mutilated person, Jackie was entitled to a discount on all train travel. "With the metal plate, I got fifty percent off, but now, with the hip replacement, it's gone up to seventy-five," he told me. "Both for me *and* the person I'm traveling with. Seventy-five percent off!"

I handed him back his ID card. "Those are some real savings."

"You know," he said, "we should maybe take a trip together. Over to Brittany, down to Marseilles—wherever we wanted."

It took a moment for his "we" to register, and another moment to come up with a fitting response. "That would be . . . something," I finally said, thinking later that at least

I didn't lie. "Where's David?" the neighbors might ask. And Hugh could say, "Oh, he and Jackie are off on vacation. You know how those two are, give them seventy-five percent off on their tickets, and the sky's the limit."

It was only after I left the house that I started feeling insulted. What made Jackie think that I'd want to travel with him? Could he possibly have believed I'd be swayed by the discount, or did he think, the way certain people might, that the two of us belonged together, the homosexual and the child molester being cousins of sorts, like ostriches and emus. I'm usually not paranoid about this kind of thing, but in a small village, you sometimes have to wonder. Why had the neighbors to our immediate left, a truck driver and his family, never said anything more than hello to us—this after years of living next door. Then there was the man two houses down, who stopped me one afternoon and asked where I slept. "I've been in that place of yours, and there's only one bedroom," he said. This is the same man who chained a goat to a tree in his backyard and let it starve to death, so in his case it was probably the craziness talking. Just as with Jackie it was the loneliness. I usually passed his hut every other day, but after the incident with his ID card I cut it back to twice a week, and then to once a week. Late that August, I traveled to Scotland, and on my return an irritated Hugh collected me at the train station. "What's eating you?" I asked, and he gunned the engine, saying, "Ask your little friend."

What happened was that Jackie had come looking for me. He'd knocked on our door while I was out of town and asked in his loud country voice if David could come out and play. Those weren't his exact words, but according to Hugh they might as well have been. Not everyone saw the child molester calling my name on our front steps, but the ones who did were pretty well connected, and it took no time at all for the story to spread.

From that day on, I always wore headphones when walking past Jackie's hut. He may have called out to me, but I neither heard him nor raised my head to look in his direction. And it went on this way for three years, until I sort of forgot about him. We didn't speak again until after he'd gotten his diagnosis. The cancer, I'd heard, was in his esophagus, and its progress was swift and merciless. In a matter of months, he was carved down to nothing, face all gaunt, pants held up with a short length of rope. I saw him on his front stoop a week before he died, and when I waved he beckoned me inside the gate, and we shook hands one last time. I found myself wondering if the cancer had upped his train discount, bumped it from seventy-five percent to something even higher, but it's a hard question to ask when you're not fluent. And I wouldn't have wanted him to take it the wrong way.

# Of Mice and Men

I've always admired people who can enter a conversation without overtaking it. My friend Evelyn, for instance. "Hello, so nice to meet you," and then she just accepts things as they come. If her new acquaintance wants to talk about plants, she might mention a few of her own, never boastfully, but with a pleasant tone of surprise, as if her parlor palm and the other person's had coincidentally attended the same high school. The secret to her social success is that she's genuinely interested—not in all subjects, maybe, but definitely in all people. I like to think that I share this quality, but when it comes to meeting strangers, I tend to get nervous and rely on a stash of pre-prepared stories. Sometimes they're based on observation or hearsay, but just as often they're taken from the newspaper: An article about a depressed Delaware woman who hung herself from a tree on October 29 and was mistaken for a Halloween decoration. The fact that it's illegal to offer a monkey a cigarette in the state of New Jersey. Each is tragic in its own particular way, and leaves the listener with a bold mental picture: Here is a dead woman dangling against a backdrop of scarlet leaves. Here is a zookeeper with an open pack of Marlboros. "Go ahead," he whispers. "Take one."

Then there was the story mailed to me by a stranger in New England, who'd clipped it from his local paper. It concerned an eighty-one-year-old Vermont man whose home was overrun by mice. The actual house was not described, but in my mind it was two stories tall and isolated on a country road. I also decided that it was painted white—not that it mattered so much, I just thought it was a nice touch. So the retired guy's house was overrun, and when he could no longer bear it, he fumigated. The mice fled into the yard and settled into a pile of dead leaves, which no doubt crackled beneath their weight. Thinking that he had them trapped, the man set the pile on fire, then watched as a single flaming mouse raced back into the basement and burned the house to the ground.

The newspaper clipping arrived in the spring of 2006, just as I was preparing to leave for the United States. There were clothes to be ironed and papers to sort, but before doing anything, I wrote the New Englander a thank-you note and said that the article had moved me in unexpected ways. I did not mention that I planned to get a lot of mileage out of it, but that was my hope, for how could you go wrong with such a story? It was, to my mind, perfect, and I couldn't wait to wedge it into whatever conversation presented itself. "Talk about eighty-one-year-olds . . . ," I imagined myself saying.

Six months earlier, my icebreaker concerned a stripper who became a quadriplegic and eventually had her vagina eaten away by bedsores, not the easiest thing to wrangle into a conversation. But if I could pull that off, I figured that a burning mouse should pose no problem.

My first chance came in New York, when I took a cab from JFK to my hotel in the West Eighties. The driver was ten to fifteen years older than I, American born, with a shaved head. There are certainly men who can pull this off, but this fellow looked like someone had taken to him with a hammer—maybe not recently, there was no blood or bruising, just a heck of a lot of lumps. The two of us got to talking, and after telling him that I lived in Paris, and listening to his subsequent remarks about what snobs and cowards the French are, I found my entrée. "Speaking of rats, or things in that general family . . ."

I thought I did a pretty good job, but when the story was finished, instead of being amazed, the cabdriver said, "So then what happened?"

"What do you mean?"

"I mean, did the guy get insurance money? Was he able to save some of his stuff?"

How to explain that this wasn't really *about* the home-owner. He figured, of course, but the lasting image is of the flaming mouse, this determined little torch, shooting back into the house and burning it to the ground. What happened after that is unimportant. That's why the newspaper left it out.

I covered these points as cheerfully as possible, and the cabdriver responded with a T-shirt slogan. "Only in New York."

"But it *didn't happen* in New York," I said. "Weren't you listening? It happened in Vermont, out in the country, where people have houses and piles of leaves in their yards."

The man shrugged. "Well, it could have happened here."

"But it *didn't*," I told him.

"Well, you never know."

That's when I thought, *OK, Lumpy, you just lost yourself a tip. The French business I was willing to overlook, but "Only in New York" and "It could have happened here" just cost you five dollars, so put that in your pipe and smoke it.*

Of course I did give him a tip, I always do. But before handing it over, I tore the bill practically in half. Passive aggression, I guess you'd call it.

I'd come to America for a lecture tour—that's what they're called, but really I just read out loud. My first date was in New Jersey, and because I don't drive the theater sent a town car, which met me in front of my hotel. Behind its wheel was a black chauffeur who wore a suit and tie and introduced himself as Mr. Davis. The man was in his early seventies, and as he lowered his visor against the setting sun, I noticed his fingernails, which were long and tapered and covered with clear polish. Above each knuckle shone a ring, and on his wrist, in addition to a watch, there hung a delicate gold chain.

I meant to plow right into my mouse story, but before I could begin, Mr. Davis started in on what he termed "the traffic situation vis-à-vis liquidity." His tone was finicky, and rather than speaking normally he tended to intone, like God addressing Moses through the clouds, only gay. After telling me that people were fools to drive in Manhattan, he looked into the surrounding cars and slandered his competition.

The woman beside us was a boob. The man in front, a chucklehead. Dimwits, dopes, dummies, and dunces: it was like he had a thesaurus on his lap and was delivering the entries in alphabetical order. He criticized a cabdriver for talking on a cell phone, and then he pulled out one of his own and left an angry message with his dispatcher, who should have known better than to send him out in this mess.

For blocks on end, Mr. Davis fumed and muttered, this until we came to Canal Street, where he pointed to a gap in the downtown skyline. "See that," he said. "That is where the World Trade Center used to be."

Out of politeness, I pretended that this information was new to me. "What do you know!"

Mr. Davis stared south and brushed a bit of lint off his shoulder. "Eleven September, two thousand and one. I was present on that fateful morning and will never forget it as long as I live."

I leaned forward in my seat. "What was it like?"

"Loud," Mr. Davis said.

One would expect a few more details, but none was offered, and so I moved on and asked what he had been doing there.

"Had myself a meeting with an import-export company," he told me. "That was my profession back then, but 9/11 killed all that. You can't ship anything now, leastwise you can't make any money at it."

I asked what he imported, and when he answered "You name it," I looked into the window of the adjacent car.

"Umm. Little stuffed animals?"

"I moved some of those," he said. "But the name of my game was mostly clothes, them and electronics."

193

"So did you travel a lot?"

"Everywhere," he told me. "Saw the world and then some."

"Did you ever go to China?"

He said that he had been more times than he could count, and when I asked what he had seen, he rolled forward a few inches. "Lots of people eating rice, mainly from bowls."

"Gosh," I said. "So it's true! And what about India? That's a place I've always wanted to visit."

"What do you think you're going to see there?" Mr. Davis asked. "Poor people? Chaos? So much garbage you can't hardly stand it?"

When I told him that I was interested in the monkeys, he said that the country was lousy with them. "I was with my driver one day, and we passed by this tree that homed over two hundred of them. Baboons, I think they were, and I'll always remember how they swarmed our car, banging on the doors and begging for peanuts." A man with a cardboard sign approached, and Mr. Davis waved him away. "Another problem with India is the heat. The last time I was there, the temperature hit one hundred and fifty degrees, saw it on the thermometer with my own eyes. Had myself an appointment with some swamis, but come time to leave the hotel, I said, 'That's it. No meeting for me today.' I'm telling you, it felt like I was burning alive."

I couldn't have dreamt for a better in. "Speaking of burning alive, there was this retired man living in Vermont, see, and his home was overrun with mice . . ."

When I had finished, Mr. Davis met my eyes in the rearview mirror. "Now, you," he said, "are just a liar."

194

"No," I told him. "The story is true. I read it in the newspaper."

"Newspaper or not, it's a load of b.s., and I will tell you why: Isn't no way that a mouse could cover all that distance without his flames going out. The wind would have snuffed them."

"Well, what about that girl in Vietnam?" I asked. "The one in the famous picture who's just been hit with napalm or whatever and is running down the road with no clothes on? I don't see the wind doing her any favors, and she just had skin, not flammable fur."

"Well, that was a dark period in our nation's history," Mr. Davis said.

"But isn't *this* a dark period?" I asked this question just as we entered the Holland Tunnel. The din of canned traffic made it impossible to talk, and so I sat back and tried to get a handle on my growing anger. Since when do politics affect a mammal's ability to sustain a flame? That aside, who *says* a burning mouse can't run a distance of twelve feet? What made this guy an authority? His fingernails? His jewelry?

What really smarted was being called a liar, and so matter-of-factly. This from someone who'd reduced the Chinese to a bunch of people eating rice from bowls. Then there was the bit about the baboons. I'd heard of them attacking people for fruit, but doing it for peanuts seemed an idea he'd picked up from the circus. I didn't believe for one moment that he was really at the World Trade Center on September 11, and as for the 150-degree heat, I'm pretty sure that at that temperature your head would just explode. All this, and *I* was the liar? Me?

Leaving the tunnel was like being freed from a clogged

drain. We were moving now, around a bend and up onto an elevated highway. Below us sat storage tanks resembling dirty aspirin, and as I wondered what they were used for, Mr. Davis pulled out his cell phone and proceeded to talk until we reached our exit. "That was my wife," he said after hanging up, and I thought, *Right. The woman you're married to. I bet he's really something.*

After New Jersey, I went to Connecticut, and then to Indiana. On and on for thirty-five days. I returned to my apartment in early May, and after closing the door behind me, I asked Hugh to go on the Internet and search for the world's highest recorded temperature. He took a seat before his computer, and I stood at his side with my fingers crossed. *Don't be 150, don't be 150, don't be 150.*

Later that day, among my receipts, I found Mr. Davis's business card. Someone needed to tell him that the hottest it's ever been is 136, and so I wrote him a short note, adding that the record was set in Libya, not India, and in the year 1922. *Before you were born,* the subtext read. *Before you could so casually call someone a liar.*

I thought I would send him the news clipping as well, and it was here that my triumph lost its luster. "Mouse gets revenge: sets home ablaze," the headline read, and then I noticed the letters "AP," and saw that while the story had been published in Vermont, it had actually taken place in New Mexico, which sort of ruined everything. Now, instead of a white, wood-frame house, I saw a kind of shack with cow skulls tacked to the outer walls. It then turned out that the homeowner had not fumigated, and that there was only one mouse, which he somehow caught alive, and threw onto a pile of leaves he'd started burning some time earlier. This would certainly qualify as thoughtless, but there was no moment when he looked at the coughing mice, running for their lives from the poisonous fumes. He did not hear the leaves crackling beneath their feet, or reach for his matches, thinking, *Aha!*

How had I so misread this story, and why? Like a dog with a table scrap, had I simply wolfed it down too quickly, or do I believe, on some subconscious level, that eastern mice are inherently more sympathetic than their western cousins? Where did the fumigation business come from, and the idea that the man's house was overrun? I recalled myself before the tour, sitting at my desk and lighting one cigarette right after the other, the way I do when time is running out. Garlands of smoke drifted into the next room and fouled the sinuses of our out-of-town guests, who'd arrived a few days earlier and were sleeping in our bed. *The house was overrun, extermination was necessary.* Had I somehow imposed my own life on the newspaper story?

Despite my embroidery, the most important facts hold true: The mouse *did* run back indoors. His flames were not extinguished by the wind. The fire spread, the house was consumed, and these are certainly dark times, both for the burning, and those who would set them alight.

# April in Paris

While watching TV one recent evening, I stumbled upon a nature program devoted to the subject of making nature programs. The cameraman's job was to catch a bird of paradise in full display, so he dug himself a hole, covered it with branches, and sat inside it for three weeks. This was in New Guinea, where the people used to wear sexy loincloths, but now stand around in T-shirts that say "Cowboys Do It with Chaps" and "I Survived the 2002 IPC Corporate Challenge Weekend." One villager might wear a pair of gym shorts and then add a fanny pack or a sun visor with the name of a riverboat casino stitched onto the brim. I suppose that these things came from a relief organization, either that or a cruise ship went down, and this was what washed up onshore.

I'll wager that quite a few sun visors found their way to Southeast Asia after the tsunami. One brutal news story after another, and it went on for weeks. The phone numbers of aid organizations would skitter across the bottom of the TV screen, and I recall thinking that if they wanted serious donations, they should have shown a puppy. Just one was all it would have taken. It could have been sleeping, its belly full of the malnourished children we'd seen on the previous night's broadcast, but none of that would have mattered. People who had never before contributed to charity emptied their pockets when a cocker spaniel was shown standing on a rooftop after Hurricane Katrina. "What choice did I have?" they asked. "That poor little thing looked into the camera and penetrated my very soul."

The eyes of the stranded grandmother, I noted, were not half as piercing. There she was, clinging to a chimney with her bra strap showing, and all anyone did was wonder if she had a dog. "I'd hate to think there's a Scottie in her house, maybe trapped on the first floor. What's the number of that canine rescue agency?"

Saying that this was everyone's reaction is, of course, an exaggeration. There were cat people too, and those whose hearts went out to the abandoned reptiles. The sight of an iguana sailing down the street on top of a refrigerator sent a herpetologist friend over the edge. "She seems to be saying, 'Where's my master?'" he speculated. "Here it is, time for our daily cuddle, and I'm stuck on the SS *Whirlpool!!!*"

I've often heard that anthropomorphizing an animal is the worst injustice you can do it. That said, I'm as guilty as anyone. In childhood stories, the snail grabs her purse and dashes out the door to put money in the meter. The rabbit cries when the blue jay makes fun of her buck teeth. The mouse loves his sister but not *that way*. And we think, *They're just like us!*

Certain nature shows only add to this misconception, but that, to me, is why they're so addictive. Take *Growing Up Camel*, a program my friend Ronnie and I watched one evening. It was set in a small privately owned zoo somewhere in Massachusetts. The camel in question was named Patsy, and the narrator reminded us several times over the next fifty minutes that she had been born on Super Bowl Sunday. While still an infant—the football stadium probably not even cleared yet—she was taken from her mother. Now she was practically grown, and as the commercials neared, the narrator announced a reunion. "Coming up, the camels reconcile after their long separation."

In the next segment, the two were reintroduced, and the grumpy old mother chased her daughter around the pen. When the opportunity arose, she bit Patsy on the backside, and pretty hard, it seemed to me. This was the camels *not* getting along, and it wasn't too terribly different from the way they acted when they did get along.

When the next break approached, the narrator hooked us with "Coming up, a tragedy that changes Patsy's life forever."

I'd have put my money on an amputated leg, but it turned out to be nothing that dramatic. What happened was that the mother got bone cancer and died. The veterinarian took it hard, but Patsy didn't seem to care one way or the other. And why would she, really? All her mom ever did was hassle her and steal her food, so wasn't she better off on her own?

The zookeepers worried that if left all alone, Patsy would forget how to be a camel, and so they imported some company, a male named Josh, and his girlfriend, Josie, who were shipped in from Texas. The final shot was of the three of them, standing in the sunshine and serenely ignoring one another. "So that's what became of the little camel who was born on Super Bowl Sunday," Ronnie said.

She turned on the light and looked me in the face. "Are you *crying?*" she asked, and I told her I had an ash in my eye.

*Growing Up Camel* had its merits, but I think I prefer the more serious type of nature show, the kind that follows its subject through the wild. This could be a forest, a puddle, or a human intestinal tract, it makes no difference. Show me a tiger or a tapeworm, and I'll watch with equal intensity. In these sorts of programs we see the creature's world reduced to its basic components: food, safety, and reproduction. It's a constant chain of desperation and heartache, the gist being that life is hard, and then it ends violently. I know I should watch these things with an air of detachment, but time and again I forget myself. The show will run its course, and afterward I'll lie on the sofa, shattered by the death of a doda or a guib, one of those four-letter antelope-type things that's forever turning up in my crossword puzzles.

Apart from leaving me spent and depressed, such programs remind me that I am rarely, if ever, alone. If there's not an insect killing time on the ceiling, there's surely a mite staring out from the bath towel, or a parasite resting on the banks of my bloodstream. I'm reminded too that, however repellent, each of these creatures is fascinating, and worthy of a nature show.

This was a lesson I learned a few summers back in Normandy. I was at my desk one afternoon, writing a letter, when I heard a faint buzzing sound, like a tiny car switching into a higher gear. Curious, I went to the window, and there, in a web, I saw what looked like an angry raisin. It was a trapped fly, and as I bent forward to get a closer look, a spider rushed forth and carried it screaming to a little woven encampment situated between the wall and the window casing. It was like watching someone you hate getting mugged: three seconds of hard-core violence, and when it was over you just wanted it to happen again.

It's hard to recall having no working knowledge of the *Tegenaria duellica,* but that's what I was back then—a greenhorn with a third-rate field guide. All I knew was that this was a spider, a big one, the shape of an unshelled peanut. In color it ranged from russet to dark brown, the shades alternating to form a mottled pattern on the abdomen. I'd later learn that the *Tegenaria* can live for up to two years, and that this was an adult female. At that moment, though, standing at the window with my mouth hanging open, all I recognized was a profound sense of wonder.

How had I spent so much time in that house and never realized what was going on around me? If the *Tegenaria* barked or went after my food, I might have picked up on them earlier, but as it was, they were as quiet and unobtrusive as Amish farmers. Outside of mating season, they pretty much stayed put, a far cry from the Carolina wolf spiders I grew up with. Those had been hunters rather than trappers. Big shaggy things the size of a baby's hand, they roamed the basement of my parents' house and evoked from my sisters the prolonged, spine-tingling screams called for in movies when the mummy invades the delicate lady's dressing room. "Kill it!" they'd yell, and then I'd hear a half-dozen shoes hitting the linoleum, followed by a world atlas or maybe a piano stool—whatever was heavy and close at hand.

I was put off by the wolf spiders as well but never thought that they were purposefully out to get me. For starters, they didn't seem that organized. Then too, I figured they had their own lives to lead. This was an attitude I picked up from my father, who squashed nothing that was not directly related to him. "You girls are afraid of your own shadows," he'd say, and no matter how big the thing was, he'd scoot it onto a newspaper and release it outside. Come bedtime I'd knock on my sisters' door and predict that the spider was now crawling to the top of the house, where he'd take a short breather before heading down the chimney. "I read in the encyclopedia that this particular breed is known for its tracking ability, and that once it's pegged its victims, almost nothing will stop it. Anyway, good night."

They'd have been horrified by the house in Normandy, as would most people, probably. Even before I joined the American Arachnological Society, the place looked haunted, cobwebs sagging like campaign bunting from the rafters and curtain rods. If one was in my way, I'd knock it down. But that all changed after I discovered that first *Tegenaria*—April, I called her. After writing her name on an index card and taping it to the wall, my interest spread to her neighbors. The window they lived in was like a tenement building, one household atop another, on either side of the frame. Above April was Marty, and then Curtis and Paula. Across the way were Linda, Russell, Big Chief Tommy, and a sexless little speck of a thing I decided to call Leslie. And this was just one window.

Seeing as I'd already broken the number one rule of a

good nature documentary—not to give names to your subjects—I went ahead and broke the next one, which was not
to get involved in their lives. "Manipulating," Hugh would
call it, but, to my mind, that was a bit too mad-scientist.
Manipulating is crossbreeding, or setting up death matches
with centipedes. What I was doing was simply called feed-
ing.

No spider, or at least none that I've observed, wants anything to do with a dead insect, even a freshly dead one. Its
food needs to be alive and struggling, and because our house
was overrun, and I had some time on my hands, I decided to
help out. In my opinion, the best place to catch flies is
against a windowpane. Something about the glass seems to
confuse them, and they get even dopier when you come at
them with an open jar. Once one was in, I'd screw on the lid
and act as though I were shaking a cocktail. The little body
would slam against the sides, and as Hugh went progressively Gandhi on me, I'd remind him that these were pests,
disease carriers who feasted upon the dead and then came
indoors to dance on our silverware. "I mean, come on," I
said. "You can't feel sorry for *everything.*"

The *Tegenaria* build what I soon learned to call "horizontal sheet webs," dense trampoline-like structures that are
most often triangular and range in size from that of a folded
handkerchief to that of a place mat. Once my prey was good
and woozy, I'd unscrew the lid and tip the jar toward the
waiting spider. The fly would drop, and, after lying still for
a moment or two, it would begin to twitch and rouse itself,
a cartoon drunk coming to after a long night. "What the
fuck . . . ?" I imagined it saying. Then it would notice the
wings and foreheads of earlier victims. "I've got to get out of

here." A whisper of footsteps off in the distance, and just as the fly tasted futility, the monster was upon him.

". . . and cut!" I would yell.

Watching this spectacle became addictive, and so, in turn, did catching flies. There were days when I'd throw a good three dozen of them to their deaths, this at the expense of whatever else I was supposed to be doing. As the spiders moved from healthy to obese, their feet tore holes in their webs. Running became a chore, and I think their legs started chafing. By this point there was no denying my emotional attachment. There were nights that first summer when I'd get out of bed at 3:00 a.m. and wander into my office with a flashlight. Everyone would be wide awake, but it was always April that I singled out. If I thought about her a hundred times a day, it seemed only fair that she thought about me as well. My name, my face: I didn't expect these things to register, but in the way that a body feels the warmth of the sun, I fully imagined that she sensed my presence, and missed it when I was away.

"That's all right," I'd tell her. "It's only me." Often I'd take out my magnifying glass and stare into the chaos that was her face.

Most people would have found it grotesque, but when you're in love nothing is so abstract or horrible that it can't be thought of as cute. It slayed me that she had eight eyes, and that none of them seemed to do her any good. They were more like decoration, really, a splay of beads crowded atop her chelicerae. These were what she used to grip her prey, and if you looked at her the right way you could see them as a pair of enormous buck teeth. This made her appear goofy rather than scary, though I'd never have said so in her presence. For a *Tegenaria,* she was quite attractive, and I was glad to see that Principal Hodges shared my view. He was a freshly molted adult male who traveled from the other side of the room and spent six days inside her inner sanctum. Why Marty or Curtis or Big Chief Tommy didn't mate with April is a mystery, and I put it on a list beside other nagging questions, such as "What was Jesus like as a teenager?" and "Why is it you never see a baby squirrel?"

As the summer progressed, so did the mysteries. Spiders relocated, both male and female, and I started noticing a lot of spare parts—a forsaken leg or palp lying in a web that used to belong to Paula or Philip or the Right Reverend Karen. Someone new would move in, and as soon as I tacked up a fresh name card, he or she would vacate without notice. What had once seemed like a fine neighborhood quickly became a dangerous one, the tenants all thuggish and transitory. Maybe April was more highly respected than anyone else in her window unit. Maybe her enemies knew that she was being watched, but, for whatever reason, she was one of the few *Tegenaria* that managed to stay put and survive. In mid-September, Hugh and I returned to the city and, at the last minute, I bought a plastic terrarium and decided to take her with me. The "April in Paris" business didn't occur to me until we were on the train, and I held her container against the window, saying, "Look, the Eiffel Tower!"

Funny, the details that slip your notice until it's too late. The fact, for instance, that we don't really have flies in Paris, at least not in our apartment. Back in Normandy, catching prey had been a breeze. I could do it barefoot and in my pajamas, but now I was forced to go outside and lurk around the trash cans in the Luxembourg Gardens. Someone would toss in a disposable diaper, and I'd stand a few feet from the bin and wait for the scent to be picked up. Then there'd be the sneak attack, the clattering jar, the little spell of cursing and foot stomping. Had the flies been gathered on a windowpane, I would have enjoyed the last laugh, but out in the open, and with an audience of French people noting my every failure, my beautiful hobby became a chore.

I'd been telling myself for months that April needed me—though of course she didn't. An adequate amount of prey stumbled into her web, and she caught it quite capably on her own—that was the case in Normandy anyway. Now, though, trapped inside a terrarium in a fourth-floor apartment, she honestly did need me, and the responsibility weighed a ton. *Tegenaria* can go without eating for three months, but whenever I returned home empty-handed, I could feel her little spider judgment seeping from the plastic box. The face that had once seemed goofy was now haughty and expectant. "Hmm," I imagined her saying. "I guess I had you figured all wrong."

In early October the weather turned cool. Then the rains came and, overnight, every fly in Paris packed up and left town. April hadn't eaten in over a week when, just by chance, I happened upon a pet store and learned that it sold live crickets, blunt little black ones that looked like bolts with legs. I bought a chirping boxful and felt very proud of myself until the next morning, when I learned something no nature show ever told me: crickets stink. They reek. Rather than dirty diapers or spoiled meat, something definite you can put your finger on, they smell like an inclination: cruelty maybe, or hatred.

No amount of incense or air freshener could diminish the stench. Any attempt only made it worse, and it was this more than anything that led me back to Normandy. April and I took the train in late October, and I released her into her old home. I guess I thought that she would move back in, but in our absence her web had fallen to ruin. One corner had come unmoored, and its ragged, fly-speckled edge drooped like a filthy petticoat onto the window ledge. "I'm pretty sure it can be fixed," I told her, but before I could elaborate, or even say goodbye, she took off running. And I never saw her again.

There have been other *Tegenaria* over the years, a new population every summer, and though I still feed them and monitor their comings and goings, it's with a growing but not unpleasant distance, an understanding that, unlike mammals, spiders do only what they're supposed to do. Whatever drives the likes of April is private and severe, and my attempts to humanize it only moved me further from its majesty. I still can't resist the fly catching, but in terms of naming and relocating I've backed off considerably, though Hugh would say not enough.

I suppose there's a place in everyone's heart that's reserved for another species. My own is covered in cobwebs rather than dog or cat hair, and, because of this, people assume it doesn't exist. It does, though, and I felt it ache when Katrina hit. The TV was on, the grandmother signaled from her rooftop, and I found myself wondering, with something akin to panic, if there were any spiders in her house.

# Crybaby

The night flight to Paris leaves JFK at 7:00 p.m. and arrives at de Gaulle the next day at about 8:45 a.m. French time. Between takeoff and landing, there's a brief parody of an evening: dinner is served, the trays are cleared, and four hours later it's time for breakfast. The idea is to trick the body into believing it has passed a night like any other—that your unsatisfying little nap was actually sleep and now you are rested and deserving of an omelet.

Hoping to make the lie more convincing, many passengers prepare for bed. I'll watch them line up outside the bathroom, some holding toothbrushes, some dressed in slippers or loose-fitting pajama-type outfits. Their slow-footed padding gives the cabin the feel of a hospital ward: the dark aisles are corridors; the flight attendants are nurses. The hospital feeling grows even stronger once you leave coach. Up front, where the seats recline almost flat, like beds, the doted-on passengers lie under their blankets and moan. I've heard, in fact, that the airline staff often refers to the business-class section as "the ICU," because the people there demand such constant attention. They want what their superiors are getting in first class, so they complain incessantly, hoping to get bumped up.

There are only two classes on the airline I normally take between France and the United States—coach and something called Business Elite. The first time I sat there, I was flown to America and back for a book tour. "Really," I kept insisting, "there's no need." The whole "first-to-board" business, I found a little embarrassing, but then they brought me a bowl of warm nuts and I began to soften. The pampering takes some getting used to. A flight attendant addresses me as "Mr. Sedaris," and I feel sorry that she's forced to memorize my name rather than, say, her granddaughter's cell phone number. On this particular airline, though, they do it in such a way that it seems perfectly natural, or at least it does after a time.

"May I bring you a drink to go with those warm nuts, Mr. Sedaris?" the woman looking after me asked—this as the people in coach were still boarding. The looks they gave me as they passed were the looks I give when the door of a limousine opens. You always expect to see a movie star, or, at the very least, someone better dressed than you, but time and time again it's just a sloppy nobody. Thus the look, which translates to, Fuck you, Sloppy Nobody, for making me turn my head.

On all my subsequent flights, the Business Elite section was a solid unit, but on this particular plane it was divided in two: four rows up front and two in the back. The flight attendant assured everyone in my section that although we were technically in the back, we shouldn't *think* of it as the back. We had the same rights and privileges as those passengers ahead of us. Yet still they were *ahead* of us, and I couldn't shake the feeling that they'd been somehow favored.

On the way to New York, I sat beside a bearded Frenchman, who popped a pill shortly after takeoff and was out until we landed. On the leg back there was no one beside me, at least not for the first half hour. Then a flight attendant knelt in the aisle beside my seat and asked if I might do her a favor. That's how they talk in Business Elite. "I'm wondering, Mr. Sedaris, if you might do me a favor?"

Chipmunk-like, my cheeks packed with warm nuts, I cocked my head.

"I've got a passenger a few rows up, and his crying is disturbing the people around him. Do you think it would be OK if he sat here?"

The woman was blond and heavily made-up. Glasses hung from a chain around her neck, and as she gestured to the empty window seat beside me, I got a pleasant whiff of what smelled like oatmeal cookies. "I believe he's Polish," she whispered. "That is to say, I think he's from Poland. The country."

"Is he a child?" I asked, and the flight attendant told me no.

"Is he drunk?"

Again she said no. "His mother just died, and he's on his way to her funeral."

"So people are upset because he's *crying over his dead mother?*"

"That's the situation," she told me.

I'd once read that a first-class passenger complained—threatened to sue, if I remember correctly—because the blind person next to him was traveling with a Seeing Eye dog. He wasn't allergic, this guy. Labrador retrievers on the street didn't bother him, but he hadn't paid thousands of dollars to sit next to one, or at least that was his argument. If that had seemed the last word in assholiness, this was a close second.

I said of course the man could sit beside me, and the flight attendant disappeared into the darkness, returning a few minutes later with the grieving passenger.

"Thank you," she mouthed.

And I said, "No problem."

The Polish man might have been in his midforties but seemed older, just as people in my parents' generation had. Foreign blood, or an abundance of responsibility, had robbed him of the prolonged adolescence currently enjoyed by Americans of the same age, so his face, though unlined, seemed older than mine, more used. His eyes were red and swollen from crying, and his nose, which was large and many-faceted, looked as if it had been roughly carved from wood and not yet sanded smooth. In the dim light, he resembled one of those elaborate, handcrafted bottle stoppers—the kindly peasant or good-natured drunk who tips his hat when you pull the string. After settling in, the man looked out the darkened window. Then he bit his lower lip, covered his face with his remarkably large hands, and proceeded to sob, deeply. I felt that I should say something, but what? And how? Perhaps it would be better, less embarrassing for him, if I were to pretend that he wasn't crying—to ignore him, basically. And so I did.

214

The Polish man didn't want dinner, just waved it away with those king-sized mitts of his, but I could feel him watching as I cut into my herb-encrusted chicken, most likely wondering how anyone could carry on at a time like this. That's how I felt when my mother died. The funeral took place on a Saturday afternoon in November. It was unseasonably warm that day, even for Raleigh, and returning from the church we passed people working on their lawns as if nothing had happened. One guy even had his shirt off. "Can you beat that?" I said to my sister Lisa, not thinking of all the funeral processions that had passed me over the years—me laughing, me throwing stones at signs, me trying to stand on my bicycle seat. Now here I was eating, and it wasn't bad, either. The best thing about this particular airline is the after-dinner sundae. The vanilla ice cream is in the bowl already, but you can choose from any number of toppings. I order the caramel and chopped nuts, and the flight attendant spoons them on before my eyes. "Is that enough sauce, Mr. Sedaris?" she'll ask, and, "Are you sure you don't want whipped cream?" It would be years before I worked up the courage to ask for seconds, and when I finally did I felt like such a dope. "Do you think, um . . . I mean, is it possible to have another one of those?"

"Well, of course it is, Mr. Sedaris! Have a third if you like!"

That's Business Elite for you. Spend eight thousand dollars on a ticket, and if you want an extra thirteen cents' worth of ice cream, all you have to do is ask. It's like buying a golf cart and having a few tees thrown in, but still it works. "Golly," I say. "Thanks!"

In the years before I asked for seconds, my sundae would

be savored—each crumb of cashew or walnut eaten separately, the way a bird might. After those were gone, I would recline a bit and start in on the caramel. By the time the ice cream itself was finished, I'd be stretched out flat, watching a movie on my private screen. The control panels for the seats are located on a shared armrest, and it would take me a good three or four flights before I got the hang of them. On this trip, for instance, I kept mashing the buttons, wondering why they failed to work: feet up, feet down, head back, head forward. I was two seconds from calling the flight attendant when I looked to my right and saw the Polish man keening and bucking against his will. It was then that I realized I had the wrong control panel. "Sorry about that," I said. And he held up his pan-sized hand, the way you do when you mean "No hard feelings."

When my empty bowl was taken away, I leafed through the in-flight magazine, biding my time until my neighbor's dizziness wore off and he could fall asleep. In an effort to appear respectful, I'd already missed the first movie cycle, but I didn't know how much longer I could hold out. Up ahead, in the cheerful part of Business Elite, someone laughed. It wasn't the practiced chuckle you offer in response to a joke, but something more genuine, a bark almost. It's the noise one makes when watching stupid movies on a plane, movies you'd probably never laugh at in the theater. I think it's the thinness of the air that weakens your resistance. A pilot will offer some shopworn joke, and even the seasoned fliers will bust a gut. The only funny announcement I've ever heard was made by a male flight attendant, a queen, who grabbed the microphone as we were taxiing down the runway in San Francisco. "Those of you standing in the aisles should have an excellent view of the Fasten Seat Belt sign," he said.

My memory of him and his stern, matronly voice was interrupted by my seatmate, who seemed to have suffered a setback. The man was crying again, not loudly but steadily, and I wondered, perhaps unfairly, if he wasn't overdoing it a bit. Stealing a glance at his blocky, tearstained profile, I thought back to when I was fifteen and a girl in my junior high died of leukemia, or "Love Story disease," as it was often referred to then. The principal made the announcement, and I, along with the rest of my friends, fell into a great show of mourning. Group hugs, bouquets laid near the flagpole. I can't imagine what it would have been like had we actually known her. Not to brag, but I think I took it hardest of all. "Why her and not me?" I wailed.

"Funny," my mother would say, "but I don't remember you ever mentioning anyone named Monica."

My friends were a lot more understanding, especially Barbara, who, a week after the funeral, announced that maybe she would kill herself as well.

None of us reminded her that Monica had died of a terminal illness, as, in a way, that didn't matter anymore. The point was that she was gone, and our lives would never be the same: we were people who knew people who died. This is to say that we had been touched by tragedy, and had been made special by it. By all appearances, I was devastated, but in fact I had never felt so purposeful and fulfilled.

The next time someone died, it was a true friend, a young woman named Dana who was hit by a car during our first year of college. My grief was genuine, yet still, no matter how hard I fought, there was an element of showmanship to it, the hope that someone might say, "You look like you just lost your best friend."

Then I could say, "As a matter of fact, I did," my voice cracked and anguished.

It was as if I'd learned to grieve by watching television: here you cry, here you throw yourself upon the bed, here you stare into the mirror and notice how good you look with a tear-drenched face.

Like most seasoned phonies, I roundly suspect that everyone is as disingenuous as I am. This Polish man for instance. Given the time it would take him to buy a ticket and get to JFK, his mother would have been dead for at least six hours, maybe longer. Wasn't he over it yet? I mean, really, who were these tears *for?* It was as if he were saying, "I loved my mother a lot more than you loved yours." No wonder his former seatmate had complained. The guy was so competitive, so self-righteous, so, well, over the top.

Another bark of laughter from a few rows up, and it occurred to me that perhaps my sympathy was misplaced. Perhaps these tears of his were the by-product of guilt rather than sorrow. I envisioned a pale, potato-nosed woman, a tube leaking fluids into her arm. Calls were placed, expensive ones, to her only son in the United States. "Come quick," she said, but he was too caught up in his own life. Such a hectic time. So many things to do. His wife was getting her stripper's license. He'd been asked to speak at his son's parole board hearing. "Tell you what," he said. "I'll come at the end of dog racing season." And then . . . this. She rides to her death on a lumpy gurney, and he flies to her funeral in Business Elite. The man killed his mother with neglect, and because of that I can't watch a movie on a plane?

I pulled my private screen from its hiding place in my armrest and had just slipped on my headphones when the flight attendant came by. "Are you sure I can't get you something to eat, Mr. . . . ?" She looked down at her clipboard and made a sound like she was gargling with stones.

The Polish man shook his head no, and she regarded me with disappointment, as if it had been my job to stoke his appetite. *I thought you were different,* her eyes seemed to say.

I wanted to point out that at least I hadn't complained. I hadn't disrespected his grief by activating my screen, either, but I did once she'd retreated back into the darkness. Of the four movies playing, I had already seen three. The other was called *Down to Earth* and starred Chris Rock as an aspiring stand-up comic. One day he gets hit and killed by a truck and, after a short spell in Heaven, he's sent back among the living in the body of an elderly white man. The reviews had been tepid at best, but I swear I've never seen anything funnier. I tried not to laugh, I really did, but that's a losing game if ever there was one. This I learned when I was growing up. I don't know why it was, exactly, but nothing irritated my father quite like the sound of his children's happiness. Group crying he could stand, but group laughter was asking for it, especially at the dinner table.

The problem was that there was so much to laugh at, particularly during the years that our Greek grandmother lived with us. Had we been older, it might have been different. "The poor thing has gas," we might have said. For children, though, nothing beats a flatulent old lady. What made it all the crazier was that she wasn't embarrassed by it—no more than our collie, Duchess, was. It sounded as if she were testing out a chain saw, yet her face remained inexpressive and unchanging.

"Something funny?" our father would ask us, this as if he hadn't heard, as if his chair, too, had not vibrated in the aftershock. "You think something's funny, do you?"

If keeping a straight face was difficult, saying no was so exacting that it caused pain.

"So you were laughing at nothing?"

"Yes," we would say. "At nothing."

Then would come another mighty rip, and what was once difficult would now be impossible. My father kept a heavy serving spoon next to his plate, and I can't remember how many times he brought it down on my head.

"You still think there's something to laugh about?"

Strange that being walloped with a heavy spoon made everything seem funnier, but there you have it. My sisters and I would be helpless, doubled over, milk spraying out of our mouths and noses, the force all the stronger for having been bottled up. There were nights when the spoon got blood on it, nights when hairs would stick to the blood, but still our grandmother farted, and still we laughed until the walls shook.

Could that really have been forty years ago? The thought of my sisters and me, so young then, and so untroubled, was sobering, and within a minute, Chris Rock or no Chris Rock, I was the one crying on the night flight to Paris. It wasn't my intention to steal anyone's thunder. A minute or two was all I needed. But in the meantime here we were: two grown men in roomy seats, each blubbering in his own elite puddle of light.

# Old Faithful

Out of nowhere I developed this lump. I think it was a cyst or a boil, one of those things you associate with trolls, and it was right on my tailbone, like a peach pit wedged into the top of my crack. That's what it felt like, anyway. I was afraid to look. At first it was just this insignificant knot, but as it grew larger it started to hurt. Sitting became difficult, and forget about lying on my back or bending over. By day five, my tailbone was throbbing, and I told myself, just as I had the day before, that if this kept up I was going to see a doctor. "I mean it," I said. I even went so far as to pull out the phone book and turn my back on it, hoping that the boil would know that I meant business and go away on its own. But of course it didn't.

All of this took place in London, which is cruelly, insanely expensive. Hugh and I went to the movies one night, and our tickets cost the equivalent of forty dollars, this after spending sixty on pizzas. And these were mini-pizzas, not much bigger than pancakes. Given the price of a simple evening out, I figured that a doctor's visit would cost around the same as a customized van. More than the money, though, I was afraid of the diagnosis. "Lower-back cancer," the doctor would say. "It looks like we'll have to remove your entire bottom."

Actually, in England he'd probably have said "bum," a word I have never really cottoned to. The sad thing is that he could remove my ass and most people wouldn't even notice. It's so insubstantial that the boil was actually an improvement, something like a bustle only filled with poison. The only real drawback was the pain.

For the first few days I kept my discomfort to myself, thinking all the while of what a good example I was setting. When Hugh feels bad, you hear about it immediately. A tiny splinter works itself into his palm, and he claims to know exactly how Jesus must have felt on the cross. He demands sympathy for insect bites and paper cuts, while I have to lose at least a quart of blood before I get so much as a pat on the hand.

One time in France we were lucky enough to catch an identical stomach virus. It was a twenty-four-hour bug, the kind that completely empties you out and takes away your will to live. You'd get yourself a glass of water, but that would involve standing, and so instead you just sort of stare toward the kitchen, hoping that maybe one of the pipes will burst and the water will come to you. We both had the exact same symptoms, yet he insisted that his virus was much more powerful than mine. I begged to differ, so there we were, competing over who was the sickest.

"You can at least move your hands," he said.

"No," I told him, "it was the wind that moved them. I have no muscle control whatsoever."

"Liar."

"Well, that's a nice thing to say to someone who'll probably die during the night. Thanks a lot, pal."

At such times you have to wonder how things got to this point. You meet someone and fall in love; then umpteen years later you're lying on the floor in a foreign country, promising, hoping, as a matter of principle, that you'll be dead by sunrise. "I'll show you," I moaned, and then I must have fallen back to sleep.

When Hugh and I bicker over who is in the most pain, I think back to my first boyfriend, whom I met while in my late twenties. Something about our combination was rotten, and as a result we competed over everything, no matter how petty. When someone laughed at one of his jokes, I would need to make that person laugh harder. If I found something half decent at a yard sale, he would have to find something better—and so on. My boyfriend's mother was a handful, and every year, just before Christmas, she would schedule a mammogram, knowing that she would not get the results until after the holidays. The remote possibility of cancer was something to hang over her children's heads, just out of reach, like mistletoe, and she took great pleasure in arranging it. The family would gather and she'd tear up, saying, "I don't want to spoil your happiness, but this may well be our last Christmas together." Other times, if somebody had something going on—a wedding, a graduation—she'd go in for exploratory surgery, anything to capture and hold attention. By the time I finally met her, she did not have a single organ that had not been touched by human hands. *Oh, my God,* I thought, watching her cry on our living room sofa, *my boyfriend's family is more fucked-up than my own.* I mean, this actually bothered me.

We were together for six years, and when we finally broke up I felt like a failure, a divorced person. I now had what the self-help books called "relationship baggage," which I would carry around for the rest of my life. The trick was to meet someone with similar baggage and form a matching set, but how would one go about finding such a person? Bars were out; I knew that much. I'd met my first boyfriend in a place called the Man Hole—not the sort of name that suggests fidelity. It was like meeting someone at fisticuffs and then complaining when he turned out to be violent. To be fair, he had never actually promised to be monogamous. That was my idea, and though I tried my hardest to convert him, the allure of other people was just too great.

Most of the gay couples I knew at that time had some sort of an arrangement. Boyfriend A could sleep with someone else as long as he didn't bring him home—or as long as he *did* bring him home. And Boyfriend B was free to do the same. It was a good setup for those who enjoyed variety and the thrill of the hunt, but to me it was just scary, and way too much work—like having one job while applying for another. One boyfriend was all I could handle, all I *wanted* to handle, really, and while I found this to be perfectly natural, my friends saw it as a form of repression and came to view me as something of a puritan. *Am I?* I wondered. But there were buckles to polish and stones to kneel upon, and so I put the question out of my mind.

I needed a boyfriend as conventional as I was, and luckily I found one—just met him one evening through a mutual friend. I was thirty-three, and Hugh had just turned thirty. Like me, he had recently broken up with someone and had moved to New York to start over. We had a few practical things in common, but what really brought us together was our mutual fear of abandonment and group sex. It was a foundation, and we built on it, adding our fears of AIDS and pierced nipples, of commitment ceremonies and the loss of self-control. In dreams sometimes I'll discover a handsome stranger waiting in my hotel room. He's usually someone I've seen earlier that day, on the street or in a television commercial, and now he's naked and beckoning me toward the bed. I look at my key, convinced that I have the wrong room, and when he springs forward and reaches for my zipper I run for the door, which is inevitably made of snakes or hot tar, one of those maddening, hard-to-clean building materials so often used in dreams. The handle moves this way and that, and while struggling to grab it I stammer an explanation as to why I can't go through with this. "I have a boyfriend, see, and, well, the thing is that he'd kill me if he ever found out I'd been, you know, unfaithful or anything."

Really, though, it's not the fear of Hugh's punishment that stops me. I remember once riding in the car with my dad. I was twelve, and it was just the two of us, coming home from the bank. We'd been silent for blocks, when out of nowhere he turned to me, saying, "I want you to know that I've never once cheated on your mother."

"Um. OK," I said. And then he turned on the radio and listened to a football game.

Years later, I mentioned this incident to a friend, who speculated that my father had said this specifically because he *had* been unfaithful. "That was a guilty conscience talking," she said, but I knew that she was wrong. More likely my father was having some problem at work and needed to remind himself that he was not completely worthless. It sounds like something you'd read on a movie poster: sometimes the sins you haven't committed are all you have to hold on to. If you're really desperate, you might need to grope, saying, for example, "I've never killed anyone *with a hammer*" or "I've never stolen from anyone *who didn't deserve it.*" But whatever his faults, my dad did not have to stoop quite that low.

I have never cheated on a boyfriend, and, as with my father, it's become part of my idea of myself. In my foiled wet dreams I can glimpse at what my life would be like without my perfect record, of how lost I'd feel without this scrap of integrity, and the fear is enough to wake me up. Once I'm awake, though, I tend to lie there, wondering if I've made a grave mistake.

In books and movies infidelity always looks so compelling, so *right*. Here are people who defy petty convention and are rewarded with only the tastiest bits of human experience. Never do they grow old or suffer the crippling panic I feel whenever Hugh gets spontaneous and suggests we go to a restaurant.

"A restaurant? But what will we talk about?"

"I don't know," he'll say. "What does it matter?"

Alone together, I enjoy our companionable silence, but it creeps me out to sit in public, propped in our chairs like a pair of mummies. At a nearby table there's always a couple in their late seventies, holding their menus with trembling, spotted hands.

"Soup's a good thing," the wife will say, and the man will nod or grunt or fool with the stem of his wineglass. Eventually he'll look my way, and I'll catch in his eye a look of grim recognition.

We are your future, he seems to say.

I'm so afraid that Hugh and I won't have anything to talk about that now, before leaving home, I'll comb the papers and jot down a half-dozen topics that might keep a conversation going at least through the entrees. The last time we ate out, I prepared by reading both the *Herald Tribune* and *The Animal Finder's Guide,* a quarterly publication devoted to exotic pets and the nuts who keep them. The waiter took our orders, and as he walked away I turned to Hugh, saying, "So, anyway, I hear that monkeys can really become surly once they reach breeding age."

"Well, I could have told you *that,*" he said. "It happened with my own monkey."

I tried to draw him out, but it saddens Hugh to discuss his childhood monkey. "Oh, Maxwell," he'll sigh, and within a minute he'll have started crying. Next on my list were the five warning signs of depression among captive camels, but I couldn't read my handwriting, and the topic crashed and burned after sign number two: an unwillingness to cush. At a nearby table an elderly woman arranged and rearranged the napkin in her lap. Her husband stared at a potted plant, and I resorted to the *Herald Tribune.* "Did you hear about those three Indian women who were burned as witches?"

"What?"

"Neighbors accused them of casting spells and burned them alive."

"Well, that's horrible," he said, slightly accusatory, as if I myself had had a hand in it. "You can't go around burning people alive, not in this day and age."

"I know it, but—"

"It's sick is what it is. I remember once when I was living in Somalia there was this woman . . ."

"Yes!" I whispered, and then I looked over at the elderly couple, thinking, *See, we're talking witch burnings!* It's work, though, and it's always *my* work. If I left it up to Hugh, we'd just sit there acting like what we are: two people so familiar with each other they could scream. Sometimes, when I find it hard to sleep, I'll think of when we first met, of the newness of each other's body, and my impatience to know everything about this person. Looking back, I should have taken it more slowly, measured him out over the course of fifty years rather than cramming him in so quickly. By the end of our first month together, he'd been so thoroughly interrogated that all I had left was breaking news—what little had happened in the few hours since I'd last seen him. Were he a cop or an emergency room doctor, there might have been a lot to catch up on, but like me Hugh works alone, so there was never much to report. "I ate some potato chips," he might say, to which I'd reply, "What kind?" or "That's funny, so did I!" More often than not, we'd just breathe into our separate receivers.

"Are you still there?"

"I'm here."

"Good. Don't hang up."

"I won't."

\*

228

In New York we slept on a futon. I took the left side and would lie awake at night, looking at the closet door. In Paris we got a real bed in a room just big enough to contain it. Hugh would fall asleep immediately, the way he's always done, and I'd stare at the blank wall, wondering about all the people who'd slept in this room before us. The building dated from the seventeenth century, and I envisioned musketeers in tall, soft boots, pleasuring the sorts of women who wouldn't complain when sword tips tore the sheets. I saw gentlemen in top hats and sleeping caps, women in bonnets and berets and beaded headbands, a swarm of phantom copulators all looking down and comparing my life with theirs.

After Paris came London, and a bedroom on the sixth floor with windows looking onto neat rows of Edwardian chimney tops. A friend characterized it as a "Peter Pan view," and now I can't see it any other way. I lie awake thinking of someone with a hook for a hand, and then, inevitably, of youth, and whether I have wasted it. Twenty-five years ago I was a young man with his whole sexual life ahead of him. How had 9,125 relatively uneventful days passed so quickly, and how can I keep it from happening again? In another twenty-five years I'll be doddering, and twenty-five years after that I'll be one of the figures haunting my Paris bedroom. Is it morally permissible, I wonder, to cheat *after* death? Is it even called cheating at that point? What are the rules? Do I have to wait a certain amount of time, or can I just jump, or, as the case may be, seep right in?

During the period that I had my boil, these questions seemed particularly relevant. The pain was always greater after dark, and by the sixth night I was fairly certain that I was dying. Hugh had gone to sleep hours earlier, and it startled me to hear his voice. "What do you say we lance that thing?" he said.

It's the sort of question that catches you off guard. "Did you just use the verb *to lance?*" I asked.

He turned on the light.

"Since when did you learn to lance boils?"

"I didn't," he said. "But I bet I could teach myself."

With anyone else I'd put up a fight, but Hugh can do just about anything he sets his mind to. This is a person who welded the plumbing pipes at his house in Normandy, then went into the cellar to make his own cheese. There's no one I trust more, and so I limped to the bathroom, that theater of home surgery, where I lowered my pajama bottoms and braced myself against the towel rack, waiting as he sterilized the needle.

"This is hurting me a lot more than it's hurting you," he said. It was his standard line, but I knew that this time he was right. Worse than the boil was the stuff that came out of it, a horrible custard streaked with blood. What got to me, and got to him even worse, was the stench, which was unbearable and unlike anything I had come across before. It was, I thought, what evil must smell like. How could a person continue to live with something so rotten inside of him? And so much of it! The first tablespoon gushed out on its own power, like something from a geyser. Then Hugh used his fingers and squeezed out the rest. "How are you doing back there?" I asked, but he was dry-heaving and couldn't answer.

When my boil was empty, he doused it with alcohol and put a bandage on it, as if it had been a minor injury, a shaving cut, a skinned knee, something normal he hadn't milked like a dead cow. And this, to me, was worth at least a hundred of the hundred and twenty nights of Sodom. Back in bed I referred to him as Sir Lance-a-Lot.

"Once is not a lot," he said.

This was true, but Sir Lance Occasionally lacks a certain ring.

"Besides," I said. "I know you'll do it again if I need you to. We're an aging monogamous couple, and this is all part of the bargain."

The thought of this kept Hugh awake that night, and still does. We go to bed and he stares toward the window as I sleep soundly beside him, my bandaged boil silently weeping onto the sheets.

# The Smoking Section

## Part I (Before)

### One

The first time someone hit me up for a cigarette I was twenty years old and had been smoking for all of two days. This was in Vancouver, British Columbia. My friend Ronnie and I had spent the previous month picking apples in Oregon, and the trip to Canada was our way of rewarding ourselves. We stayed that week in a cheap residence hotel, and I remember being enchanted by the Murphy bed, which was something I had heard about but never seen in person. During the time we were there, my greatest pleasure came in folding it away and then looking at the empty spot where it had been. Pull it out, fold it away, pull it out, fold it away. Over and over until my arm got tired.

It was in a little store a block from our hotel that I

bought my first pack of cigarettes. The ones I'd smoked earlier had been Ronnie's—Pall Malls, I think—and though they tasted no better or worse than I thought they would, I felt that in the name of individuality I should find my own brand, something separate. Something me. Carltons, Kents, Alpines: it was like choosing a religion, for weren't Vantage people fundamentally different from those who'd taken to Larks or Newports? What I didn't realize was that you could convert, that you were allowed to. The Kent person could, with very little effort, *become* a Vantage person, though it was harder to go from menthol to regular, or from regular-sized to ultralong. All rules had their exceptions, but the way I came to see things, they generally went like this: Kools and Newports were for black people and lower-class whites. Camels were for procrastinators, those who wrote bad poetry, and those who put off writing bad poetry. Merits were for sex addicts, Salems were for alcoholics, and Mores were for people who considered themselves to be outrageous but really weren't. One should never loan money to a Marlboro menthol smoker, though you could usually count on a regular Marlboro person to pay you back. The eventual subclasses of milds, lights, and ultra-lights would not only throw a wrench into the works, but make it nearly impossible for anyone to keep your brand straight, but that all came later, along with warning labels and American Spirits.

The pack I bought that day in Vancouver were Viceroys. I'd often noticed them in the shirt pockets of gas station attendants, and no doubt thought that they made me appear masculine, or at least as masculine as one *could* look in a beret and a pair of gabardine pants that buttoned at the ankle. Throw in Ronnie's white silk scarf, and I needed all the Viceroy I could get, especially in the neighborhood where this residence hotel was.

It was odd. I'd always heard how clean Canada was, how peaceful, but perhaps people had been talking about a different part, the middle maybe, or those rocky islands off the eastern coast. Here it was just one creepy drunk after another. The ones who were passed out I didn't mind so much, but those on their way to passing out—those who could still totter and flail their arms—made me afraid for my life.

Take this guy who approached me after I left the store, this guy with a long black braid. It wasn't the gentle, ropy kind you'd have if you played the flute, but something more akin to a bullwhip: *a prison braid,* I told myself. A month earlier I might have simply cowered, but now I put a cigarette in my mouth, the way one might if he were about to be executed. This man was going to rob me, then lash me with his braid and set me on fire—but no. "Give me one of those," he said, and he pointed to the pack I was holding. I handed him a Viceroy, and when he thanked me, I smiled and thanked him back.

It was, I later thought, as if I'd been carrying a bouquet, and he'd asked me for a single daisy. He loved flowers, I loved flowers, and wasn't it beautiful that our mutual appreciation could transcend our various differences and somehow bring us together? I must have thought too that had the situation been reversed, he'd have been happy to give *me* a cigarette, though my theory was never tested. I may have been a Boy Scout for only two years, but the motto stuck with me forever: Be Prepared. This does not mean "Be

Prepared to Ask People for Shit," but "Think Ahead, and Plan Accordingly, Especially in Regard to Your Vices."

**Two**

When I was in the fourth grade, my class took a field trip to the American Tobacco plant in nearby Durham. There we witnessed the making of cigarettes and were given free packs to take home to our parents. I tell people this, and they ask me how old I am, thinking, I guess, that I went to the world's first elementary school, one where we wrote on cave walls and hunted our lunch with clubs. I date myself again when I mention the smoking lounge at my high school. It was outdoors, but still, you'd never find anything like that now, not even if the school was in a prison.

I recall seeing ashtrays in movie theaters and grocery stores, but they didn't make me want to smoke. In fact, it was just the opposite. Once I drove an embroidery needle into my mother's carton of Winstons, over and over, as if it were a voodoo doll. She then beat me for twenty seconds, at which point she ran out of breath and stood there panting, "That's . . . not . . . funny."

A few years later, while sitting around the breakfast table, she invited me to take a puff. I did. Then I ran to the kitchen and drained a carton of orange juice, drinking so furiously that half of it ran down my chin and onto my shirt. How could she, could anyone, really, make a habit of something so fundamentally unpleasant? When my sister Lisa started smoking, I forbade her to enter my bedroom with a lit cigarette. She could talk to me, but only from the other side of the threshold, and she had to avert her head when she exhaled. I did the same when my sister Gretchen started.

It wasn't the smoke but the smell of it that bothered me. In later years I wouldn't care so much, but at the time I found it depressing: the scent of neglect is how I thought of it. It wasn't so noticeable in the rest of the house, but then again, the rest of the house was neglected. My room was clean and orderly, and if I'd had my way it would have smelled like an album jacket the moment you removed the plastic. That is to say, it would have smelled like anticipation.

**Three**

At the age of fourteen I accompanied a classmate to a Raleigh park. There we met with some friends of his and smoked a joint by the light of the moon. I don't recall being high, but I do recall pretending to be high. My behavior was modeled on the whacked-out hippies I'd seen in movies and on TV, so basically I just laughed a lot, regardless of whether anything was funny. When I got home I woke my sisters and had them sniff my fingers. "Smell that?" I said. "It's marijuana, or 'grass,' as we sometimes call it."

I was proud to be the first in my family to smoke a joint, but once I had claimed the title, I became vehemently antidrug and remained that way until my freshman year of college. Throughout the first semester, I railed against my dorm mates: Pot was for losers. It pickled your brain and forced you into crummy state universities like this one.

I'd later think of how satisfying it must have been to them—how biblical, almost—to witness my complete turnaround. The reverend mother becomes the town slut, the prohibitionist a drunkard, and me a total pothead, and so quickly! It was just like you'd see in a made-for-TV movie:

FRIENDLY FELLOW FROM DOWN THE HALL: Oh, come on. One puff's not going to hurt you.

ME: The heck it won't! I've got some studying to do.

HANDSOME ROOMMATE OF THE FRIENDLY FELLOW DOWN THE HALL: Just let me give you a shotgun.

ME: A shotgun? What's that?

AGAIN THE HANDSOME ROOMMATE: You lie back while I blow smoke into your mouth.

ME: Where do you want me to lie?

I remember returning to my room that night and covering my lamp with a silk scarf. The desk, the bed, the heavy, misshapen pottery projects: nothing was new, but everything was different; fresh somehow and worthy of interest. Grant a blind person the ability to see, and he might have behaved the way I did, slowly advancing across the room and marveling at everything before me: a folded shirt, a stack of books, a piece of corn bread wrapped in foil. "Amazing." The tour ended with the mirror, and me standing in front of it with a turban on my head. *Well, hello there, you,* I thought.

I let a college kid give me a shotgun, and for the next twenty-three years my life revolved around getting high. It was pot, in fact, that led me to smoking tobacco. Ronnie and I were by the side of the highway, making our way to Canada, and I was whining about having no marijuana. The sameness of everything was getting on my nerves, and I asked if cigarettes made you feel any different.

Ronnie lit one and thought for a minute. "I guess they leave you sort of light-headed," she told me.

"You mean, like, nauseous?"

"A little," she said. And I decided that was good enough for me.

**Four**

As with pot, it was astonishing how quickly I took to cigarettes. It was as if my life was a play, and the prop mistress had finally shown up. Suddenly there were packs to unwrap, matches to strike, ashtrays to fill and then empty. My hands were at one with their labor, the way a cook's might be, or a knitter's.

"Well, that's a hell of a reason to poison yourself," my father said.

My mother, however, looked at the bright side. "Now I'll know what to put in your Christmas stocking!" She put them in my Easter basket as well, entire cartons. Today it might seem trashy to see a young man accepting a light from his mom, but smoking didn't always mean something. A cigarette wasn't always a statement. Back when I started, you could still smoke at work, even if you worked in a hospital where kids with no legs were hooked up to machines. If a character smoked on a TV show, it did not necessarily mean that he was weak or evil. It was like seeing someone who wore a striped tie or parted his hair on the left—a detail, but not a telling one.

I didn't much notice my fellow smokers until the mid-eighties, when we began to be cordoned off. Now there were separate sections in waiting rooms and restaurants, and I'd often look around and evaluate what I'd come to think of as "my team." At first they seemed normal enough—regular people, but with cigarettes in their hands. Then the campaign began in earnest, and it seemed that if there were ten

239

adults on my side of the room, at least one of them was smoking through a hole in his throat.

"Still think it's so cool?" the other side said. But coolness, for most of us, had nothing to do with it. It's popular to believe that every smoker was brainwashed, sucked in by product placements and subliminal print ads. This argument comes in handy when you want to assign blame, but it discounts the fact that smoking is often wonderful. For people like me, people who twitched and jerked and cried out in tiny voices, cigarettes were a godsend. Not only that, but they tasted good, especially that first one in the morning, and the seven or eight that immediately followed it. By late afternoon, after I'd finished a pack or so, I'd generally feel a heaviness in my lungs, especially in the 1980s, when I worked with hazardous chemicals. I should have worn a respirator, but it interfered with my smoking, and so I set it aside.

I once admitted this to a forensic pathologist. We were in the autopsy suite of a medical examiner's office, and he responded by handing me a lung. It had belonged to an obese, light-skinned black man, an obvious heavy smoker who was lying on a table not three feet away. His sternum had been sawed through, and the way his chest cavity was opened, the unearthed fat like so much sour cream, made me think of a baked potato. "So," the pathologist said. "What do you say to *this?*"

He'd obviously hoped to create a moment, the kind that leads you to change your life, but it didn't quite work. If you are a doctor and someone hands you a diseased lung, you might very well examine it and consequently make some very radical changes. If, on the other hand, you are *not* a doctor, you're liable to do what I did, which was to stand there thinking, *Damn, this lung is heavy.*

**Five**

When New York banned smoking in restaurants, I stopped eating out. When they banned it in the workplace I quit working, and when they raised the price of cigarettes to seven dollars a pack, I gathered all my stuff together and went to France. It was hard to find my brand there, but no matter. At least twice a year I returned to the United States. Duty-free cartons were only twenty dollars each, and I'd buy fifteen of them before boarding the plane back to Paris. Added to these were the cigarettes brought by visiting friends, who acted as mules, and the ones I continued to receive for Christmas and Easter, even after my mom died. Ever prepared for the possibility of fire or theft, at my peak I had thirty-four cartons stockpiled in three different locations. "My inventory," I called it, as in, "The only thing standing between me and a complete nervous breakdown is my inventory."

It is here that I'll identify myself as a Kool Mild smoker. This, to some, is like reading the confessions of a wine enthusiast and discovering midway through that his drink of choice is Lancers, but so be it. It was my sister Gretchen who introduced me to menthol cigarettes. She'd worked at a cafeteria throughout high school and had gotten on to Kools by way of a line cook named Dewberry. I never met the guy, but in those first few years, whenever I found myself short of breath, I'd think of him and wonder what my life would be like had he smoked Tareytons.

People were saying that Kools had fiberglass in them, but

surely that was just a rumor, started, most likely, by the Salem or Newport people. I'd heard too that menthols were worse for you than regular cigarettes, but that also seemed suspect. Just after she started chemotherapy, my mom sent me three cartons of Kool Milds. "They were on sale," she croaked. Dying or not, she should have known that I smoked Filter Kings, but then I looked at them and thought, Well, they *are* free.

For people who don't smoke, a mild or light cigarette is like a regular one with a pinhole in it. With Kools it's the difference between being kicked by a donkey and being kicked by a donkey that has socks on. It took some getting used to, but by the time my mother was cremated, I'd converted.

**Six**

Over the years, I've had quite a few essays reprinted in textbooks. When the students are high schoolers or younger, the editors will sometimes ask if they can replace or eliminate a certain filthy word or phrase, which makes sense, I suppose. What didn't make sense, at least to me, was a similar request to eliminate a cigarette, to essentially blank it out. The same is done with photographs now, and the effect is disconcerting. Here is Marlene Dietrich in repose, her fingers spread apart for no reason, her eyes staring at the burning tip of nothing.

This particular textbook was for tenth graders. *Horizons,* it was called, or maybe *Perspectives.* The line that the editors wanted to erase did not glamorize smoking. In fact it was just the opposite. The cigarette in question belonged to my mother and was referred to as an irritant, something invasive that had given me a headache. I suppose I could have replaced the irritating Winston with an irritating Roman candle, but the story was supposed to be true, and my mother never sat around with fireworks in her mouth. The point I argued is that certain people smoke. It's part of what makes them who they are, and though you certainly don't have to like it, altering someone's character seems a bit harsh, especially when that someone is your mother, and picturing her without a cigarette is unimaginable. "It's like she was a windup toy and that was her key," I said.

It seems crazy to cut smoking mothers out of textbooks, but within a few years they won't be allowed in movies either. A woman can throw her newborn child from the roof of a high-rise building. She can then retrieve the body and stomp on it while shooting into the windows of a day care center, but to celebrate these murders by lighting a cigarette is to send a harmful message. There are, after all, young people watching, and we wouldn't want them to get the wrong idea.

We're forever being warned about secondhand smoke, but if it's really as dangerous as they claim it is, I'd have been dead before my first birthday. My brother and sisters would be dead as well, or maybe we'd never have lived to begin with, our mother having been snuffed out by her own parents' cigarettes.

My grandparents on my father's side didn't smoke, but as owners of a newsstand and tobacco shop, they profited from other people doing it. My dad started smoking when he went to college, but he quit when my older sister and I were still young. "It's a filthy, stinking habit." He said this fifty times a day, not that it did any good. Even before the warnings were printed, anyone could see that smoking was bad for you. My mother's sister, Joyce, was married to a surgeon, and every time I stayed at their house I was awoken at dawn by my uncle's hacking, which was mucky and painful-sounding and suggested imminent death. Later, at the breakfast table I'd see him with a cigarette in his mouth and think, Well, *he's* the doctor.

Uncle Dick died of lung cancer, and a few years later my mother developed a nearly identical cough. You'd think that being a woman, hers would be softer, a delicate lady's hack, but no. I remember lying in bed and thinking with shame, *My mom coughs like a man.*

By the time my embarrassment ripened to concern, I knew there was no point in lecturing her. I had become a smoker myself, so what could I say, really? Eventually she dropped her Winstons in favor of something light and then ultralight. "It's like sucking on a straw," she'd complain. "Give me one of yours, why don't you?"

My mother visited twice when I lived in Chicago. The first time was when I graduated from college, and the second was a few years later. She had just turned sixty, and I remember having to slow down when walking with her. Climbing to the elevated train meant stopping every fifth step or so while she wheezed and sputtered and pounded her chest with her fist. *Come on,* I remember thinking. *Hurry it up.*

Toward the end of her life, she managed two weeks without a cigarette. "That's half a month, practically," she said to me on the phone. "Can you believe it?"

I was in New York at the time and tried to imagine her going about her business: driving to the bank, putting in a load of laundry, watching the portable TV in the kitchen, nothing in her mouth besides her tongue and her teeth. At that time in her life, my mother had a part-time job at a consignment shop. Easy Elegance, the place was called, and she was quick to remind me that they didn't take just anything. "It has to be classy."

The owner didn't allow smoking, so once every hour my mother would step out the back door. I think it was there, standing on gravel in the hot parking lot, that she came to think of smoking as unsophisticated. I'd never heard her talk about quitting, but when she called after two weeks without a cigarette, I could hear a tone of accomplishment in her voice. "It's hardest in the mornings," she said. "And then, of course, later on, when you're having your drink."

I don't know what got her started again: stress, force of habit, or perhaps she decided that she was too old to quit. I'd probably have agreed with her, though now, of course, sixty-one, that's nothing.

There would be other attempts to stop smoking, but none of them lasted more than a few days. Lisa would tell me that Mom hadn't had a cigarette in eighteen hours. Then, when my mother called, I'd hear the click of her lighter, followed by a ragged intake of breath. "What's new, pussycat?"

**Seven**

Somewhere between my first cigarette and my last one, I became a business traveler. The business I conduct is reading out loud, but still I cover a lot of territory. At first I was happy to stay in any old place, be it a Holiday Inn or a Ramada near the airport. Bedspreads were usually slick to the touch, and patterned in dark, stain-concealing colors. Parked here and there on the hallway carpets were any number of cockeyed trays, each with a hamburger bun or a crust of French toast on it. *Room service,* I'd think. *How fancy can you get?*

It didn't take long to become more discriminating. It seems that when you're paying for yourself, any third-rate chain will do. But if someone else is footing the bill, you sort of need the best. The places that made me the insufferable snob I am today ranged from the fine to the ridiculously fine. Sheets had the snap of freshly minted money, and there was always some little gift waiting on the coffee table: fruit, maybe, or a bottle of wine. Beside the gift was a handwritten note from the manager, who wanted to say how pleased he was to have me as a guest. "Should you need anything, anything at all, please phone me at the following number," he would write.

The temptation was to call and demand a pony—"and be quick about it, man, this mood of mine won't last forever"— but of course I never did. Too shy, I guess. Too certain that I would be bothering someone.

More than a decade into my snobitude, I'm still reluctant to put anyone out. Once someone sent a cake to my room, and rather than call downstairs and ask for silverware I cut it with my credit card and ate the pieces with my fingers.

When I first started traveling for business, it was still possible to smoke. Not *as* possible as it had been in the eighties, but most places allowed it. I remember complaining when, in order to have a cigarette, I had to walk to the other end of the terminal, but in retrospect that was nothing. As the nineties progressed, my life grew increasingly difficult. Airport bars and restaurants became "clean-air zones," and those few cities that continued to allow smoking constructed hideous tanks.

The ones in Salt Lake City were kept in good condition, but those in St. Louis and Atlanta were miniature, glass-walled slums: ashtrays never emptied, trash on the ground, air ducts exposed and sagging from the caramel-colored ceiling. Then there were the people. My old friend with the hole in his throat was always there, as was his wife, who had a suitcase in one hand and an oxygen tank in the other. Alongside her were the servicemen from Abu Ghraib, two prisoners handcuffed to federal agents, and the Joad family. It was a live antismoking commercial, and those passing by would often stop and point, especially if they were with children. "See that lady with the tube taped to her nose? Is that what you want to happen to you?"

In one of these tanks, I sat beside a woman whose two-year-old son was confined to a wheelchair. This drew the sort of crowd that normally waves torches, and I admired the way the mother ignored it. After hot-boxing three quarters of her Salem, she tossed the butt in the direction of the ashtray, saying, "Damn, that was good."

As nasty as the tanks could be, I never turned my back on one. The only other choice was to go outside, which became increasingly complicated and time-consuming after September 11. In a big-city airport, it would likely take half an hour just to reach the main entrance, after which you'd have to walk ten, then twenty, then fifty yards from the door. Cars the size of school buses would pass, and the driver, who was most often the only person on board, would give you that particular look, meaning, "Hey, Mr. Puffing on Your Cigarette, thanks a lot for ruining our air."

As the new century advanced, more and more places went completely smoke-free. This included all the Marriott hotels. That in itself didn't bother me so much—*Screw them*, I thought—but Marriott owns the Ritz-Carltons, and when they followed suit I sat on my suitcase and cried.

Not just businesses, but entire towns have since banned smoking. They're generally not the most vital places on the map, but still they wanted to send a message. If you thought you could enjoy a cigarette in one of their bars or restaurants, then think again, and the same goes for their hotel rooms. Knowing that a traveler would not be smoking while sitting at his desk at the Palookaville Hyatt: I guess this allowed the townspeople to sleep a little easier at night. For me it marked the beginning of the end.

I don't know why bad ideas spread faster than good ones, but they do. Across the board, smoking bans came into effect, and I began to find myself outside the city limits, on that ubiquitous commercial strip between the waffle restaurant and the muffler shop. You may not have noticed, but there's a hotel there. It doesn't have a pool, yet still the lobby smells like chlorine, with just a slight trace of French fries. Should you order the latter off the room service menu, and find yourself in need of more ketchup, just wipe some off your telephone, or off the knob to the wall-mounted heating and air-conditioning unit. There's mustard there too. I've seen it.

The only thing worse than a room in this hotel is a smoking room in this hotel. With a little fresh air, it wouldn't be quite so awful, but, nine times out of ten, the windows have been soldered shut. Either that, or they open only a quarter of an inch, this in case you need to toss out a slice of toast. The trapped and stagnant smoke is treated with an aerosol spray, the effectiveness of which tends to vary. At best it recalls a loaded ashtray, the butts soaking in a shallow pool of lemonade. At worst it smells like a burning mummy.

The hotels I found myself reduced to had posters hanging in the elevators. "Our Deep Dish Pizza Is *Pan*tastic!!!" one of them read. Others mentioned steak fingers or "appeteazers," available until 10:00 at Perspectives or Horizons, always billed as "The place to see and be seen!" Go to your room, and there are more pictures of food, most in the form of three-dimensional flyers propped beside the telephone and clock radio. If it's rare to find a really good photograph of bacon, it's rarer still to find one on your bedside table. The same is true of nachos. They're just not photogenic.

When my room is on the ground floor, the view out my window is of a parked eighteen-wheel truck, but if I'm higher up I can sometimes see the waffle restaurant parking lot, and beyond that the interstate. The landscape is best described as "pedestrian hostile." It's pointless to try to take a walk, so I generally just stay in the room and think about shooting myself in the head. In a decent hotel there's always a bath to look forward to, but here the tub is shallow and made of fiberglass. When the stopper is gone—and it usually is—I plug the drain with a balled-up plastic bag. The hot water runs out after three minutes or so, and then I just lie there, me and a bar of biscuit-sized soap that smells just like the carpet.

I told myself that if this was where I needed to stay in

order to smoke, then so be it. To hell with the Ritz-Carltons and the puritanical town councils. I'd gone without decent sheets for close to forty years, and now I would do so again. My resolve lasted through the autumn of 2006 but was never terribly strong. By the time I found a wad of semen on the buttons of my remote control, I had already begun to consider the unthinkable.

**Eight**

If the first step in quitting was to make up my mind, the second was to fill my eventual void. I hated leaving a hole in the smoking world, and so I recruited someone to take my place. People have given me a lot of grief, but I'm pretty sure that after high school, this girl would have started anyway, especially if she chose the army over community college.

After crossing "replacement" off my list, I moved on to step three. According to the experts, the best way to quit smoking is to change your environment, shake up your routine a little. For people with serious jobs and responsibilities, this might amount to moving your sofa, or driving to work in a rental car. For those with less serious jobs and responsibilities, the solution was to run away for a few months: new view, new schedule, new lease on life.

As I searched the atlas for somewhere to run to, Hugh made a case for his old stomping grounds. His first suggestion was Beirut, where he went to nursery school. His family left there in the midsixties and moved to the Congo. After that, it was Ethiopia, and then Somalia, all fine places in his opinion.

"Let's save Africa and the Middle East for when I decide to quit living," I said.

In the end, we settled on Tokyo, a place we had gone the previous summer. The city has any number of things to recommend it, but what first hooked me was the dentistry. People looked as if they'd been chewing on rusty bolts. If a tooth was whole, it most likely protruded, or was wired to a crazy-looking bridge. In America I smile with my mouth shut. Even in France and England I'm self-conscious, but in Tokyo, for the first time in years, I felt normal. I loved the department stores too and the way the employees would greet their customers. *"Irrasshimase!"* They sounded like cats, and when a group would call out in unison, the din was fantastic. When I looked back on our short, three-day visit, I thought mainly of the curiosities: a young woman dressed for no reason like Bo Peep, a man riding a bike while holding a tray. It had a bowl of noodles on it, and though the broth went right up to the rim, he hadn't spilled so much as a drop.

I'd thought of Japan as a smoker's paradise, but, like everywhere else, it had gotten more restrictive. In most areas of Tokyo, it is illegal to walk the streets with a lit cigarette in your hand. This doesn't mean that you can't smoke, just that you can't move and smoke at the same time. Outdoor ashtrays have been set up, and while they're not as numerous as one might wish, still they exist. Most are marked with metal signs, the Japanese and English messages accompanied by simple illustrations: "Please mind your manners." "Don't throw butts into the street." "Use portable ashtrays in consideration of others around you."

At a smoking station in the neighborhood of Shibuya, the messages were more thought-provoking, as were the pictures that accompanied them: "I carry a 700-degree fire in my hand with people walking all around me!" "Before I pass gas, I look behind me, but I don't bother when I'm smoking." "A lit cigarette is held at the height of a child's face."

All of the messages were related to civics. Smoking leads to litter. Smoking can possibly burn or partially blind those around you. There was none of the finger wagging you see in America, none of the "shouldn't you know better?" and the "how could you?" admonitions that ultimately ignite more cigarettes than they extinguish.

When it came to restrictions, Japan was just the opposite of everywhere else. Instead of sending its smokers outdoors, it herded them inside where there was money to be made. In coffee shops and restaurants, in cabs and offices and hotel rooms, life was like a black-and-white movie. Compared to the United States, it was shocking, but compared to France it seemed fairly normal, the most telling difference being the warning labels on the sides of the packs. In France they read, "SMOKING WILL KILL YOU," the letters so big they can be read from space. In Japan both the writing and the message were more discreet: "Be careful of how much you smoke so as not to damage your health."

There was no mention of cancer or emphysema and certainly no pictures of diseased organs. They do that in Canada, and while I don't know that it encourages people to quit, I do know that it makes for one ugly package.

What with all the indoor smoking, Japan was something of a throwback. It might seem the place to start rather than stop, but when I finally thought of quitting, I thought of Tokyo. Its foreignness would take me out of myself, I hoped, and give me something to concentrate on besides my own suffering.

## Nine

We decided on Tokyo in early November, and before I could back out, Hugh found us an apartment in the neighborhood of Minato-ku. The building was a high-rise, and most of the tenants were short term. The real estate agent sent pictures, and I viewed them with mixed feelings. Tokyo I was excited about, but the idea of not smoking—of actually going through with this—made me a little sick. The longest I'd ever gone without a cigarette was twelve hours, but that was on an airplane so it probably didn't count.

On an average day I'd smoke around a pack and a half, more if I was drunk or on drugs, and more still if I was up all night, working against a deadline. The next morning I'd have what amounted to a nicotine hangover, my head all stuffy, my tongue like some filthy sandal crammed into my mouth—not that it prevented me from starting all over again the moment I got out of bed. I used to wait until I had a cup of coffee in my hand, but by the early 1990s, that had gone by the wayside. The only rule now was that I had to be awake.

In preparing myself to quit, I started looking at this or that individual cigarette, wondering why I'd lit it in the first place. Some you just flat-out need—the ones you reach for after leaving the dentist's office or the movie theater—but others were smoked as a kind of hedge. "Only if I light this will my bus appear," I'd tell myself. "Only if I light this will the ATM give me small bills." There were cigarettes lit because the phone was ringing, because the doorbell was ringing, even a passing ambulance was an excuse. There would certainly be bells and sirens in Tokyo, but I doubted that anyone would come to our door. What with the time difference, I wasn't expecting many calls either. When not panicking, I could sometimes congratulate myself on what was actually a pretty decent plan.

## Ten

In the summer of 2006, shortly before our three-day trip to Tokyo, I bought a Japanese-language CD. It was just the basics: "Good morning," "May I have a fork?" that type of thing. The person giving the English translation spoke at a normal pace, but the one speaking Japanese, a woman, was remarkably slow and hesitant. *"Koooonniiiichiii waaa,"* she'd say. *"Ooooohaaaayooooo goooooo . . . zaimasssssuuu."* I memorized everything she said and arrived in Japan feeling pretty good about myself. A bellman escorted Hugh and me to our hotel room and, without too much trouble, I was able to tell him that I liked it. *"Korrree gaaa sukiii dessssu."* The following morning I offered a few pleasantries to the concierge, who politely told me that I was talking like a lady, an old, rich one, apparently. "You might want to speed it up a little," he suggested.

A lot of people laughed at my Japanese on that trip, but I never felt that I was being made fun of. Rather, it was like I'd performed a trick, something perverse and unexpected, like pulling a sausage out of my ear. When I first came to France, I was afraid to open my mouth, but in Tokyo, trying was fun. The five dozen phrases I'd memorized before coming served me in good stead, and I left the country wanting to learn more.

This led me to a second, much more serious instructional program—forty-five CDs as opposed to just one. The speakers were young, a guy and a girl, and they didn't slow down for anybody. The idea here was to listen and repeat—no writing whatsoever—but that, to me, sounded too good to be true. It wasn't advised, but at the end of each lesson I'd copy all the new words and phrases onto index cards. These allowed me to review, and, even better, to be quizzed. Hugh has no patience for that sort of thing, so I had my sisters Amy and Lisa do it. The two of them came to Paris for Christmas, and at the end of every day I'd hand one or the other of them my stack of cards.

"All right," Lisa might say. "How do you ask if I'm a second-grade reading teacher?"

"I haven't learned that yet. If it's not written down, I don't know how to say it."

"Oh, really?" She'd then pull a card from the stack and frown at it. "All right, say this: 'As for this afternoon, what are you going to do?'"

"*Gogo wa, nani o shimasu ka?*"

"'What *did* you do this afternoon?' Can you say that in Japanese?"

"Well, no—"

"Can you say that you and your older sister saw a bad movie with a dragon in it? Can you at least say 'dragon'?"

"No."

"I see," she said, and as she reached for another card, I felt a mounting hopelessness.

It was even worse when Amy quizzed me. "How do you ask someone for a cigarette?"

"I don't know."

"How do you say, 'I tried to quit, but it's not working'?"

"I have no idea."

"Say 'I'll give you a blow job if you'll give me a cigarette.'"

"Just stick to the index cards."

"Say 'Goodness, how fat I've become! Can you believe how much weight I've gained since I quit smoking'?"

"Actually," I said, "I think I'll just do this on my own."

## Eleven

In the months preceding our trip to Tokyo, I spoke to quite a few people who had either quit smoking or tried to. A number of them had stopped for years. Then their step-grandmother died or their dog grew a crooked tooth, and they picked up where they'd left off.

"Do you think you were maybe *looking* for a reason to start again?" I asked.

All of them said no.

The message was that you were never really safe. An entire decade without a cigarette, and then . . . wham! My sister Lisa started again after six years, and told me, as had others, that quitting was much more difficult the second time around.

When asked how they made it through the first few weeks, a lot of people mentioned the patch. Others spoke of gum and lozenges, of acupuncture, hypnosis, and some new drug everyone had heard about but no one could remember the name of. Then there were the books. The problem with most so-called quit lit is that there are only so many times you can repeat the words "smoking" and "cigarettes." The trick is to alternate them, not to reach for your thesaurus. It bothers me to read that so-and-so "inhaled a cancer stick," that he "sucked up a coffin nail." I don't know anyone who refers to tobacco as "the evil weed." People in the UK gen-uinely say "fags," but in America it's just embarrassing and self-consciously naughty, like calling a cat a pussy.

The book I was given used all of these terms and more. I read the first hundred pages and then offered Hugh the following summary: "The guy says that choking down lung busters is a filthy, disgusting habit."

"No it's not," he said.

After years of throwing open the windows and telling me I smelled like a casino, it seemed that Hugh didn't want me to quit. "You just need to cut back a little," he told me.

Not being a smoker himself, he didn't understand how agonizing that would be. It had been the same with alcohol; easier to stop altogether than to test myself every day. As far as getting wasted was concerned, I was definitely minor league. All I know is that I drank to get drunk, and I succeeded every night for over twenty years. For the most part, I was very predictable and bourgeois about it. I always waited until 8:00 p.m. to start drinking, and I almost always did it at home, most often at the typewriter. What began at age twenty-two as one beer per night eventually became five, followed by two tall Scotches, all on an empty stomach and within a period of ninety minutes. Dinner would sober me up a little and, after eating, I'd start smoking pot.

Worse than anything was the dullness of it, night after night the exact same story. Hugh didn't smoke pot, and though he might have a cocktail, and maybe some wine with dinner, he's never seemed dependent on it. At 11:00 you could talk to him on the phone, and he'd sound no different from the way he would at noon. Call me at 11:00, and after a minute or so I'd forget who I was talking to. Then I'd remember, and celebrate by taking another bong hit. Even worse was when *I* placed the call. "Yes," I'd

257

say. "May I please speak to . . . oh, you know. He has brownish hair? He drives a van with his name written on it?"

"Is this David?"

"Yes."

"And you want to speak to your brother, Paul?"

"That's it. Could you put him on, please?"

Most often I'd stay up until 3:00, rocking back and forth in my chair and thinking of the things I could do if I weren't so fucked up. Hugh would go to bed at around midnight, and after he'd fallen asleep I would have dinner all over again. Physically I couldn't have been hungry. It was just the pot talking. "Fry me an egg," it would demand. "Make me a sandwich." "Cut a piece of cheese and smear it with whatever's on that shelf there." We couldn't keep a condiment for longer than a week, no matter how horrid or ridiculous it was.

"Where's that Nigerian tica-tica sauce Oomafata brought us from Lagos last Tuesday?" Hugh would ask, and I'd say, "Tica-tica sauce? Never saw it."

In New York I got my marijuana through a service. You called a number, recited your code name, and twenty minutes later an apple-cheeked NYU student would show up at your door. In his knapsack would be eight varieties of pot, each with its own clever name and distinctive flavor. Getting high on Thompson Street was the easiest thing in the world, but in Paris, I had no idea where to find such a college student. I knew a part of town where people lurked in the shadows. The way they whispered and beckoned was familiar, but as a foreigner I didn't dare risk getting arrested. Then too, they were most likely selling moss, or the innards of horsehair sofas. The things I've bought from strangers in the dark would curl your hair.

You don't withdraw from marijuana the way you do from speed or cocaine. The body doesn't miss it, but the rest of you sure does. "I wonder what this would look like stoned." I said this to myself twenty times a day, referring to everything from Notre Dame to the high-beamed ceiling in our new apartment. Pot made the normal look ten times better, so I could only imagine what it did to the extraordinary.

If I survived in Paris without getting high, it was only because I still had drinking to look forward to. The bottles in France are smaller than they are in the States, but the alcohol content is much higher. I'm no good at math but figured that five American beers equaled nine French ones. This meant I had to be vigilant about the recycling. Skip a day, and it would look like I'd had Belgium over.

In time I knew that my quota would increase, and then increase again. I wanted to quit before that happened, but practical concerns kept getting in the way. When drinking and working went hand in hand, it was easy to sit at your desk every night. Without it, though, how could a person write? What would be the incentive? Then there was the mess of quitting: the treatment center with the chatterbox roommate, the AA meetings where you'd have to hold hands.

In the end, I stopped on my own. One night without a drink became two nights, and so on and so on. The first few weeks were kind of shaky, but a lot of it was just me being dramatic. As for the writing, I simply changed my schedule and worked in the daytime rather than in the evening. When other people drank, I tried to be happy for them, and when they got drunk and fell down, I found that I didn't have to try. My happiness was genuine and unforced. *Look at what I'm missing,* I'd think.

Turn down a drink in the United States, and people get the message without your having to explain. "Oh," they say, ashamed of themselves for presuming otherwise. "Right. I should probably . . . quit too." In Europe, though, you're not an alcoholic unless you're living half-naked on the street, drinking antifreeze from a cast-off shoe. Anything shy of this is just "fun-loving" or "rascally." Cover your glass in France or Germany—even worse, in England—and in the voice of someone who has been personally affronted, your host will ask why you're not drinking.

"Oh, I just don't feel like it this morning."

"Why not?"

"I guess I'm not in the mood?"

"Well, this'll put you in the mood. Here. Drink up."

"No, really, I'm OK."

"Just taste it."

"Actually, I'm sort of . . . well, I sort of have a problem with it."

"Then how about *half* a glass?"

I was at a French wedding a few years back, and when it came time to toast the couple, the bride's mother approached me with a bottle of Veuve Clicquot.

"That's all right," I told her, "I'm happy with my water."

"But you have to have champagne!"

"Really," I said, "I'm fine the way I am."

"But . . ."

Just then the toast was delivered. I raised my glass into the air, and as I was bringing it to my lips someone jabbed a champagne-soaked finger into my mouth. It was the bride's mother. "I'm sorry," she said, "but those are the rules. You're not supposed to toast with Perrier."

In America I'm pretty sure you could sue somebody for this. But the woman had meant well, and at least her nails had been short. In the years since the wedding, I've learned to accept the glass of champagne. It's easier to take it, then quietly pass it to Hugh, than it is to make a big deal about it. Other than that, I don't give much thought to alcohol anymore. I don't think about drugs, either, not unless something new comes along, something I never got a chance to try. The point, I guess, is that I was able to quit. And if I was able to quit drinking and taking drugs, perhaps I'd be able to quit smoking as well. The trick was not to get all sensitive about it, lest you give abstinence a worse name that it already has.

## Twelve

My last cigarette was smoked in a bar at Charles de Gaulle Airport. It was January 3, a Wednesday morning, and though we would be changing planes in London and would have a layover of close to two hours, I thought it best to quit while I was still ahead.

"All right," I said to Hugh. "This is it, my final one." Six minutes later I pulled out my pack and said the same thing. Then I did it one more time. "This is it. I mean it." All around me, people were enjoying cigarettes: the ruddy Irish couple, the Spaniards with their glasses of beer. There were the Russians, the Italians, even some Chinese. Together we formed a foul little congress: the United Tarnations, the Fellowship of the Smoke Ring. These were my people, and now I would be betraying them, turning my back just when they needed me most. Though I wish it were otherwise, I'm actually a very intolerant person. When I see a drunk or a drug addict begging for money, I don't think, *There but for the grace of God go I,* but, *I quit, and so can you. Now get that cup of nickels out of my face.*

It's one thing to give up smoking, and another to become a former smoker. That's what I would be the moment I left the bar, and so I lingered awhile, looking at my garish disposable lighter, and the crudded-up aluminum ashtray. When I eventually got up to leave, Hugh pointed out that I still had five cigarettes left in my pack.

"Are you just going to leave them there on the table?"

I answered with a line I'd gotten years ago from a German woman. Her name was Tini Haffmans, and though she often apologized for the state of her English, I wouldn't have wanted it to be any better. When it came to verb conjugation she was beyond reproach, but every so often she'd get a word wrong. The effect was not a loss of meaning, but a heightening of it. I once asked if her neighbor smoked, and she thought for a moment before saying, "Karl has . . . finished with his smoking."

She meant, of course, that he had quit, but I much preferred her mistaken version. "Finished" made it sound as if he'd been allotted a certain number of cigarettes, three hundred thousand, say, delivered at the time of his birth. If he'd started a year later or smoked more slowly, he might still be at it, but as it stood he had worked his way to the last one, and then moved on with his life. This, I thought, was how *I* would look at it. Yes, there were five more Kool Milds in that particular pack, and twenty-six cartons stashed away at

262

home, but those were extras, an accounting mistake. In terms of my smoking, I had just finished with it.

## Part II (Japan)

### January 5

The first time we flew to Tokyo, I ran outside immediately after clearing customs. I had just gone half a day without a cigarette, and the one I would light out on the curb would leave me so woozy I'd come close to toppling over. To most people, this sounds unpleasant, but to a smoker it's about as good as it gets—the first cigarette in the morning times ten. This was always my reward for traveling, and without it I wasn't sure what to do with myself. After clearing customs on this most recent flight, I set down my suitcase and turned to Hugh. "What happens next?" I asked. And with no fanfare, he led us toward the train.

That was yesterday morning, which seems like months ago. It's been thirty-eight hours since my last cigarette, and I have to say that while it hasn't been completely painless, neither is it as ghastly as I thought it would be. I expected a complete meltdown, but strangely it's Hugh who's become moody and irritable. If I'm no different than ever, it might have something to do with the patch I applied three hours into our flight. I hadn't planned on buying any, but a few days ago, while passing a pharmacy, I changed my mind and got eighty of them. If I'd never used one in the past, it's because I'd thought of smoking as just that—an activity that produces smoke. Patches don't satisfy the urge to stick something in your mouth and set it on fire, but they are oddly

263

calming. While I was at it, I also bought five boxes of nicotine lozenges. I haven't opened them yet, but knowing they're available—perhaps that calms me as well.

More than my products, I think it helps that everything is so new and different: our electric toilet, for instance. There's a control panel attached to the seat, and on it are a dozen buttons. Each is labeled in Japanese and marked with a simple illustration. What looks like a lowercase *w* is a bottom. A capital *Y* is a vagina. If you have both, you can occupy yourself for hours, but even for guys there's a lot to have done. "May I wash that for you?" the toilet silently asks. "Regarding the water, would you prefer the steady stream or the staccato burst? What temperature? Might I offer my blow-dry service as well?" On and on.

Along with everything else in the apartment, the electric toilet was pointed out by the building manager. Super-san, I call him. The man is a few inches shorter than me and seems to speak no English other than "hello." Two months of instructional CDs allowed me to confidently introduce both myself and Hugh, and to comment on the pleasant weather as we boarded the elevator to the twenty-sixth floor.

ME: *Ii o tenki desu ne?*
HIM: *So desu ne!*

Just inside our door, Super-san pulled off his loafers. Hugh did the same and then he kicked me with his stockinged foot. "No shoes allowed."

"But it's *our* apartment," I whispered.

"It doesn't matter."

At the end of the short entryway, just where the carpet

begins, there's a low metal tree with slippers hanging off it. They're brand-new, a mix of men's and women's, and all of them still have price tags on the soles. Super-san stepped into the smallest pair and then gave us a tour of what will be our home for the next three months.

I knew how to say that the apartment was big, and good, but not that it smelled new and reminded me of one of those midlevel residence hotels. In the living room are two framed pictures. They look like the color samples you get at the paint store, nameless, though, and matted in white. These hang above an empty console that faces an empty bookshelf. There's an empty, glass-doored cabinet as well, along with two sofas, a table and chairs, and a complicated-looking TV. While the apartment itself is unremarkable, outside it's a wonderland. Off the living room there's a shallow balcony, and from it we can see the Tokyo Tower. There's a balcony in the bedroom as well, and it overlooks a network of canals, some with little boats in them. Then there's a train yard and, beyond that, a sewage treatment plant. I said to Super-san, "Good. Good. Our place is good." When he smiled, we smiled. When he bowed, we bowed. When he left, we took his slippers and hung them on the low metal tree.

**January 6**
Our high-rise is on a busy but not unpleasant street lined with similar tall buildings, some business and others residential. There's a post office on one side of us, and a chain restaurant on the other. Outside our front door there are trees decorated with festive lights, and across the street there's a convenience store called Lawson. When writing a

foreign word, the Japanese use the katakana alphabet, but this sign, just like the one at the 7-Eleven, is in English. They sell my brand of cigarettes at Lawson, but if I wanted them even quicker I could get them at the Peacock, a good-sized supermarket located in the basement of our building. Their sign is also in English, but I don't know why. If you're catering to Westerners, the first thing you need are the Westerners. There are Hugh and me, but other than us, I haven't seen a single one, not on the streets, and certainly not at the Peacock. We went there twice yesterday and found ourselves completely lost. The milk I recognized by the red carton and by the little silhouette of the cow, but how do you find soy sauce when everything on the shelves looks like soy sauce? How do you differentiate between sugar and salt, between regular coffee and decaf?

In Paris the cashiers sit rather than stand. They run your goods over a scanner, tally up the price, and then ask you for exact change. The story they give is that there aren't enough euros to go around. "The entire EU is short on coins."

And I say, "Really?" because there are plenty of them in Germany. I'm never asked for exact change in Spain or Holland or Italy, so I think the real problem lies with the Parisian cashiers, who are, in a word, lazy. Here in Tokyo they're not just hardworking but almost violently cheerful. Down at the Peacock, the change flows like tap water. The women behind the registers bow to you, and I don't mean that they lower their heads a little, the way you might if passing someone on the street. These cashiers press their hands together and bend from the waist. Then they say what sounds to me like "We, the people of this store, worship you as we might a god."

**January 7**

A Japanese woman we'd met in Paris came to the apartment yesterday and spent several hours explaining our appliances. The microwave, the water kettle, the electric bathtub: everything blinks and bleeps and calls out in the middle of the night. I'd wondered what the rice maker was carrying on about, and Reiko told us that it was on a timer and simply wanted us to know that it was present and ready for duty. That was the kettle's story as well, while the tub was just being an asshole and waking us up for no reason.

**January 8**

I peeled away my patch last night and was disgusted by the cruddy shadow it left. It feels like I've been wearing a bumper sticker, so instead of replacing the one I took off, I think I'll just go without and see what happens. As for my three hundred dollars' worth of lozenges, I still haven't opened them, and don't think I'm going to. What I've been doing instead is rolling index cards into little tubes. I put one in my mouth when I sit down to write, and then I slowly chew it to a paste and swallow it. I'm now up to six a day and am wondering if I should switch to a lighter, unlined brand.

**January 9**

In the grocery section of Seibu department store, I saw a whole chicken priced at the equivalent of forty-four dollars. This seemed excessive until I went to another department store and saw fourteen strawberries for forty-two dollars. They were pretty big, but still. Forty-two dollars—you could almost buy a chicken for that.

**January 10**

I dropped by a Japanese-language school to ask about classes, and the woman at the front desk suggested that as long as I was there, I might as well take the placement exam. "Why not?" she said. "This a good a time as any!" I hadn't planned on staying that long, but I liked how fun and easy she made it sound. A test! In Japanese! I was just thinking the exact same thing!

A minute later I was seated behind a closed door in a small white room.

Q: *Ueno koen __ ____ desu ka?*
A: *Asoko desu!*

I had been fine all morning—in the apartment, on the subway, standing in line at the post office. It wasn't as if I had never smoked, but I was able to put *not* smoking on a back burner. Now, though, under pressure to answer a dozen and a half test questions, I'd have gladly traded one of my eyes for a cigarette, even one that was not my brand. I've found that it helps to gently chew on my tongue, but that works only during standard cravings. For this one I needed to chew on someone else's tongue—until it came off.

Sitting there in that hot little room, I wished I'd taken the advice of my friend Janet, who filled a baby food jar with an inch of water and a half-dozen butts. This she carried around in her purse, and whenever she wanted a cigarette, she'd just unscrew the lid and take a whiff of what even the most enthusiastic smoker has to admit is pretty damn nasty. In times of weakness, it's easy to forget why you ever wanted to quit. That's why I should have kept that remote control.

Even when the semen dried and flaked off, I think it would have served as a good reminder.

*Breathe in. Breathe out.* It took a few minutes, but eventually I calmed down and realized that, thanks to my instructional CDs, I knew quite a few of these answers, at least in the fill-in-the-blank section. Then came the multiple-choice part, and I found myself blindly guessing. Capping it all off was an essay question, the subject being, "My Country, an Introduction."

"I am American, but now I live in other places sometimes," I wrote. "America is big and not very expensive."

Then I sat with my hands folded until an instructor came and led me back to the lobby. My test was graded in less than a minute, and when the woman behind the counter assigned me to the beginner's class, I tried to act flattered, as if there was a *sub*-beginner's class, and it had just been decided that I was too good for it.

## January 12

In terms of stress and its connection to smoking, language school is probably not the best idea in the world. I thought of this yesterday morning as I headed to my first class. Our session ran from 9:00 to 12:45, and during that time we had two different teachers, both women and both remarkably kind. With Ishikawa-sensei we began at the beginning: Hello. Nice to meet you. I am Lee Chung Ha, Keith, Matthieu, and so on. Out of ten students, four are Korean, three are French, two are American, and one is Indonesian. I was luckily not the oldest person in the room. That's a distinction that went to Claude, a history professor from Dijon.

It's sad, really. Put me in a classroom, and within five minutes it all comes back: the brownnosing, the jealousy, the desire to be the best student, and the reality that I've never been smart enough. "Stop talking," I write in my notebook. "It's only the first day. Don't exhaust people yet."

I like Sang Lee, the seventeen-year-old Korean girl who sits in the second row. Actually, "like" is probably not the right word. More than that, I need her, need someone who's worse than I am, someone I can look down on. Because this class is for beginners, I didn't think that anyone would know the hiragana alphabet. A character or two, maybe, but certainly not the entire thing. When it turned out that *everyone* knew it, everyone but me and this little idiot Sang Lee, I was devastated.

"Where did you learn this?" I asked one of the French students.

And he said, very matter-of-factly, "Oh, I just picked it up."

"A flu is something you 'just pick up,'" I told him. "The words to a song in Spanish. But a forty-six character alphabet isn't learned unless you specifically sit down and stuff it inside your head."

"Picked it up," indeed. I know two characters. That's it. Only two. This puts me two ahead of that lovable nitwit, Sang Lee, but still, it's not much of a lead.


**January 13**

As school continues, so does the parade of new teachers. We had two different ones yesterday, Ayuba-sensei and Komito-sensei. Both were patient and enthusiastic, but neither could match the exuberance of Thursday's Miki-sensei. At one point, she asked me how to say the number *six*. I hesitated a little too long, and out of the corner of her mouth, she whispered, "Roku."

"Come again?"

She whispered it a second time, and when I successfully repeated after her, she applauded with what looked like genuine sincerity and told me I had done really, really well.

## January 16

Just before 3:00 a.m. I awoke to find our bed moving. "Earthquake!" I yelled. Hugh sat up at the sound of my voice, and together we gawked at the gently swaying curtains. There was no time to stand, much less run for cover, but I remember thinking how unfair it would be to die two weeks after I quit smoking.

## January 17

I was in the school break room with Christophe-san yesterday, and the two of us got to talking about vending machines, not just the ones before us, but the ones outside as well. "Can you believe it?" he asked. "In the subway station, on the street, they just stand there, completely unmolested."

"I know it," I said.

Our Indonesian classmate came up, and after listening to us go on, he asked what the big deal was.

"In New York or Paris, these machines would be trashed," I told him.

The Indonesian raised his eyebrows.

"He means destroyed," Christophe said. "Persons would break the glass and cover everything with graffiti."

The Indonesian student asked why, and we were hard put to explain.

"It's something to do?" I offered.

"But you can read a newspaper," the Indonesian said.

"Yes," I explained, "but that wouldn't satisfy your basic need to tear something apart."

Eventually, he said, "Oh, OK," the way I do when moving on seems more important than understanding. Then we all went back to class.

I reflected on our conversation after school, as I hurried down a skyway connecting two train stations. Windows flanked the moving sidewalks, and on their ledges sat potted flowers. No one had pulled the petals off. No one had thrown trash into the pots or dashed them to the floor. How different life looks when people behave themselves—the windows not barred, the walls not covered with graffiti-repellent paint. And those vending machines, right out in the open, lined up on the sidewalk like people waiting for a bus.

**January 18**

In my how-to-quit-smoking book, the author writes that eating is not a substitute for cigarettes. He repeats this something like thirty times, over and over, like a hypnotist. "Eating is not a substitute for smoking. Eating is not a substitute for smoking . . ." I repeat it myself while looking through the refrigerator and grimacing at the crazy stuff Hugh brought home yesterday: things like pickled sticks, or at least that's what they look like. Everything is dark brown and floating in murky syrup. Then there's this fish wrapped up in paper. It's supposed to be dead, but I can't shake the feeling that it's simply been paralyzed. My new thing is the Cozy Corner, a Western-style coffee shop next to the Tamachi train station. I pointed to something in the bakery case last Saturday, and the woman behind the counter identified it as *shotokeki*. This, I've come to realize, is Japanese for shortcake.

## January 19

We were given a dictation quiz yesterday, and I found myself wanting to cry. It's not just that I'm the worst student in the class, it's that I'm *clearly* the worst student in the class, miles behind that former dope, Sang Lee. What makes it that much harder to bear is the teacher's kindness, which has come to feel like pity. "You can keep your book open," Miki-sensei told me, but even that didn't help. Instead of *kyoshi* I wrote *quichi*. Instead of *Tokyo*, I wrote *doki*, as in *tokidoki*, which means "sometimes." "It's all right," Miki-sensei said. "You'll get it eventually."

After dictation we opened our books and read out loud. Mae Li breezed right along, as did Indri and Claude. Then came my turn. "Who . . . whose . . . book . . . is . . ."

"This," Sang Lee whispered.

"Whose book is this?" I continued.

"Good," the teacher said. "Try the next line."

I could hear the rest of the class groan.

"Is . . . it . . . you . . . your book . . ."

Buying a bottle of shampoo and discovering later that it's actually baby oil is bad, but at least that's a private humiliation. This is public, and it hurts everyone around me. *Don't call on David-san, don't call on David-san,* I can feel my classmates thinking. When we team up for exercises, I see that

273

look, meaning, "But it's not fair. I had to be with him *last* time."

I went through this with French school but never knew how easy I had it. Certain letters might not be pronounced, but at least it's the same alphabet. I was younger then, too, and obviously more resilient. I left yesterday's class with one goal—to find a secluded place, sit down, and treat myself to a nice long cry. Unfortunately, this is Tokyo, and there is no secluded place—no church to duck into, no park bench hidden in the shadows.

It didn't help any that I got off the subway at Shin-juku. Two million people a day pass through the station. Then they scatter to office towers and department stores, to clogged streets and harshly lit underground malls. I'm always wanting to compare an area to Times Square. Then I walk a mile or so, and come to another, even more crowded area. On and on, and with each new neighborhood I feel ever more insignificant. It's like looking at a sky full of stars and knowing for a fact that each one is not just inhabited, but overpopulated, the message being: you are less than nothing.

It's probably for the best that I didn't cry. A lot of people feel that smoking and drinking go together. "The two are inseparable," they insist. I guess I feel the same way about tears. Unless you can follow a good weep with a cigarette, there's really no use doing it.

## January 21

Every so often I forget that I've quit smoking. I'll be on the subway or in a store and think, *Ah, a cigarette, that should solve everything*. Then I'll put my hand to my pocket and, after the panic that comes with finding nothing, I'll remember that I've given it up, and I'll feel a crushing little blow. It's like being told some piece of horrible news, but on a smaller scale, not "the baby is going to die," but "not all of the baby's hair is going to make it." Ten times a day this happens. I forget and then I remember.

## January 23

"If you want to quit smoking, you have to return to the person you were before you started." Someone told me this a few months ago, and I assumed that he was joking. Now I see that, like it or not, I am reverting to my twenty-year-old self, at least scholastically. Yesterday morning we took a hiragana test. Out of a possible 100 points, I received 39. It was the worst grade in the class, but still the teacher decorated my paper with a fanciful sticker and the message, "Cheers up!!!"

"That's a very bad score," Claude-san told me. He himself had received a perfect 100, and as he headed off to celebrate with a cigarette, I looked at him and thought, *Loser.*

## January 25

According to the book I read, after three weeks without smoking, I'm supposed to feel elation. *Yippee,* I should be thinking. *I'm free!* Yesterday marked my three-week anniversary, but instead of feeling joyful I felt weak and opened my mind to the possibility of having a cigarette. *Just one,* I thought. *Just to prove that they're not as good as I remember them being.*

Then I thought of the supermarket in the basement, and of the convenience store across the street. I could buy a pack of Kool Milds, take just one, and throw the rest away.

Imagining how it would taste—the almost medicinal punch at the back of my throat—literally made my mouth water, and for the first time since quitting I saw the hopelessness of it. A person gives up smoking, and then what? Spends the rest of his miserable life wanting a cigarette? It wasn't like that with drinking, but then again, I have a life to lead, things to do, and being drunk kept getting in the way. Unlike alcohol, a cigarette casts no immediate shadow. Smoke one, smoke five or twenty, and you can not only function, you can function better, unless, I mean, you're chopping down trees or resuscitating someone, two things I hardly ever do anymore. *Just one cigarette,* I thought. *Just one.*

It's embarrassing, but what got me through my moment of weakness was the thought of the Four Seasons in Santa Barbara. Its regular rooms are pretty swank, but even better are the private cottages. I stayed in one once, back when you could still smoke, and was struck by how comfortable it felt, how much like a real home. Most hotels are fairly spartan. Anything not nailed down is likely to be stolen, so it's just the bed, the desk, the mindless abstract print bolted to the wall: the basics. These cottages, though, they look like little houses lived in by gentle rich people. Cashmere lap blankets, Arts and Crafts bowls—it's not exactly my taste, but who cares? My cottage had a fireplace, and, if I remember correctly, there was an iron poker and a pair of tongs hanging from a rack beside the hearth. It's such a faggy thing to think about—the fireplace tongs at the Four Seasons in Santa Barbara—but there you have it. I thought of them for a minute or two, and then I was fine, the craving had passed, which is another thing they told me in the book I read: just hold on.

**January 26**

It's hard to put a finger on our neighborhood. Crammed between the office towers are a good number of apartment buildings. I just can't figure out who lives in them. Are the people wealthy? Middle class? A woman can wear a tattered dress over two pairs of pants, and it looks to me like Comme des Garçons, last season maybe, but still smart and expensive. Along the canals there are simple two- and three-story houses. Were they in America, you could casually peep through the windows, but here, on the off chance that the curtains are open, you're likely to see the back side of a dresser or bookshelf. Even in homes facing the park, people have their windows obscured. Either that, or the glass is textured. I noticed the same thing when we went to the country. Here's a village of twenty houses, and you can't look into a single one of them.

Likewise, people cover their books with patterned, decorative jackets so you can't see what they're reading. In the rest of the world, if you're curious about someone, all you have to do is follow him for a while. Within a few minutes his cell phone will ring, and you'll learn more than you ever wanted to know. Here, of course, there's a considerable language barrier, but even if I were fluent it wouldn't help me any. After three weeks I have yet to see a single bus or subway passenger talking on a cell phone. People do it on the street sometimes, but even there they whisper and cover their mouths with their free hands. I see this and wonder, *What are you hiding?*

**January 27**

It might be different for actual Japanese people, but as a visitor I am regularly overwhelmed by how kind and accommodating everyone is. This woman at our local flower shop, for instance. I asked her for directions to the monorail, and after she patiently gave them to me I decided to buy a Hello Kitty bouquet. What it basically amounts to is a carnation with pointed ears. Add two plastic dots for the eyes and one more for the nose, and you've got a twenty-dollar cat. "Cute," I said, and when the florist agreed, I supersized the compliment to "very cute."

"You speak with skill," she told me.

Drunk with praise, I then observed that the weather was nice. She said that it certainly was, and after paying I headed for the door. Anywhere else I'd say goodbye when exiting a shop or restaurant. Here, though, I use a phrase I learned from my instructional CD. "Now I am leaving," I announce, and the people around me laugh, perhaps because I am stating the obvious.

**January 30**

Following yesterday's midmorning break, the teacher approached me in the hallway. "David-san," she said, "I think you homework *chotto . . .*"

This means "a little" and is used when you don't want to hurt someone's feelings.

"You think it's *chotto* what?" I asked. "*Chotto* bad?"

"No."

"*Chotto* sloppy? *Chotto* lazy?"

The teacher pressed her hands together and regarded them for a moment before continuing. "Maybe, ah, maybe you don't understand it so much," she said.

I used to laugh at this Japanese indirectness, but now I see that there's a real skill, not just to using it, but to interpreting it. At 11:00 we changed teachers. Miki-sensei walked in carrying her books and visual aids and went on to explain how to ask for things. If you want, for example, to borrow some money, you ask the other person if he or she has any. If you want to know the time, you ask if the other person has a watch.

I raised my hand. "Why not just ask for the time?"

"Too much directness," Miki-sensei said.

"But the time is free."

"Maybe. But in Japan, not a good idea."

After school I went to the Cozy Corner with Akira, who spent many years in California and now works as a book translator. We both ordered *shotokeki,* and as we ate he observed that, as opposed to English, Japanese is a listener's language. "What's not being mentioned is usually more important than what is."

I asked him how I'd compliment someone on, say, his shirt. "Do I say, 'I like the shirt you're wearing' or 'I like your shirt'?"

"Neither," he told me. "Instead of wasting time with the object, you'd just say 'I like,' and let the other person figure out what you're talking about."

Our teachers offer much the same advice. Give them a sentence, and they'll immediately trim off the fat. "No need to begin with *I,* as it is clear that you are the one talking," they'll say.

The next session of Japanese class begins on February 8, and I've just decided not to sign up for it. Should I announce this in advance, I wonder, or would that be too wordy and direct? Maybe it's best just to walk out the door and never return. I'll feel guilty for a day or two, but in time

I'll get over it. The way I see it, I came here to quit smoking. That's my first priority, and, as long as I don't start again, I can consider myself, if not a success, then at least not a complete failure.

## January 31
Four weeks without a cigarette.

Given the state of my Japanese it seems unfair to criticize some of the English I've been seeing. A sign outside a beauty parlor reads "Eye Rash Tint," and instead of laughing, I should give them credit for at least coming close. What gets me are the mass-produced mistakes, the ones made at Lawson, for example. A huge, nationwide chain of convenience stores, and this is what's printed on the wrappers of their ready-made sandwiches: "We have sandwiches which you can enjoy different tastes. So you can find your favorite one from our sandwiches. We hope you can choose the best one for yourself."

It's not that horribly off the mark, but still you'd think that someone, maybe someone in management, might say, "I've got a cousin who lives in America. What do you say I give him a call and run this by him before we slap it on tens of millions of wrappers?" But no.

Among Hugh's birthday gifts were two handmade teacups I bought at Mitsukoshi, a department store. Included in the box was a profile of the craftswoman, who has, for many years, been enchanted by "the warmth of Cray." I thought that this was another craftsperson, the beloved Cray-san, but Hugh figured out that what they meant to say was "clay." The sentence, in its entirety, reads, "With being enchanted by the warmth of Cray and the traditional of pottery over the period so far she is playing active parts widely as a coordinator who not only produce and design hers own pottery firstly but suggest filling Human's whole life with fun and joyful mind."

## February 5

Beside the Imperial Palace, there's a park, with a big koi-filled pond in it. Hugh and I were just nearing the gate yesterday when a pair of young men approached, saying, "Yes. Hello. A minute please?"

Both were students at a local university and were wondering if they might show us the sights, "Not for money," explained the larger of the two, "but to help improve our Engarish."

"I don't think so," Hugh told him, and the young man who had spoken, and whose name turned out to be Naomichi, turned to his friend. "He is saying to us, 'No, thank you.'"

Then I piped up. "Oh, what the heck," I said to Hugh. "Come on, it'll be fun."

"Are you saying, 'Yes, please'?" Naomichi asked. And I told him that I was.

For the first five minutes of our guided tour, we talked about the ruined buildings. "If this is the shell of the guardhouse, where's the place the guards were guarding?" I asked.

"Burned down," Student No. 2 told me.

Except for a few walls, it seemed that everything had burned. "Why didn't you build stuff with stone?" I asked, this as if I were scolding one of the three pigs. "If fires were a problem, and they obviously were, why not move on to fire*proof*."

"Not our way," Naomichi said.

"We did not then have the skills," his friend added.

It was here that we lost interest in the park and began asking the students about their lives. "What's your major?" "Do you live with your parents?" "How long have you been studying English?" While Hugh and Naomichi talked about the declining popularity of sumo wrestling, Student No. 2 and I discussed the majesty of nature. "What wild animals do you have in Tokyo?" I asked.

"Wild animal?"

"Do you have squirrels?"

No response.

I pretended to fill my cheeks with nuts, and the young man said, "Ah, *sukaworra!*"

I then moved on to snakes and asked if he was afraid of them.

"No. I think that they are very cute."

*Surely,* I thought, *he's misunderstood me.* "Snake," I repeated, and I turned my arm into a striking cobra. "Horrible. Dangerous. Snake."

"No," he said. "The only thing I am afraid of is moutha."

"The snake's mouth?"

"No," he said, "*moutha.* I maybe saying it wrong, but *moutha. Moutha.*"

I was on the verge of faking it when he pulled out an electronic dictionary and typed in the word he was looking for, *ga,* which translates, strangely enough, to "moth."

"You're afraid of moths?"

He nodded yes and winced a little.

"But nobody's afraid of moths."

"I am," he whispered, and he looked behind us, as if afraid that one might be listening.

"Are you afraid of butterflies too?" I asked.

The young man cocked his head.

"Butterfly," I said, "colorful cousin of the moth. Are you afraid that he too will attack?"

Hugh overheard me saying this and turned around. "What the hell are you two talking about?"

And Student No. 2 said, "The wildness."

## February 6

I thought before coming here that every afternoon I would grab my iPod and my index cards and take a long walk. It's what I did in Paris, and, as a result, whenever I use a particular phrase, I recall where I was when I learned it. Yesterday morning, for instance, I ran into Super-san, and when I asked how many children he had, I thought of the Boulevard Daumesnil, just as it reaches the Viaduct des Arts. It had rained heavily the day I learned Lesson No. 13, and the last leaves of the season, russet-colored and as big as pot holders, stuck to the sidewalk as if they had been glued down and covered with varnish. I walked for two hours that afternoon, and the phrases I learned stayed learned, or at least they have so far. I think it helped that I was smoking. Back in December, I could light a cigarette without thinking. Now I *don't* light it and think so hard about what I'm missing that there isn't room for anything else.

A bigger problem is that it's difficult to walk here, at least in the way that I can in London or Paris. Take Ginza, a neighborhood of fancy shops and department stores. It's the sort of place I feel guilty for liking, the sort that offers menus in English. There's a stand there that sells black ice cream

and another that sells pizza in a cone. On Sunday after-
noons, the main street is closed to traffic and beautifully
dressed people parade about in their finery.

Ginza is a mile from our apartment, and in order to reach
it I have to cross umpteen lanes of traffic, often using pedestrian bridges. Then there are the elevated highways and
overhead train tracks, the off-ramps and construction sites.
It's not just in this neighborhood, but everywhere I go. The
arrangement of buildings is higglety-pigglety as well, the
mirrored cube between the high-rise and the one-story
house made of cobbled-together planks.

As a child I once found an ant, running a crazy path
across my family's basement. I meant to open the door and
herd the thing out, but then I got a better idea and dropped
him through the ventilation grate in the back of our TV.
What the ant saw then and what I see now are likely very
similar: a chaotic vision of the future, heavy on marvels, but
curiously devoid of charm. No lake, no parkland, no leafy
avenues, and it stretches on forever.

**February 7**
I tried on a swimsuit at one of the Ginza department stores
and made the mistake of walking fully dressed into the car-
peted changing room. The saleswoman saw me and called
out in the only shrill voice I've heard since my arrival. "Stop.
Wait! Your shoes!"

It hadn't occurred to me that I needed to remove them,
but after all this time I suppose that it should have. At a
small shop I went to last weekend, I had to change into slippers in order to look into the display case. Then I put my
shoes back on and had to remove them again to climb the

stairs to the second level, which was designated as a sock-only zone.

Then there was our recent visit to the Asakura Choso Museum, the restored home and studio of the late, noted sculptor. Upon entering, you change into slippers, which are then exchanged for other slippers if you want to step onto the patio. Slippers are removed entirely for the second floor, but put back on for the third, and then changed again for the rooftop garden. The artist's sculptures were displayed throughout the house, and though there were quite a few of them he could have completed twice as many if he hadn't had to change his goddamn shoes every three minutes.

## February 8

Yesterday was my last day of school, and once again I had second thoughts about defecting. Our first teacher was Ayuba-sensei, one of my favorites. With her we spend a lot of time repeating things, which is fine by me. Talking is the only part I'm any good at, and she'll occasionally reward me with a little *"Ii desu,"* meaning "Good."

At the end of the session, she moved her fingers down her cheeks, imitating tears. I started to think that I was making a terrible mistake, but then we had our break, followed by two hours with Miki-sensei. She's a lovely woman, but I died a little when she handed out lined sheets of paper and asked us to write an essay titled *"Watashi No Nihon No Seikatsu"* (My Japanese Life).

My final product was fairly simple, but it involved no cheating and it was all written in hiragana. "My Japanese life is entertaining but very busy. My place is tall—28 stories—and all the time I am riding on the elevator. Sometimes I go

285

to the movies with my friend Hugh-san. Every day I do homework but always I make bad tests. Now I will go to England and talk English. Maybe later I will study Japanese."

**February 9**
To celebrate the end of school, Hugh and I went out to dinner. I ordered the tasting menu, which consisted of eight courses, none of them large enough to fill a saucer. The second—a stunted radish carved to resemble a flower, a bit of fish, a potato the size of a marble—was served in a deep wooden box and accompanied by a hand-calligraphed sign. The presentation was beautiful, each plate a different size, a different shape, a different texture. The food was good too. There just wasn't enough of it.

We ate at the counter, not far from a man who was just finishing a bottle of wine. "Do you mind if I light a cigarette?" he asked, and I told him to go ahead. "Have three, why don't you, and blow the smoke this way?" I think he read my remark as sarcasm, but I was being completely sincere. Back when I was smoking myself, I was often irritated by the smell of other people's cigarettes. Now for some reason, I love it. Especially when I'm eating.

**February 12**
Late yesterday morning, Hugh and I took our new swimsuits and headed to a nearby municipal building. There, on the seventh floor, is an Olympic-sized pool. I liked that I could see our apartment from the floor-to-ceiling windows behind the lifeguard stand. I liked the dressing room and the quiet way people moved about. The only thing I didn't care for was the actual swimming.

As opposed to Hugh, who's always had a bathing cap and a pair of goggles drying in the bathroom, I haven't attempted a lap in over thirty years. Bike riding I can manage, but three strokes in the water and I feel as if my heart might burst. It took awhile, but I eventually got from one end of the pool to the other. Then I did it again and again, each length terminating in an extended howl. While groaning and panting, I gripped the edge of the pool and screwed my eyes shut, looking, I imagine, like a half-dead monkey. Out of everyone in that room, I was the only person with hair on his chest. This was bad enough, but to have it on my back as well—I could actually feel myself disgusting people.

**February 14**
I quit smoking only six weeks ago, but already my skin looks different. It used to be gray, but now it's gray with a little pink in it. I also notice how much easier it is to move around, to climb stairs, to run for a bus. I've often heard cigarettes compared to friends. They can't loan you money, but they are, in a sense, there for you, these mute little comfort merchants always ready to lift your spirits. It's how I now feel about macadamia nuts, and these strange little crackers I've been buying lately. I can't make out the list of ingredients, but they taste vaguely of penis.

**February 15**
It is now official: there is no place on earth where you will not find a Peruvian band. Leaving Tamachi Station last night, I heard the familiar sounds of Simon and Garfunkel's "El Condor Pasa." Up the escalator, and there they were: five men in ponchos, blowing the pipes of Pan into cordless

microphones. "Didn't I just see you in Dublin?" I wanted to ask. "Or, no, wait, maybe it was Hong Kong, Oxford, Milan, Budapest, Toronto, Sioux Falls, South Dakota."

**February 16**
On my way home from the park yesterday, I decided to stop and get my hair cut. The barber was just sitting around watching TV when I entered, and he invited me to set my bags on one of his three empty chairs. He then gestured for me to sit. I did, and as he covered me with a cloth I came to realize that the man had shit on his hands, a swipe or whatever, most likely on the palm. The smell was unmistakable, and every time he raised the scissors I recoiled. Spotting it would have set my mind to rest, but because he was busy, and most often gripping something, it was hard to get a good look. Then too I was preoccupied by our conversation, which required a great deal of concentration.

Shit on his hands or no shit on his hands, you couldn't deny that he was a remarkably friendly barber, and a talented one to boot. Early in his career he'd won some sort of a competition. I know this because he showed me a photo: him, fifty years younger, being presented with a medal. "Number one-o champ," he said, and as he held up his index finger, I bent forward and squinted at it. "Not number two-o?"

He knew, by my count, eight words of English, and after he had used them, we spoke exclusively in Japanese.

"Last night for dinner I ate pork," I told him. "What did you have?"

"*Yakitori,*" he said, and I wondered how I might ask if some of that *yakitori,* the digested version, might not have come back to haunt him.

*"Mimi,"* I said, and I pointed to my ear.

"Very good." And he pointed to his own ear. *"Mimi!"*

I then touched the tip of my nose *"Hana."*

"That's right, *hana,"* the barber said, and he touched his own.

Next I raised my hand, fanned out the fingers, and slowly turned it this way and that, as if it were modeling jewelry on the shopping channel. *"Te."*

"Excellent," the barber said, but rather than displaying his own hand, he simply raised it a little.

It went on like this for twenty minutes, and when he had finished cutting my hair, the barber covered my head with a damp towel. He then proceeded to punch me about the ears. I've gone back and forth on this, wondering if "punch" is too strong a word, but I really don't think it is. He didn't fracture my skull or break any of his knuckles, he never actually drew back his arm, but it really did hurt.

"Hey," I said, but he just laughed and landed another blow above my right *mimi.* Luckily the towel was there, or in addition to the pain I'd have obsessed about the shit he was pounding into my new haircut. Of course I washed it anyway, twice as a matter of fact. Hugh had his hair cut a few weeks ago, and so I asked if his barber had punched him in the head as well.

"Sure did," he said. So at least that part was normal.

**February 19**

According to Amy's friend Helen Ann, it takes thirty days to break a habit and forty-five to break an addiction. On my forty-fifth day without a cigarette, I was in Kyoto and didn't think about smoking until we left a temple and came across a group of men gathered around an outdoor ashtray. This was at about 4:00 in the afternoon, during a brief break in the rain.

Our weekend trip was a package deal—train fare and two nights in a slightly shabby hotel. I don't know if it's common or not, but all of the bellhops were women. Not one of them weighed over ninety pounds, so it felt very strange to hand over my suitcase. It also felt weird not to offer a tip, but, according to Reiko, that's never done.

The hotel wasn't very busy, and its relative emptiness made it all the more depressing. Our Western-style breakfast was served on the ground floor, in a plain, harshly lit banquet room. It was there that I saw a Japanese woman eat a croissant with chopsticks. The food was self-serve, and I wonder who they consulted before deciding on the menu. Eggs and sausage made sense, as did toast, cereal, and fruit. But who eats a green salad for breakfast? Who eats mushroom soup, corn chowder, or steamed broccoli? On our second morning we went to an equally sad room and had the Japanese breakfast, which was served by women in kimonos. This, too, was something of a nightmare, and while shuddering I imagined a mother scolding her son. "Oh, no you don't," she might say. "This is the most important meal of the day, and you're not going anywhere until you finish your pickles. That's right, and your seaweed too. Then I want you to eat your cold poached egg submerged in broth and at least half of that cross-eyed fish."

**February 22**

Lying in bed this morning, I realized that since leaving Paris I have not seen a single person on Rollerblades. Neither have

I seen anyone on one of those push-along scooters that were a five-minute fad for the rest of the world but remain inexplicably popular in France. The problem here is bikes, which people ride on the sidewalks rather than in the streets. Elsewhere this is done with a sense of entitlement—"Get out of my way, you"—but the cyclists of Tokyo seem content to slowly, silently creep along behind you, "Don't mind me" being the general attitude. I also notice that of the hundreds of bikes parked outside the subway station, hardly any of them are locked. This makes me wonder if people lock their cars or the front doors to their apartments.

**February 23**

Every time I return from the basement supermarket, Hugh asks me what music was playing. I wondered why he wanted to know, and then I started paying attention and realized that it's a really good question. A few days ago, I stood in line and listened to an English rendition of "For He's a Jolly Good Fellow." Since then I've heard "Rock-a-bye Baby," "Supercalifragilisticexpialidocious," "The Bear Went Over the Mountain," and what may well be the Mormon Tabernacle Choir singing, "Heigh-ho, heigh-ho, it's home from work we go."

**February 27**

In the spotless restroom of the Tamachi station, I noticed that beside each urinal there's a hook for your umbrella. It's just another of those personal touches that keep you coming back.

**March 3**

In the lobby of our building, there are four leather sofas and two coffee tables. People occasionally sit down there, but not too often. "Maybe because of this," Hugh said yesterday, and he pointed to a sheet of rules written in Japanese. "No smoking" was clear enough, just a cigarette with a slash through it. Then there was "no drinking milk from a carton" and what was either "no eating candy hearts" or "no falling in love."

**March 4**

I'd always thought of myself as a careful smoker, but last night, while watching a burning building on the evening news, I remembered the afternoon I started a fire in a hotel room. What happened was that I'd emptied my ashtray too soon. One of the butts must have been smoldering, and it ignited the great wads of paper in my trash can. Flames licked the edge of my desk and would have claimed the curtains had I not acted quickly.

Then there was the time I was taking a walk in Normandy, and the tip of my lit cigarette brushed the cuff of my jacket. One moment my wrist felt hot, and the next thing I knew I was like the Scarecrow in *The Wizard of Oz*. Flames leapt from my sleeve and I jumped from foot to foot, batting at them and calling out for help.

In all the excitement, my half-smoked cigarette dropped from my hand and rolled to the edge of the road. Once the fire was out and I'd halfway regained my composure, I picked it up, brushed off the dirt, and stuck it back in my mouth, just happy to be alive.

**March 6**

I took the train to Yokohama yesterday and was at
Shinagawa Station when a couple got on with their young
son, who was maybe a year and a half old. For the first few
minutes the boy sat on his mother's lap. Then he started
fussing and made it clear that he wanted to look out the
window. The father said something that sounded, in tone,
like, "You just looked out the window two days ago." Then
he sighed and bent forward to remove his son's shoes. The
mother, meanwhile, went through her bag and pulled out a
small towel, which she then spread upon the seat. The boy
stood upon it in his stocking feet, and as he considered the
passing landscape he smacked his palms against the glass.
"Ba," he said, and I wondered if that was a word or just a
sound. "Ba, ba."

We all rode along for a pleasant ten minutes, and, shortly
before the train reached their stop, the father put the boy's
shoes back on. His wife returned the towel to her purse, and
then, using a special wipe, she cleaned her son's fingerprints
off the glass. Coming from France where people regularly
put their feet on the train seats, and from America where
they not only pound the windows, but carve their initials
into them, the family's display of consideration was almost
freakish. Ba, I've since decided, is Japanese for "Watch carefully, and do what we do."

**March 7**

Four hours into *Yoshitsune and the Thousand Cherry Trees,*
and I wondered how I had survived all these many years
without Kabuki. It helped, I think, that we rented those
little radio transmitters. Hugh's and mine were in English,

and Akira's was in Japanese. The play was in Japanese as well, but the stylized manner in which people spoke made them very difficult to understand. The equivalent, in English, might be Margaret Hamilton as the Wicked Witch of the West calling out that she's melting, only slower, and with frequent pauses.

If I hadn't had the radio transmitter, I would have been perfectly happy watching the sets and the elaborately costumed actors. I would have noticed that most of the women were on the homely side, some of them strikingly so, but I wouldn't have known that these roles were played by men, which is one of the rules, apparently: no girls allowed, just like in Shakespeare's day.

The story of *Yoshitsune and the Thousand Cherry Trees* was both simple and complicated. Simple in that things never change: people are consistently jealous or secretive or bravehearted. As for the rest, it all came down to a series of misunderstandings, the type that could happen to anyone, really. You assume that the sushi bucket is full of gold coins, but instead it's got Kokingo's head in it. You think you know everything about your faithful follower, but it turns out that he's actually an orphaned fox who can change his shape at will. It was he who spoke my favorite line of the evening, five words that perfectly conveyed just how enchanting and full of surprises this Kabuki business really is: "That drum is my parents."

There was a lot of sobbing in last night's presentation. Lots of teeth gnashing, lots of dying. Our transmitters explained that the playwrights wanted to end on a dramatic note, so at the close of act six, after Kakuhan reveals himself as Noritsune and vows to one day meet Yoshitsune on the field of battle, he climbs a two-step staircase, turns to the audience, and crosses his eyes. What with his fist clenching and a hairstyle that might be best described as a Beefeater shag, you had to laugh, but at the same time you couldn't help being moved. And that, I think, is pretty much the essence of a good show.

**March 9**

Riding the high-speed train—the Shin-kansen—to Hiroshima, I supposed that to the untrained eye, all French cities might look alike, as might all German and American ones. To a Japanese person, Kobe and Osaka might be as different as Santa Fe and Chicago, but I sure don't see it. To me it's just concrete, some gray and some bleached a headachy white. Occasionally you'll pass a tree, but rarely a crowd of them. The Shin-kansen moves so fast you can't really concentrate on much. It's all a whoosh, and before you know it one city is behind you and another is coming up.

If the world outside the train is fast and bleak, the world inside is just the opposite. I like the girl in uniform who pushes the snack cart down the aisle and the two girls in brighter, shorter uniforms who come by every so often and cheerfully collect your trash. Nobody talks on his cell phone, or allows music to bleed from an iPod. You don't see any slobs either. On the first leg of our trip, we sat across from a man I guessed to be in his midfifties. His lower face was obscured by a mask, the type people wear when they have a cold. But his hair was oiled and carefully combed. The man wore a black suit, matching black shoes, and canary yellow socks that looked to be made of wool rather than cotton. It was such a small thing, these socks, but I couldn't take my eyes off them. "Hugh," I said. "Do you think I would look good in yellow socks?"

He thought for a moment before saying, "No," this without a trace of doubt, as if I asked if I'd look good in a body stocking.

**March 10**

Having written that so many Japanese cities look alike, I couldn't help noticing that Hiroshima was clearly different: greener, more open. We caught a cab at the station, and after telling the driver where we were going I explained that my friend and I were Europeans, visiting from our home in Paris.

"Oh," the driver said. "That's far."

"Yes it is," I agreed.

The trip to the hotel took maybe ten minutes, and Hugh and I spent most of it speaking French. We did this a lot during our time in Hiroshima, especially at the memorial museum, which was torturous. Just when you'd think that it couldn't get any sadder, you'd come upon another display case, one in particular with a tag reading, "Nails and skin left by a twelve-year-old boy." This boy, we learned, was burned in the blast, and subsequently grew so thirsty that he tried to drink the pus from his infected fingers. He died, and his mother kept his nails and the surrounding skin to show to her husband, who'd gone off to work the day the bomb was dropped but never came home.

The museum was full of stories like this, narratives that ended with the words "But he died / but she died." This came to seem like something of a blessing, especially after we passed the diorama. The figures were life-sized and three-dimensional, a ragged group of civilians, children mainly, staggering across a landscape of rubble. The sky behind them was the color of glowing embers, and burnt skin hung in sheets from their arms and faces. You couldn't fathom how they could still be upright, let alone walking. One hundred forty thousand people were killed in Hiroshima, and more died later of hideous diseases.

There were a dozen or so displays devoted to the aftereffects of radiation, and in one of them a pair of two-inch-long black rods, curled, and the circumference of a pencil, sat on a pedestal. It seemed that a young man had his arm out the window when the bomb went off, and that some time later, after most of his wounds had healed, these rods grew from his fingertips and took the place of his nails. Worse still is that they had blood vessels inside of them, and when they broke off they hurt and bled and were ultimately replaced by new rods. The narrative was fairly short, no more than a paragraph, so a lot of my questions went unanswered.

The museum was crowded during our visit, and nobody spoke above a whisper. I spotted two Westerners standing before a photograph of charred bodies, but because they were speechless, I have no idea where they were from. After leaving the main exhibit, we exited into a sunny hallway filled with drawings and video monitors. The drawings were done by survivors and were ultimately more haunting than any of the melted bottles or burnt clothing displayed in the previous rooms. "Jr. High Students' Corpses Stacked Like Lumber" was the title of one of them.

## March 11

A booklet in our hotel room includes a section on safety awkwardly titled *Best Knowledge of Disaster Damage Prevention and Favors to Ask of You.* What follows are three paragraphs, each written beneath a separate, boldfaced heading: "When you check in the hotel room," "When you find a fire," and, my favorite, "When you are engulfed in flames."

Further weird English from our trip:

- On an apron picturing a dog asleep in a basket: "I'm glad I caught you today. Enjoy mama."
- On decorative paper bags a person might put a gift in: "When I think about the life in my own way I need gentle conversations."
- On another gift bag: "Today is a special day for you. I have considered what article of present is nice to make you happy. Come to open now, OK?"
- On yet another gift bag: "Only imflowing you don't flowing imflowing." (This last one actually gave me a headache.)

## March 12

Saturday night's dinner included small pieces of raw horse meat served on chipped ice. It wasn't the first time I've eaten horse, or even raw horse, for that matter, but it *was* the first time I've done it while dressed in a traditional robe, two robes actually, the first one amounting to a kind of slip. The woman who served us was a little on the heavy side, young, with big crooked teeth. After showing us to our table on the floor, she handed us steaming towels and then looked from Hugh to me and back again. "He is you brother?" she asked, and I recalled Lesson 8 of my instructional CD. "He is my friend," I told her.

This same thing happened last month at a department store. "Brothers traveling together?" the clerk had asked.

Westerners often think all Asians look alike, and you don't see the ridiculousness of it until it's turned in reverse. Back home, Hugh and I couldn't even pass for stepbrothers.

## March 19

It was cold yesterday, and after lunch, armed with an out-of-date guidebook, Hugh and I went to Shinjuku Station and then changed trains. The neighborhood we wound up in was supposed to be packed with antique stores, but that, most likely, was back in the eighties. Now there was just a handful of places, most selling stuff from France and Italy: pitchers with "Campari" written on them, that type of thing. Still, it was well worth the trip. Few of the buildings were more than three stories tall. Architecturally, they weren't that interesting, but their scale gave the area a cozy, almost familiar feeling.

We wandered around until it started getting dark and were heading back toward the subway station when we came upon what looked like a garage. The door was open, and leaning against a counter was a naive painting of a beaver, not the kind you'd see on all fours, building a dam or whatever, but breezy and cartoonish, wearing a shirt and trousers. I had just stepped forward to admire it when a man appeared and held an electronic wand to his throat. The voice it created was completely flat, never varying in tone or volume. Robotic, I guess you'd call it. Otherworldly. It's how movie aliens used to sound when they asked to be taken to our leader.

The man was so difficult to understand that for the first

minute, I couldn't tell if he was speaking English or Japanese. I sensed that he was asking a question, though, and, not wanting to offend him, I agreed in both languages. "Yes," I said. "Hai."

I'd guess the guy was about seventy, but youthful-looking. He wore a baseball cap and a collarless leather coat that left his throat unobstructed and open to the cold. I pointed once more to the painting, and after I said how much I liked it, he brought me a brochure. On its cover was this same cartoon beaver, only smaller and less charming.

This time I said, "Ahhh. OK."

It was hard to tell what this shop was all about. One entire wall was open to the street, and most of the shelves were lined with what looked like junk: used newspapers, grocery bags, a championship cup made out of plastic. "My daughter," the man droned in English, and he held the cup aloft and gave it a little shake. "She win."

I was then shown a photo of a smiling fat guy with his hair in a bun. "Amateur sumo champion," the shopkeeper told me.

And I said, in Japanese, "He is a big boy."

The man nodded, and as he returned the photo to its shelf, I asked him what he sold. "Ah," he said. "Yes. My business." Then he led me to the street and pointed to the roof, where a handmade sign read, "Cancer Out Tea."

"I have cancer," he announced.

"And you cured it with tea?"

He made a face I took to mean "Well . . . kind of."

I was going to ask what kind of cancer he had, but then I thought better of it. When my mom got sick, people would often push for details. It was their way of setting her at ease, of saying, "Look, I'm acknowledging it. I'm not freaked out." But when they learned that she had lung cancer, the mood tended to change, the way it wouldn't have if the tumor was in her breast or brain.

Because of the electronic wand, I assumed the man had cancer of the larynx. I also assumed, perhaps unfairly, that it was prompted by smoking. What shocked me, standing in that ice-cold garage, was my certainty that the same thing will not happen to me. It's so queer how that works. Two months without a cigarette, and I'm convinced that all the damage has reversed itself. I might get Hodgkin's disease or renal cell carcinoma, but not anything related to smoking. The way I see it, my lungs are like sweatshirts in a detergent commercial, the before and after so fundamentally different that they constitute a miracle. I never truly thought that I would die the way my mother did, but now I really, *really* don't think it. I'm middle-aged, and, for the first time in thirty years, I feel invincible.

## Part III (After)

### One
On the return flight from Tokyo, I pulled out my notebook and did a little calculating. Between the plane tickets, the three-month apartment rental, the school tuition, and the unused patches and lozenges, it had cost close to twenty thousand dollars to quit smoking. That's 2 million yen and, if things keep going the way they have been, around 18 euros.

Figuring that I bought most of my cigarettes duty-free,

and annually paid about twelve hundred dollars for them, in order to realize any savings I'd have to live for another seventeen years, by which time I'd be sixty-eight and clinging to life by a thread. It's safe to assume that by 2025, guns will be sold in vending machines, but you won't be able to smoke anywhere in America. I don't imagine Europe will allow it either, at least not the western part. During the months I'd been gone, France had outlawed smoking in public buildings. In a year's time it would be forbidden in all bars and restaurants, just as it was in Ireland. Italy, Spain, Norway; country by country, the continent was falling.

Hugh and I flew British Airways to Tokyo and back. Most of the flight attendants were English, and as one of them roamed the aisle with the duty-free cart, I flagged her down. "Ordinarily I'd be buying cigarettes," I told her. "This time I'm not, though, because I quit."

"Oh," she said. "Well, that's all right then."

As she turned to leave, I stopped her again. "For three decades I smoked. Now I don't anymore."

"Lovely."

"Cold turkey, that's how I did it."

Then she said, "Brilliant," and hurried off down the aisle.

"Why did you do that?" Hugh asked.

"Do what?" I said, and I turned back to the movie I'd been watching. The truth, of course, is that I'd wanted some praise. I'd denied myself. I'd done something hard, and now I wanted everyone to congratulate me. It was the same in 2000 when I lost twenty pounds. "Notice anything different?" I'd say—this to people who had never seen me before.

**Two**

It was one thing to be a quitter, but I didn't have to call myself a nonsmoker—to formally define myself as one—until I returned to the United States. By the time I landed, I hadn't had a cigarette in exactly three months, almost an entire season. My hotel had been booked in advance and, upon my arrival, the desk clerk confirmed the reservation, saying, "That's 'King Nonsmoking,' right?"

The first word referred to the size of the bed, but I chose to hear it as a title.

Adjusting my imaginary crown, I said, "Yes, that's me."

Now when I travel, I like the hotel to have a pool, or, better yet, a deal with the local YMCA. That's been one thing to come out of this: a new hobby, something to replace my halfhearted study of Japanese. Though I haven't yet learned to enjoy the actual swimming part, I like all the stuff around it. Finding a lap pool, figuring out the locker system. Then there's the etiquette of passing someone, of spending time alongside them in the water.

In Tokyo once I complimented a fellow Westerner on the gracefulness of his backstroke. "It's like you were raised by otters," I said, and the way he nodded and moved into the next lane suggested that I had overstepped some fundamental boundary. It's the same in the locker room, apparently. Someone can have a leech stuck to his ass, but unless it's a talking one, and unless it personally asks you a question, you should say nothing.

I was in El Paso one afternoon, changing out of my swimsuit, and a young man said, "Excuse me, but aren't you . . ." When I say I was changing out of my swimsuit, I mean that I had nothing on. No socks, no T-shirt. My underpants were in my hand. I guess the guy recognized me from my book jacket photo. The full-length naked one on the back cover of my braille editions.

My other bad experience took place in London, at a community pool I used to go to. It was a Saturday afternoon and very crowded. I'd just reached the end of my lane and was coming up for air when I heard the sound of a whistle and noticed that I was the only one left in the water. "What's the problem?" I asked, and the lifeguard said something I couldn't quite understand.

"What?"

"Poo," he repeated. "Everybody out while we clean the water."

As I walked toward the changing room, a second lifeguard fished out the turds. There were four of them, each the size and shape of a cat's hair ball. "Third time today that's happened," the person at the desk told me.

At the pool I currently go to, one of the regulars is a woman with Down syndrome. She's fairly heavy and wears an old-fashioned swimsuit, the sort with a ruffled skirt. Then there's this bathing cap that straps beneath her chin and is decorated with rubber flowers. Odd is the great satisfaction I take whenever I beat her from one end to the other. "I won three out of four," I told Hugh the first time she and I swam together. "I mean I really creamed her."

"Let me get this straight," he said. "She's obese. She's as old as you are. *And* she has Down syndrome?"

"Yes, and I beat her. Isn't that great!"

"Did she even know you were having a race?"

I hate it when he gets like this. Anything to burst my bubble.

I no longer tell him about the old people I defeat. Older than I am, I mean—women in their late seventies and eighties. Then there are the children. I was in Washington State, at a small-town YMCA, when a boy wandered into the lap lane and popped his head, seal-like, out of the water. I would later learn that he was nine, but at the time he was just this kid, slightly pudgy, with a stern haircut. It's like he went to a barbershop with a picture of Hitler, that's how severe it was. We got to talking, and when I told him I wasn't a very good swimmer, he challenged me to a race. I think he assumed that, like most adults, I'd slow down and intentionally let him win, but he didn't know who he was dealing with. I need all the confidence I can get, and one victory is just as good as any other. Thus I swam for my very life and beat the pants off him. I thought this was it—he'd accept his defeat and move on with his life—but five minutes later he stopped me again and asked if I believed in God.

"No," I told him.

"Why?"

I thought for a second. "Because I have hair on my back, and a lot of other people, people who kill and rob and make life miserable, don't. A real God wouldn't let that happen."

I was happy to leave it at that, but before I could resume he blocked his path. "It was God who let you win that race," he said. "He touched you on the leg and made you go faster, and that's how come you beat me."

He really looked like Hitler then, eyes blazing like two little coals.

"If God knows that I don't believe in him, why would he go out of his way to help me?" I asked. "Maybe instead of making *me* win, God reached down and made *you* lose. Did you ever think of that?"

I continued my swimming but was stopped once again at the end of the next lap. "You're going to go to hell," the boy said.

"Is this still about me winning that race?"

"No," he told me. "It's about God, and if you don't believe in Him you're going to burn for the rest of eternity."

I thanked him for the tip and then I went back to my laps, grateful that at the church I had attended, the service was entirely in Greek. My sisters and I had no idea what the priest was saying, and when you're young that's probably for the best. Lil' Hitler was only in the third grade, and already he was planning for his afterlife. Even worse, he was planning for mine. While changing out of my suit, it occurred to me that I probably shouldn't have contradicted him. It's insane to discuss religion with a child. Especially at the Y. What bugged me was his insistence that I'd had unfair help, that God had stepped in and pushed me over the finish line. I mean, really. Can I not beat a nine-year-old on my own?

**Three**
When I look back on my many years of smoking, the only real regret I have is all the litter I generated, all those hundreds of thousands of butts crushed underfoot. I was always outraged when a driver would empty his ashtray onto the asphalt. "What a pig!" I'd think. But he only did in bulk what I did piecemeal. In a city you tell yourself that someone will clean it up, someone who wouldn't *have* a job unless you dropped that butt onto the sidewalk. In that respect you're good, you're helping. Then too, it never felt like real litter,

like tossing down, say, a broken lightbulb. No one was going to cut his foot on a cigarette butt, and because of its earthy color it pretty much disappeared into the landscape, the way a peanut shell might. This made it "organic" or "biodegradable"—one of those words that meant "all right."

I didn't stop throwing my cigarette butts down until, at the age of forty-eight, I was arrested for it. This was in Thailand, which makes it all the more embarrassing. Tell someone the police picked you up in Bangkok, and they reasonably assume that, after having sex with the eight-year-old, you turned her inside out and roasted her over hot coals, this last part, the cooking without a permit, being illegal under Thai law. "Anything goes," that's the impression I had, and so it surprised me when, out of nowhere, two policemen approached. One took my right arm, the other took my left, and they led me toward a brown tent. "Hugh!" I called, but as usual he was twenty paces ahead of me and wouldn't notice I was gone for another ten minutes. The officers seated me at a long table and made a motion for me to stay put. They then walked away, leaving me to wonder what I had possibly done to offend them.

Before my run-in with the police, Hugh and I had visited the criminology museum, a sad sort of homemade affair, its highlight being a dead man suspended in a glass box and dripping amber-colored fluid into a shallow enameled pan. The sign, which was written in Thai and translated into English, read, simply, "Rapist and Murderer." It was the way they'd mark a stuffed or pickled cobra at a natural history museum, a way of saying, "This is what this creature looks like. Keep your eyes peeled."

Except for the amber fluid, the rapist-murderer was

actually quite pleasant-looking, a lot like the policemen who'd picked me off the street and the man who'd sold us our lunch. It was only 300 degrees outside, so after leaving the criminology museum Hugh thought we might eat some piping-hot soup cooked in what amounted to a roving cauldron. There were no tables, so we lowered ourselves onto overturned buckets and put the scalding bowls in our laps. "Let's sit in the blistering sun and burn the skin off our tongues!" That's a Hamrick's idea of a good time.

From there we'd gone to a grand palace. It wasn't my sort of thing, but I hadn't complained or insulted the royal family. Nothing had been stolen or written on with Magic Marker, so, again, what was the problem?

When the officers returned, they handed me a pen and placed a sheet of paper before me. The document was in Thai, a language that looks like cake decoration to me. "What did I do?" I asked, and the men pointed behind me, where a sign announced a thousand-baht fine for littering.

"Littering?" I said, and one of the officers, the more handsome of the two, took an invisible cigarette from his mouth, and threw it to the ground.

I wanted to ask if, instead of paying the fine, he could maybe cane me, but I think that's done in Singapore, not Thailand, and I didn't want to come off as unsophisticated. In the end I signed my name, handed over the equivalent of thirty dollars, and stepped outside to look for my cigarette butt, which I eventually found lying in the gutter between a severed duck head and a fly-covered plastic bag half full of coconut milk.

*That's right,* I thought. *Fine the Westerner.* Really, though, wasn't I just as guilty as these other litterers? You either trash up the landscape, or you don't, and I was clearly a member of Group A, a crowd I'd always viewed, perhaps unfairly, as foreign or uneducated. This was a notion I picked up from my Greek grandmother. Yiayia lived with us while I was growing up and was hands down the worst litterbug I had ever seen. Cans, bottles, fat Sunday newspapers, anything that could fit through the car window was thrown through the car window. "What the hell are you doing?" my father would shout. "Throwing crap onto the road, we don't do that in this country."

Yiayia would blink at him through her thick-lensed glasses. Then she'd say, "Oh," and do it again two minutes later, this as if the grocery receipt was litter but the *Time* magazine wasn't. I think she actually saved her used tissues and empty medicine bottles, stuck them in her purse until she was back in the moving station wagon.

"That's a Greek for you," our mother would say, adding that her mother would never throw anything from a car window. "Not even a peach pit."

During the period that our grandmother lived with us, litter was very much on our minds, in part the result of TV. The "Keep America Beautiful" commercials featured a crying Indian, his composure shattered by the sight of a trash-strewn creek bed.

"See that?" I'd say to Yiayia. "All that garbage and stuff in the water, that's wrong."

"Awwww, you're wasting your time," Lisa would say. "She doesn't even get that the guy is an Indian."

Our father worried that our grandmother was setting a bad example, but, actually, it worked the other way. None of us would ever think of throwing something out a car window, unless, of course, it was a cigarette butt, which is not just trash, but red-tipped, flaming trash. "Shame about that forest fire," we'd say. "You really have to wonder about people who do things like that. It's a sickness of the mind."

I can't say that after leaving Bangkok I never again crushed a cigarette underfoot. I can say, though, that I never did it comfortably. If a trash can was around, I'd use it, and if not, I'd either tuck the butt into the cuff of my pants or try to hide it under something, a leaf, maybe, or some bit of paper cast down by somebody else, as if the shade would allow it to disintegrate faster.

Now that I've quit, I've started collecting trash—not tons, but a little bit every day. If, for example, I see a beer bottle left on a park bench I'll pick it up and toss it into the nearest garbage can, which is usually no more than a few feet away. Then I say, "Stupid lazy asshole couldn't be bothered to throw away his own fucking bottle."

I wish I could do my penitence with grace, but I doubt that will happen any time soon. People see me picking up garbage and figure, with reason, that I'm being paid for it. They wouldn't want to put me out of a job, so instead of throwing their plastic fork away, they drop it, leaving me with even more to clean up. Empty bags that used to hold French fries, paper cups, used bus tickets . . . it's funny, but the only thing I *won't* pick up are discarded butts. It's not their germs that put me off. I'm simply afraid that on taking one between my fingers, I'll somehow snap to and remember, with clarity, just how good a cigarette would taste right now.